Lecture Notes in Computer Science 11998

More information about this subseries at http://www.springer.com/series/7407

Santosh Pande · Vivek Sarkar (Eds.)

Languages and Compilers for Parallel Computing

32nd International Workshop, LCPC 2019
Atlanta, GA, USA, October 22–24, 2019
Revised Selected Papers

 Springer

Editors
Santosh Pande
Georgia Institute of Technology
Atlanta, GA, USA

Vivek Sarkar
Georgia Institute of Technology
Atlanta, GA, USA

ISSN 0302-9743   ISSN 1611-3349   (electronic)
Lecture Notes in Computer Science
ISBN 978-3-030-72788-8   ISBN 978-3-030-72789-5   (eBook)
https://doi.org/10.1007/978-3-030-72789-5

LNCS Sublibrary: SL1 – Theoretical Computer Science and General Issues

This Springer imprint is published by the registered company Springer Nature Switzerland AG
The registered company address is: Gewerbestrasse 11, 6330 Cham, Switzerland

Preface

The **32nd Workshop on Languages and Compilers for Parallel Computing (LCPC)** was held during **October 22–24, 2019 at Georgia Institute of Technology, Atlanta**. LCPC is the longest-running workshop in the intersection of programming systems and parallel computing. Since its inception, LCPC has been a leading venue for disseminating cutting-edge research on all aspects of parallel programming systems – including programming models, languages, compilers, runtime systems, and tools – for a diverse range of application domains and computing platforms. The scope of LCPC 2019 spanned a wide variety of topics related to parallel computing, including current domains and platforms, such as scientific computing, batch/streaming/real-time data analytics, machine learning, cognitive computing, heterogeneous/reconfigurable computing, mobile computing, cloud computing, IoT; as well as forward-looking domains such as analog and quantum computing. Bold new ideas in programming systems are critical for the success of computing platforms in the Moore's Law end-game and post-Moore eras. LCPC 2019 offered a highly interactive forum for the dissemination of innovative research contributions as well as in-depth discussions of novel and emerging ideas. As in past years, LCPC 2019 brought together researchers from academia, national labs, and industry with the aim of creating and strengthening research collaborations. LCPC 2019 also hosted a co-located event on October 21, 2019 – a special workshop on MLIR for HPC organized by Prof. Mary Hall.

We were fortunate to have a diverse set of expert program committee (PC) members, spanning junior and senior researchers, women and under-represented groups, and researchers from different cross sections of the community, including academia, industry, and national labs. The details of the PC can be found at https://lcpc19.cc. gatech.edu/committee. Two types of papers were invited for submission:

- **Full papers** on innovative and original research that describe new research contributions. 15 pages limit.
- **Short papers** on preliminary results, surveys, demonstrations, or vision for future research. 8 pages limit.

The review process was guided by novelty; reviewers were given explicit instructions to look for novel, intriguing ideas in the submissions. The inclusion of papers that propose new ideas – a new problem, a new research topic, radical insight into an existing topic, surprising results, etc. – was one of the key goals in devising the workshop program. Another important consideration was whether the paper could provoke interesting discussions during the workshop. The PC ensured that each paper received at least 4 reviews. Each paper was discussed in an online PC meeting, and the final selection of the papers was based on the degree of novelty and quality. Regardless of acceptance or rejection, authors were provided with detailed feedback. Out of 17 submissions, 8 were accepted as regular papers and 3 were accepted as short papers. As in past LCPC workshops, a two-tier revision process was followed for the accepted papers: first, the authors were asked to incorporate the reviewers' feedback and prepare a pre-proceedings version of the paper, which was made available at the workshop. Next, the authors were asked to incorporate the feedback received during the workshop and prepare a final camera-ready version, which is included in these proceedings.

Apart from the accepted papers, the workshop program included two exciting keynote talks, one on resource-efficient quantum computing by Prof. Fred Chong, University of Chicago, and another on the role of compilers in supporting modern cryptography-based computations by Dr. Madan Musuvathi from Microsoft Research. The program also included eight invited talks and a panel that covered a variety of frontiers and emerging topics in the field. The full program of the workshop can be found at https://lcpc19.cc.gatech.edu/program. The eight invited talks were:

1. 'HPVM: Performance, Portability, Programmability and Approximation for Heterogeneous Parallel Systems' by Vikram Adve, UIUC
2. 'Optimization in the Sparse Tensor Algebra Compiler' by Fredrik Kjolstad, MIT
3. 'Optimizing Data Movement and Achieving Performance Portability with Brick Data Layouts' by Mary Hall, University of Utah
4. 'DPC++: A Direct Programming Model for Diverse Architectures' by Xinmin Tian, Intel
5. 'Model-driven multi-level tiling for tensor contractions' by P. (Saday) Sadayappan, University of Utah
6. 'A framework for compositional transformations of recursions and loops' by Milind Kulkarni, Purdue University
7. 'A Lightweight Polyhedral Abstraction for MLIR' by Albert Cohen, Google
8. 'Filling in the gaps between applications and OpenMP for in-node programming on exascale systems' by Oscar Hernandez, Oak Ridge National Laboratory

The social part of the workshop included an excursion to Georgia Aquarium, the largest aquarium in the United States and in the Western Hemisphere. It is home to whale sharks, beluga whales, California sea lions, bottlenose dolphins, and manta rays that reside in 10 million gallons of fresh and saltwater (workshop photos are available at: https://lcpc19.cc.gatech.edu/photos).

A total of 48 students, faculty, and researchers participated in LCPC 2019. They contributed to interesting discussions in a close-knit setting during the workshop sessions, breaks, lunches, excursion, and dinner, while enjoying beautiful fall weather in Atlanta.

The LCPC 2019 organizers would like to thank our sponsors, Futurewei and Intel, for their generous support. We are grateful to the keynote and invited speakers, the authors, and all the participants for making LCPC 2019 a great success. We would especially like to thank Sri Raj Paul (Publicity and Web Chair) and Francella Tonge (Administrative Support), without whose hard work the workshop would not have been possible. We would also like to thank all the student volunteers. We thank Georgia Tech and GT Hotel for the use of their conference facilities and Springer-Verlag for providing publication support for the workshop proceedings through their LNCS series. Finally, we would like to thank the LCPC steering committee for providing us the opportunity to organize LCPC 2019, and for their guidance and support throughout the entire process.

Sincerely,

Santosh Pande
Vivek Sarkar

Organization

Workshop Chairs

Santosh Pande   Georgia Tech
Vivek Sarkar   Georgia Tech

Steering Committee

Rudolf Eigenmann   U. Delaware
Alex Nicolau   UC Irvine
David Padua   UIUC
Lawrence Rauchwerger   TAMU, UIUC
Vivek Sarkar   Georgia Tech

Keynote/Panel Chair

Oscar Hernandez   Oak Ridge National Labs

Program Committee

Milind Chabbi   Scalable Machines Research, Uber
Tiago Cogumbreiro   UMass Boston
Damian Dechev   University of Central Florida
Chen Ding   University of Rochester
Yufei Ding   UC Santa Barbara
Mary Hall   University of Utah
Akihiro Hayashi   Rice University
Changhee Jung   Purdue University
Martin Kong   University of Oklahoma
Tushar Kumar   Google
Seyong Lee   Oak Ridge National Laboratory
Zhiyuan Li   Purdue University
Lawrence Rauchwerger   TAMU, UIUC
Hari Sundar   University of Utah
Rishi Surendran   Xilinx Inc

Publicity/Web Chair

Sri Raj Paul   Georgia Tech

Contents

Performance of Static and Dynamic Task Scheduling for Real-Time Engine
Control System on Embedded Multicore Processor   1
    Yoshitake Oki, Hiroki Mikami, Hikaru Nishida, Dan Umeda,
    Keiji Kimura, and Hironori Kasahara

PostSLP: Cross-Region Vectorization of Fully or Partially
Vectorized Code   15
    Vasileios Porpodas and Pushkar Ratnalikar

FLARE: Flexibly Sharing Commodity GPUs to Enforce QoS
and Improve Utilization   32
    Wei Han, Daniel Mawhirter, Bo Wu, Lin Ma, and Chen Tian

Foundations of Consistency Types for a Higher-Order
Distributed Language   49
    Xin Zhao and Philipp Haller

Common Subexpression Convergence: A New Code Optimization
for SIMT Processors   64
    Sana Damani and Vivek Sarkar

Using Performance Event Profiles to Deduce an Execution Model
of MATLAB with Just-In-Time Compilation   74
    Patryk Kiepas, Corinne Ancourt, Claude Tadonki, and Jarosław Koźlak

CLAM: Compiler Leasing of Accelerator Memory   89
    Dong Chen, Chen Ding, and Dorin Patru

Abstractions for Polyhedral Topology-Aware Tasking [Position Paper]   98
    Martin Kong

SWIRL ++ : Evaluating Performance Models to Guide Code
Transformation in Convolutional Neural Networks   108
    Tharindu R. Patabandi, Anand Venkat, Rajkishore Barik, and Mary Hall

A Structured Grid Solver with Polyhedral+Dataflow Representation   127
    Eddie C. Davis, Catherine R. M. Olschanowsky, and Brian Van Straalen

CubeGen: Code Generation for Accelerated GEMM-Based Convolution
with Tiling.   147
    Amarin Phaosawasdi, Christopher Rodrigues, Long Chen, and Peng Wu

Author Index   165

Performance of Static and Dynamic Task Scheduling for Real-Time Engine Control System on Embedded Multicore Processor

Yoshitake Oki, Hiroki Mikami, Hikaru Nishida, Dan Umeda, Keiji Kimura$^{(\boxtimes)}$, and Hironori Kasahara

Department of Computer Science and Engineering, Waseda University, Tokyo, Japan
keiji@waseda.jp
http://www.kasahara.cs.waseda.ac.jp

Abstract. Embedded multicore processors running hard real-time applications such as engine control programs require an appropriate scheduling routine to meet the real-time deadline constraints. These applications typically consist of various conditional branches which change the flow of the program and the task executions based on sensors inputs and vehicle status information. Conventionally, dynamic on-line scheduling was the only option for such applications that have unpredictable runtime behaviors. However, techniques for compilers and schedulers allow static off-line scheduling to be applied to engine control programs by utilizing execution profile feedback methods to feed task execution time information to the compiler. This paper is the first to compare dynamic scheduling and static scheduling schemes through the OSCAR multi-grain automatic parallelizing compiler and its overheads on an actual engine control program using an embedded multicore processor implemented on an FPGA. Evaluations and analysis on the engine control program indicate promising results for static scheduling, recording a 2.53× speedup on 4 cores compared to single core execution. In contrast, speedup on dynamic scheduling with 4 cores was only 0.86x compared to sequential execution. The evaluation shows that static scheduling with execution profile feedback methods is an effective tool for real hard-real time control applications that have task granularity that is too fine for dynamic scheduling on embedded multicore processors.

Keywords: Parallelizing compiler · Multicore · Dynamic scheduling · Static scheduling · Scheduling overhead · Performance comparison · Hard real-time control systems

1 Introduction

The performance requirements for modern embedded systems have increased significantly to deal with large and complex programs that have hard deadline constraints, such as automobile engine control systems and cyber physical

© Springer Nature Switzerland AG 2021
S. Pande and V. Sarkar (Eds.): LCPC 2019, LNCS 11998, pp. 1–14, 2021.
https://doi.org/10.1007/978-3-030-72789-5_1

systems. In these environments, various periodic and non-periodic tasks with specific hard deadlines are invoked by inputs such as sensor and vehicle status data. Moreover, the control flow of the program depends on the value of these inputs. Failure to meet these task deadlines may lead to accidents, and must be avoided.

Research in task scheduling has been focused on offline static scheduling and on-line dynamic scheduling schemes. Both types of methods deal with creating scheduling results that guarantee the deadline requirements of the target application.

With static scheduling, scheduling results of the program are computed by off-line software solutions such as compilers [11,12]. Static scheduling has the advantage of knowing the execution timings of the tasks of the program before runtime, allowing the processor to explicitly determine when and where the tasks would be executed and reducing any data transfer overheads. This predictability of task execution timing is favorable for applications that have hard deadline constraints, making static scheduling a potential option for embedded multicore processor systems.

In contrast, dynamic scheduling is a scheduling approach that decides the task execution timings during the runtime of the application [13]. By deciding which tasks to execute on-the-fly, dynamic scheduling can load-balance the tasks onto the processor. However, if the data transfer and memory access overhead between tasks becomes large relative to the task execution times, the load-balancing benefits diminishes. The on-line characteristics of dynamic scheduling make it a viable scheduling option for OS and packet routing systems where tasks arrive at arbitrary intervals. As a hybrid approach, there are dynamic scheduling algorithms which consider data locality among tasks by scheduling specific tasks onto the same processor core [16].

Performance of multicore processors for embedded systems is achieved by applying appropriate scheduling schemes that match the target application. For applications such as engine control programs where task executions are based on inputs and conditional branches, dynamic scheduling was the only scheduling algorithm applicable since the control flow of the program is undefined before runtime. However, through compiler techniques with execution profile feedback methods, static scheduling is also applicable to programs with conditional branches.

The scheduling algorithm for embedded multicore systems must be chosen based on the target application's parallelism, task sizes, and the scheduling overheads. In this paper, the problem of static and dynamic scheduling for embedded systems is discussed, and compares the performance of the two scheduling schemes on an engine control program running on an embedded multicore processor implemented on an FPGA [15].

The contributions of the paper are as follows.

1. Applies static and dynamic scheduling on an engine control program using the same compiling and scheduling framework.

2. Compares the performance of the two scheduling schemes running on an embedded multicore processor implemented FPGA and shows the effectiveness of static scheduling for engine control applications.

The rest of the paper is organized as follows. Section 2 presents related works. Section 3 introduces a motivational problem for task scheduling. Section 4 introduces the static and dynamic scheduling schemes. Section 5 shows evaluation results of the scheduling algorithms on an engine control program. Section 6 concludes the paper.

2   Related Works

There is significant research on scheduling methods that target embedded systems and periodic tasks.

For periodic task scheduling on single core environments, Liu et al. reported a Rate Monotonic Algorithm for hard real-time environments that prioritize tasks with high request rates [1]. Kalogeraki et al. proposed a dynamic scheduling scheme based on laxity values of periodic tasks and utilizes a global and local scheduler for each processor [3]. Han et al. proposed a fault-tolerant scheduling scheme that schedules primary and alternate tasks using fixed priority-driven algorithms [2]. Fohler reported a method that utilizes both static and dynamic scheduling techniques to allocate periodic tasks to processors [4]. Fohler's scheduling approach initially creates a static scheduling result, and utilizes an on-line mechanism to shift tasks within scheduling windows to create space for dynamically allocated tasks. Moreover, there are dynamic scheduling methods that target heterogeneous systems [6–8]. These methods schedule kernels to host CPUs or GPUs at runtime of the program. For compiler assisted scheduling, Baskaran et al. proposed a dynamic scheduling scheme for loop tiles on multicore processors [5]. For dynamic scheduling methods that consider scheduling overhead, Kasahara et al. proposed a dynamic scheduling scheme to reduce scheduling overhead by generating scheduling routine codes through a parallelizing compiler [13].

As presented in this section, scheduling methods for embedded systems are mainly based on dynamic scheduling approaches. However, compiler techniques with execution profile feedback methods have allowed embedded systems with conditional branches, varying task execution times, and small task granularities to utilize static scheduling as an alternative to dynamic scheduling [14]. Moreover, a performance analysis of dynamic scheduling and static scheduling for embedded systems has not been attempted so far. This paper is the first research that compares the performance of dynamic and static scheduling, and the applicability of the two scheduling schemes on a real automobile engine control system with an embedded multicore processor implemented on an FPGA.

3   Motivation

Due to varying task execution times and unpredictable control flow, scheduling methods for embedded applications mainly utilize dynamic scheduling. Engine control programs are a typical example of such applications.

3.1   Engine Control Program

Engine control programs are mainly composed with conditional branches and few loops with small task granularities. The tasks of engine control programs include crank shaft related tasks as well as periodic tasks which are activated every few milliseconds. Typical deadlines of the tasks for engine control programs are 1 ms, 5 ms, and 50 ms.

The outputs and the resulting control flow of the conditional branches are decided by the input sensors and the vehicle status data given to the application. Since the conditional branches are either taken or not taken during execution, it is unknown at compile time whether a task is executed or not. Conventionally, this unpredictability of tasks makes dynamic scheduling the only feasible scheduling algorithm for engine control programs.

3.2   The OSCAR Multi-grain Parallelization Compiler for Scheduling Routine Generation [10]

To generate scheduling results for applications of embedded systems, this paper utilizes the multi-grain parallelization and scheduling scheme of the OSCAR multi-grain and multi-platform automatic parallelizing compiler. The OSCAR compiler is a source-to-source compiler developed since 1991 [10]. The compiler takes sequential C and Fortran programs as input, and transforms them into parallelized code for a wide variety of multicore processors which can then be further compiled to executables through conventional compilers.

To generate scheduling results for multicore processors, the input program must first be parallelized. The OSCAR compiler detects parallelism at multiple levels of granularity. These granularities are loop parallelism, coarse grain parallelism, and fine grain parallelism.

The parallelization process of the OSCAR compiler begins by dividing the input program into three types of coarse-grain tasks, or Macro Tasks (MT): Basic Blocks (BB), Repetition Blocks (RB), and Subroutine Blocks (SB). RBs and SBs can recursively be decomposed into smaller MTs if coarse-grain task parallelism still exists within those blocks. Once all MTs for the input program are generated, the compiler then analyzes the produced MTs to generate a Macro Flow Graph (MFG). MFGs depict the control flow of the MTs that have data dependence edges. MFGs do not show any parallelism among tasks. Subsequently, a Macro Task Graph (MTG) is generated by analyzing the earliest execution time of every MT and tracing the control flow of the MFG. Based on the generated MTs on the MTG, the OSCAR compiler can produce either static or dynamic scheduling codes from the same input application. For static scheduling, the scheduling codes for each processor core are inserted between MT codes. For dynamic scheduling, each processor core has scheduling codes that gets the next available task and updates the common ready queue.

The details of the parallelizing techniques and the utilized structures of the OSCAR compiler are beyond the scope of this paper.

4   Task Scheduling Algorithms

The goal of this paper is to compare the static and dynamic scheduling performances on embedded multicore systems. This section presents the details of the two scheduling schemes presented by the OSCAR Compiler [10].

4.1   Static Scheduling of the OSCAR Compiler

The main idea of the static scheduling routine of the OSCAR compiler is to generate scheduling results and codes during the compilation phase of the input program. For multicore processors, the scheduling results for each processor and its corresponding code are generated at compile time. Since the execution schedules of the tasks are chosen before runtime, the tasks on each processor core can be executed with no scheduling overhead.

To generate static scheduling results, the compiler analyzes the flow graph of the input application. For the OSCAR compiler, this corresponds to the MTG of the application. The MTG depicts the data dependence and the control flow of the program. From the MTG, the OSCAR compiler detects which tasks, or MTs, can be executed in parallel.

The OSCAR compiler utilizes a heuristic static scheduling algorithm called CP/DT/MISF (Critical Path/Data Transfer/Most Immediate Successors First) [11,12], which is an improved version of the CP/MISF [9] algorithm by considering data transfer times.

The steps of the CP/DT/MISF algorithm are shown below.

1. For each task on the MTG, determine the longest path to the exit node.
2. Calculate data transfer time required for all available tasks when mapped to processor cores.
3. Choose the assignment of the task to processor cores that have the minimum data transfer time, and add it to the schedule.

4.2   Task Execution Feedback with Conditional Branches and Memory Mapping of the OSCAR Compiler

For static scheduling, knowing the execution times of the scheduling tasks at compile time is critical to generate a scheduling result that meets deadline requirements. However, the scheduling results may be insufficient by using compiler calculated costs. To address this, the OSCAR compiler utilizes task execution feedback information to improve scheduling results. By using feedback information, the compiler generates an improved estimation of the execution times of each task.

To enable static scheduling and task execution feedback, the compiler must know the control flow of the program at compile time. If the control flow of the program changes during runtime due to uncertainties such as conditional branches, successor tasks must wait longer than the decided scheduling results, making static scheduling an infeasible scheduling scheme.

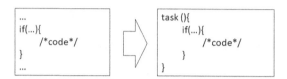

Fig. 1. Example of hiding conditional branches into a task

To allow static scheduling to be applied to programs with conditional branches, an effective approach is to combine conditional branches into a larger task to hide the conditional branches and increase the task granularities. An example of hiding conditional branches into tasks is shown in Fig. 1. By hiding conditional branches, the target program becomes simpler with only task blocks, allowing compilers or schedulers to create static scheduling results at compile time. An example of hiding conditional branches into tasks is Macro Task Fusion [14].

After hiding the conditional branches into tasks, the compiler initially estimates the cost of the tasks based on the number of instructions in the tasks. When task execution feedback is applied, the compiler generates profiling codes to gather task execution times of each task. These codes are inserted before and after tasks. Subsequently, the generated profiling and application codes are executed with 1 processor core to collect runtime profile information. The collected information is the average execution time or the worst case execution time of the tasks. For real-time applications, the method utilizes the worst case execution times of the tasks to guarantee the completion of the application by the generated scheduling result.

Once collected, the profile information is fed to the compiler to generate a static scheduling result based on the collected execution times of the tasks, and distributes the tasks to each processor core based on the dependence and the parallelism available among the tasks. Since the process utilizes the actual execution time of the tasks as costs rather than the estimated costs, the compiler can generate an accurate scheduling result. This is critical especially if the application contains conditional branches that change the costs of the tasks. If required, synchronization barriers are inserted before and after tasks if a task has to wait for another task to begin execution.

Additionally, the compiler also creates a mapping result for each variable onto each memory section of the available memory types of the target architecture in a way that require the least latency for all variables for each processor core. Since the scheduling results of the tasks would not change for each invocation, the feedback and the memory mapping process are only applicable to static scheduling schemes.

4.3 Dynamic Scheduling of the OSCAR Compiler

In dynamic scheduling, tasks are dynamically scheduled to idle processor cores at runtime to deal with runtime uncertainties. The main idea of dynamic scheduling is to map executable tasks to available processor cores. By mapping tasks to processor cores on-the-fly, dynamic scheduling can load balance the tasks and prevent processors to become idle.

However, the drawback of dynamic scheduling is the task scheduling overhead. Whenever a processor core becomes available, the core must search for the next ready task of the program. Since the information of the ready tasks is shared among processor cores, the accesses to the tasks incur scheduling overhead during runtime.

In the OSCAR compiler, the tasks of the MTGs are coarse-grain tasks. Utilizing coarse-grain tasks help keep the relative scheduling overhead small compared to the actual task execution time. Moreover, the scheduling scheme by the OSCAR compiler does not utilize OS calls, but rather generates scheduling codes from the MTG for each processor core to reduce scheduling overhead. In other words, the processor cores execute core-exclusive scheduling code and acts like a dynamic scheduler.

The dynamic scheduling algorithm adopted by the OSCAR compiler is the Dynamic-CP algorithm [13]. The Dynamic-CP algorithm assigns tasks to processor cores based on the task's priority calculated during compilation. The priority of the tasks is the estimated longest path length from each task to the exit node in the MTG.

The Dynamic-CP Scheduling algorithm utilizes the scheduling variables shown in Table 1. These scheduling variables are initialized on the initialization step of the algorithm. The Dynamic-CP Scheduling algorithm for multicore processors of the OSCAR compiler is shown below.

Table 1. Scheduling Variables of the Dynamic-CP Scheduling Algorithm

Scheduling variables	Description
Ready queue	A queue for execution ready tasks. Placed on memory which can be accessed by all processor cores
Task queues	Task queues for each processor core which stores execution ready tasks. Placed on memory close to each processor core
Task counters	Counter variables corresponding to each task. Task counters indicate the number of predecessor tasks the task has to wait to become an execution ready task
Ready queue lock variable	Lock variable for the Ready Queue. Processor cores atomically access this variable to perform operations to the Ready Queue
Task lock variables	Lock variables for each task. Processor cores atomically access these variables to update the Task Counters of the corresponding tasks

1. An initialization step is performed by a single processor core to define and set queues, lock variables, and scheduling variables.
2. Tasks that are ready at this point are copied into a common Ready Queue, which would be shared among all processor cores.
3. Each core gathers tasks from the Ready Queue atomically and copies the task into its own core-exclusive Task Queue.
4. Each core executes the tasks in its own Task Queue.
5. Each core atomically decrements the counter variables of the successor tasks of the executed task in the previous step. These counters indicate the number of dependent tasks each successor tasks must wait for in order to be ready. If a successor task's counter becomes 0, that task is atomically moved into the Ready Queue.
6. Each core updates its own Task Queue's pointer to signify the next ready task.
7. Each core performs step 3 to 5 until the Ready Queue becomes empty.

In the parallelized program generated by the OSCAR compiler, the scheduling program codes for each processor cores are inserted between the task codes. The scheduling variables are shared and atomically updated among processor cores to search and gather tasks that are ready to execute.

4.4   Scheduling Overhead of Dynamic Scheduling

Table 2. Scheduling Overheads of the Dynamic-CP Scheduling Algorithm

Scheduling overheads	Description
Initialization	Initialization of synchronization variables, such as Ready Queue, Task Queues, and lock variables (Corresponds to step 1 of the Dynamic-CP Algorithm in Sect. 4.3)
Gettask	Atomically gathers a task from the Ready Queue using lock and unlock operations to the lock variables (Corresponds to step 3 of the Dynamic-CP Algorithm in Sect. 4.3)
SetState	Decrements the successor task's counters, and moves that tasks to the Ready Queue if the counter becomes 0. Locks are required for both decrementing counters and moving tasks (Corresponds to step 5 of the Dynamic-CP Algorithm in Sect. 4.3)
FinishMT	Updates each processor core's Task Queue's pointer (Corresponds to step 6 of the Dynamic-CP Algorithm in Sect. 4.3)

Although dynamic scheduling for multicore processors can load balance the tasks among processor cores, the scheduling overhead during execution becomes a critical bottleneck. Overheads for dynamic scheduling include atomic access to a common ready queue and updates to various scheduling variables. This especially becomes a problem when there are many processor cores waiting for the ready queue or a scheduling variable to become unlocked. In the generated dynamic scheduling routine of the OSCAR compiler, the scheduling overheads are defined in Table 2.

5   Performance Comparison of Dynamic Scheduling and Static Scheduling

In this section, the performance of the two scheduling schemes is shown through evaluation results on a real engine control program written in C provided by an automobile company. The target application includes a 5 ms periodic task, and conditional branches are hidden inside task blocks before parallelizing and generating scheduling results. The scheduling is done with MT granularity. For static scheduling, task execution information of the MTs were used for task execution feedback, and variables were mapped to specific memory locations for each processor core. The scheduling results and codes were generated by the OSCAR automatic parallelizing compiler. The output parallelized C programs were compiled by the Renesas Compiler as the backend compiler, and executed on the Renesas RH850 8-core multicore processor FPGA system.

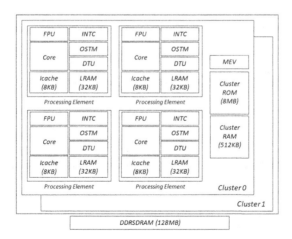

Fig. 2. Architecture diagram of the RH850 multicore processor

5.1   The RH850 Multicore Processor

The Renesas RH850 multicore processor is an embedded processor developed by Renesas Electronics [15]. The RH850 processor is equipped with two SMP clusters, each with 4 processor cores. Each processor core runs with a frequency of 24 MHz. Each processor core has access to a 32 KB local RAM, and each cluster has access to a 512 KB cluster RAM. The processors and the memory structures are connected with a bus. For the evaluation, an FPGA implementation of the RH850 processor was used. A diagram of the RH850 Mutlicore Processor is shown in Fig. 2.

5.2   Comparison of Execution Time and Overhead of Dynamic Scheduling and Static Scheduling

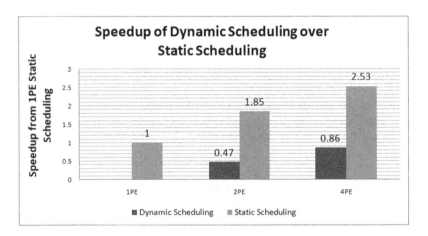

Fig. 3. Speedups of dynamic scheduling over static scheduling on an engine control program

Figure 3 shows the evaluation results of an engine control program on the RH850 processor FPGA system. The results compare executions of the applications that utilize static scheduling and dynamic scheduling. The average clock cycle of the tasks is 607.68 cycles.

The results utilizing dynamic scheduling recorded speedups of 0.47× for 2 cores and 0.86× for 4 cores compared to single core environment. In contrast, the speedups with static scheduling were 1.85× for 2 cores and 2.53× for 4 cores against sequential execution.

With the evaluated RH850 processor environment, static scheduling versions execute in 2.9 ms for 2 cores and 2.1 ms for 4 cores, which meet the 5 ms deadline of the application. However, for dynamic scheduling, the execution takes 11.3 ms for 2 cores and 6.1 ms for 4 cores. Although the 4 core execution shows speedup

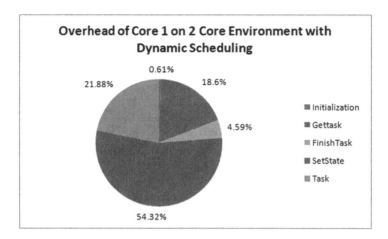

Fig. 4. Overhead of core 1 on 2 core environments utilizing dynamic scheduling

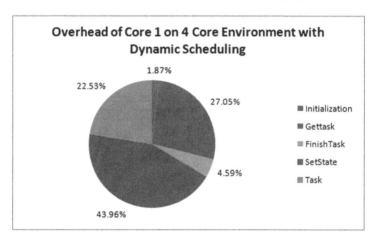

Fig. 5. Overhead of core 1 on 4 core environments utilizing dynamic scheduling

compared to the 2 core execution, the dynamic scheduling versions misses the deadline of the application running on the RH850 environment.

Figure 4 and Fig. 5 show the scheduling overhead of the engine control program of core 1 with dynamic scheduling applied under 2 and 4 core environments. The scheduling overheads such as gathering tasks from the ReadyQueue (Gettask) and decrementing the successor task counters to set the next available task (SetState) are the scheduling codes generated by the OSCAR compiler. The details of the overheads are shown in Sect. 4.4.

With 2 core, the task execution time covers only 21.88% of the entire program execution. For 4 cores, this task execution rate has a similar trend of 22.53%. The Gettask step for 2 cores is 18.6% and increases to 27.05% for 4 cores. By adding more cores to the execution, the cores tries to gain access to the common Ready Queue, creating lock contentions among processor cores and adding more waiting time to the lock access times.

On the other hand, the SetState step overhead reduces from 54.32% for 2 cores to 43.96% for 4 cores. In this step, each core decrements the successor task counters, and copies ready tasks into the Ready Queue atomically. By having more cores, tasks are distributed among each core, thus reducing the number of times each processor core calls the SetState step.

The results also show that the total scheduling overhead of dynamic scheduling covers 78.12% for 2 core environments and 77.47% for 4 core environments. By eliminating scheduling overheads, static scheduling can achieve higher speedup rates for programs that have task granularities with only an average of 607.68 clock cycles compared to its dynamic scheduling counterparts.

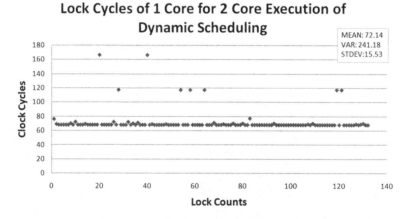

Fig. 6. Lock Cycles of core 1 on 2 core environments utilizing dynamic scheduling

Figure 6 and Fig. 7 show the lock overhead of the Gettask step of core 1 with dynamic scheduling for 2 and 4 core environments. The horizontal axis represents the lock counts, and the vertical axis represents the clock cycles for each acquired lock. The lock cycle average is 72.14 cycles for 2 cores, and 93.3 cycles for 4 cores. However, the number of lock counts is 132 for the 2-core environment, and 80 for the 4-core environment. As more processor cores are executed, the total lock counts reduce, but the clock cycles per lock show an increasing trend. This growth in lock clock cycles from 2 cores to 4 cores comes from the increased lock contentions and the sequential access to the common Ready Queue.

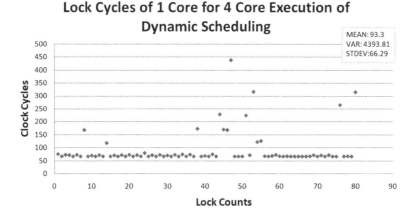

Fig. 7. Lock Cycles of core 1 on 4 core environments utilizing dynamic scheduling

6   Conclusions

This paper compares the performance of the OSCAR multi-grain automatic parallelizing compiler's dynamic and static scheduling schemes on a real engine control program running on an embedded multicore processor implemented on an FPGA. For embedded real-time systems such as cyber physical systems and automobile engine control programs, properties such as conditional branches depending on sensor inputs and vehicle status, tasks with small granularities, and program structures with few loops made dynamic scheduling the only viable option for execution. However, through task execution profile feedback methods that alleviate task execution variances, static scheduling also becomes an effective scheduling method for embedded real-time systems. With static scheduling, scheduling overheads of dynamic scheduling methods such as task ready queue and lock variable updates can be eliminated. To compare the effectiveness of the two scheduling methods, this paper evaluates the OSCAR compiler's dynamic and newly implemented static scheduling scheme on a real engine control program provided by an automobile company, and analyzes the performance of the two schemes. Evaluations were performed on the RH850 multicore processor FPGA system. For the engine control program, static scheduling achieved speedups of 1.85× for 2 cores and 2.53× for 4 cores against sequential execution. In contrast, dynamic scheduling achieved smaller speedups of 0.47× for 2 cores and 0.86× for 4 cores compared to single core execution. The results indicate that static scheduling with execution profile feedback methods is effective for reducing execution times for embedded hard-real time control systems with multicore processors.

Acknowledgments. The authors wish to thank Mr. Hirokazu Komori of Denso Corporation for his cooperation and support for the evaluation application.

References

1. Liu, C.L., Layland, J.W.: Scheduling algorithms for multiprogramming in a hard-real-time environment. J. ACM (JACM) **20**(1), 46–61 (1973)
2. Han, C.-C., Shin, K.G., Jian, W.: A fault-tolerant scheduling algorithm for real-time periodic tasks with possible software faults. IEEE Trans. Comput. **52**(3), 362–372 (2003)
3. Kalogeraki, V., Melliar-Smith, P.M., Moser, L.E.: Dynamic scheduling for soft real-time distributed object systems. In: Proceedings Third IEEE International Symposium on Object-Oriented Real-Time Distributed Computing (ISORC 2000) (Cat. No. PR00607). IEEE (2000)
4. Fohler, G.: Joint scheduling of distributed complex periodic and hard aperiodic tasks in statically scheduled systems. In: Proceedings 16th IEEE Real-Time Systems Symposium. IEEE (1995)
5. Baskaran, M.M., et al.: Compiler-assisted dynamic scheduling for effective parallelization of loop nests on multicore processors. ACM SIGPLAN Not. **44**(4), 219–228 (2009)
6. Gregg, C., et al.: Dynamic heterogeneous scheduling decisions using historical run-time data" In: Workshop on Applications for Multi-and Many-Core Processors (A4MMC) (2011)
7. Hamidzadeh, B., Atif, Y., Lilja, D.J.: Dynamic scheduling techniques for heterogeneous computing systems. Concurr. Pract. Exp. **7**(7), 633–652 (1995)
8. Anson, H.T., et al.: Dynamic scheduling Monte-Carlo framework for multi-accelerator heterogeneous clusters. In: 2010 International Conference on Field-Programmable Technology. IEEE (2010)
9. Kasahara, H., Narita, S.: Practical multiprocessor scheduling algorithms for efficient parallel processing. IEEE Trans. Comput. **11**, 1023–1029 (1984)
10. Kasahara, H., et al.: A multigrain parallelizing compilation scheme for OSCAR (optimally scheduled advanced multiprocessor). In: International Workshop on Languages and Compilers for Parallel Computing (1991)
11. Kimura, K., Kasahara, H.: Near fine grain parallel processing using static scheduling on single chip multiprocessors. In: Innovative Architecture for Future Generation High-Performance Processors and Systems (Cat. No. PR00650). IEEE (1999)
12. Kasahara, H., Honda, H., Narita, S.: Parallel processing of near fine grain tasks using static scheduling on OSCAR (optimally scheduled advanced multiprocessor). In: Supercomputing 1990: Proceedings of the 1990 ACM/IEEE Conference on Supercomputing. IEEE (1990)
13. Kasahara, H., Honda, H., Mogi, A., Ogura, A., Fujiwara, K., Narita, S.: A multigrain parallelizing compilation scheme for OSCAR (optimally scheduled advanced multiprocessor). In: Banerjee, U., Gelernter, D., Nicolau, A., Padua, D. (eds.) LCPC 1991. LNCS, vol. 589, pp. 283–297. Springer, Heidelberg (1992). https://doi.org/10.1007/BFb0038671
14. Umeda, D., et al.: Automatic parallelization of hand written automotive engine control codes using OSCAR compiler. In: 17th Workshop on Compilers for Parallel Computing (CPC2013) (2013)
15. https://www.renesas.com/en-in/products/microcontrollers-microprocessors/v850/v850e2mx/v850e2mx4.html
16. Yoshida, A., Koshizuka, K., Kasahara, H.: Data-localization for Fortran macro-dataflow computation using partial static task assignment. In: Proceedings of the 10th International Conference on Supercomputing. ACM (1996)

PostSLP: Cross-Region Vectorization of Fully or Partially Vectorized Code

Vasileios Porpodas$^{(\boxtimes)}$ and Pushkar Ratnalikar

Intel Corporation, Santa Clara, USA
{vasileios.porpodas,pushkar.v.ratnalikar}@intel.com

Abstract. Modern optimizing compilers rely on auto-vectorization algorithms for generating high-performance code. Both loop and straight-line code vectorization algorithms generate SIMD vector instructions out of scalar code, with no intervention from the programmer.

In this work, we show that the existing auto-vectorization algorithms operate on restricted code regions and therefore are missing out vectorization opportunities by either generating narrower vectors than those possible for the target architecture or are completely failing and leaving some of the code in scalar form. We show the need for a specialized post-processing re-vectorization pass, called PostSLP, that has the ability to span across multiple regions, and to generate more effective vector code. PostSLP is designed to convert already vectorized, or partially vectorized code into wider forms that perform better on the target architecture. We implemented PostSLP in LLVM and our evaluation shows significant performance improvements in SPEC CPU2006.

1 Introduction

Software applications increasingly rely on SIMD vector-hardware for high performance. This reliance on vector-units for performance has also led to the throughput improvements and refinements of vector instruction sets (ISAs), such as the Intel®AVX-512. Software developers have a few options for exploiting the full potential of vector-hardware: They can use target-specific intrinsics, they can call high-performance libraries, or they can use programming models like OpenMP [19]. All of these approaches require additional effort by the software developer, and they can lead to non-portable code or code with non-portable performance. Compiler auto-vectorization aims at automatically converting scalar code into vector code, tuned for the target hardware.

There are two primary approaches for vectorizing scalar code. *Loop vectorization* widens the operations within a loop body [1,8,18], while *SLP vectorization* [10,29] replaces groups of isomorphic instructions with their corresponding vector instructions. Most production compilers including GCC [5] and LLVM [11] implement both.

V. Porpodas—Currently at Google.

© Springer Nature Switzerland AG 2021
S. Pande and V. Sarkar (Eds.): LCPC 2019, LNCS 11998, pp. 15–31, 2021.
https://doi.org/10.1007/978-3-030-72789-5_2

The main motivation for this work is the observation that current Loop and SLP vectorization algorithms miss out vectorization opportunities and, in several cases, generate narrower vectors than are possible. Loop vectorizers, like the one in LLVM, are restricted to vectorizing within a set of consecutive iterations, combining consecutive iterations of a loop to a vector form. It does not check whether these could be combined with instructions from subsequent iterations that belong to the next region. Opportunities like these show up when the loop-body contains instructions of different bit-widths, as explained in Sect. 3.3. The SLP vectorizer also operates on regions which terminate on one end at the *seed* instructions (stores to consecutive memory locations, reduction tree, etc.) and at the other end at either load or gathering points where isomorphism no longer holds. Current approaches do not consider cross-region vectorization, resulting in generation of smaller vectors, often leaving some code in scalar form.

In this paper we introduce a new post-vectorization technique called PostSLP that can successfully vectorize code that is not vectorized by existing state-of-the-art auto-vectorization algorithms. It specifically focuses on vectorization of operations across vectorized regions or at the boundaries of those regions. We show that that PostSLP can successfully form wider vectors out of either partially vectorized code (i.e., code with some scalars and some vectors), or out of fully vectorized code but with narrower vectors. This results in generation of wider vectors out of either partially vectorized code or already vectorized code but with narrower vectors. Our contributions include:

1. Highlighting a major weakness in existing SLP and loop-vectorization approaches with respect to their ability to maximize the vector length.
2. Proposing a new compiler post-vectorization pass, to be placed after both auto-vectorization passes in the pipeline, that vectorizes code (i) cross vector regions horizontally, and (ii) can seamlessly handle both vector and scalar instructions.
3. Evaluating our algorithm in an industrial compiler and showing that the proposed pass pipeline, with PostSLP, can consideralby improve performance of real-world workloads.

2   Background on Auto-vectorization

Auto-Vectorization is a performance-critical optimization in modern compilers. Its goal is to replace scalar code with equivalent vector code, which has higher performance when the target architecture supports SIMD vector units. Modern compilers typically have two approaches to auto-vectorization,

1. Loop-based auto-vectorization - This approach primarily targets loops and depends on dependence analysis to determine legality of the transforms that would generate vector-code that is faster but semantically equivalent to the scalar version. Classical Loop-based auto-vectorization strategies are described in [8], while approaches described in [17,18] are relatively recent advances in auto-vectorization of loops.

2. Straight-line code auto-vectorization - These include SLP-style algorithms, e.g. [10,26,29]. They identify sets of scalar instructions and replace them with vector instructions. These algorithms operate on any straight-line code, anywhere within the program including loop-bodies after loop-optimizations are unable to vectorize the code.

2.1 SLP Vectorization

Since PostSLP is inspired by SLP, we will provide a high-level overview of SLP in this section. SLP (Superword Level Parallelism) performs straight-line code vectorization. It does not require a loop structure, instead it can analyze any straight-line piece of code including loop bodies. It collects instructions that can be grouped together into vectors and replaces them with the corresponding vector instructions. For example, given the code on the left hand side of Fig. 1, SLP will generate the code at the right hand side.

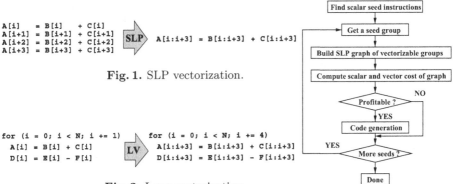

Fig. 1. SLP vectorization.

Fig. 2. Loop-vectorization.

Fig. 3. SLP algorithm

The SLP-algorithm begins by identifying set of *seed* instructions. An overview of the algorithm is shown in Fig. 3. These sets of instructions are good starting point for vectorization, e.g., stores to consecutive memory addresses, or instructions which form reduction trees. More specifically, the set of *seeds* contains at least 2 instructions, which: 1. have the same bit-width and type; 2. have no dependencies among them; 3. access adjacent locations if they are memory instructions, or form a reduction tree (e.g., a reduction tree of additions). The *seed* instructions are the starting point of the vectorizable graph, i.e., they form the root group node.

Using these *seed* instructions as the root node, the compiler follows the use-def chains towards the definitions, looking for instructions that can form more group nodes. This bottom-up approach of building the graph is followed by most state-of-the-art implementations of SLP-algorithms including LLVM and GCC. When it encounters an instruction that cannot be part of the group, it stops extending the group.

After the SLP graph is built, the algorithm performs profitability analysis of the code, by comparing the cost of leaving the graph in scalar form and cost of vectorizing the instructions in the graph. The analysis should also account for execution of additional instructions that have to be generated. An example would be, if the group generated <4 x i32> instructions, but there are external scalar i32 uses, we have to generate extractelement instructions that will move the data from the vectors to the scalars. The accuracy of the target-specific cost-analysis is critical in determining the profitability of the group. Once all the *seed* instructions of the code are exhausted, the process stops.

2.2 Loop Vectorization

Unlike SLP, the loop vectorizer can only operate on loops. It is an inherently different vectorization approach, as it does not work by searching the code for vectorization candidates. Instead, it relies on the semantics of the loop: An instruction in a loop will repeat across the loop iterations. Therefore, the loop vectorizer will widen each instruction in the loop, vectorizing across consecutive loop iterations. Obviously, just like in SLP, vectorization is not always legal, so the loop dependence analysis needs to be queried for the necessary checks. Finally, similarly to SLP, loop vectorization is not always profitable, so the cost model needs to decide on whether the loop should get vectorized or not. In the example of Fig. 2, the statement on the left hand side will be vectorized as shown on the right.

3   Motivation

3.1   Restrictive Regions

The example of Fig. 4 shows how we can improve the code generated by the state-of-the-art compiler with the help of PostSLP.

Given the code of Fig. 4(a), the SLP auto-vectorizer will first notice that the scalar stores A[i+0] and A[i+1] are consecutive, and the same for the stores to A[i+3] and A[i+4]. There is a gap between these two group stores, as there is no store to A[i+2] in the code. Please note that such code is more commonly a result of struct accesses, rather than array accesses, but we are using the array access notation for better readability of the example.

The SLP vectorizer will form two separate groups out of these two sets of consecutive stores, and will therefore operate on these two seeds independently. Each seed group becomes a separate bottom-up region, as shown in Fig. 4(b). Region 1 includes the stores to A[i+0] and A[i+1] and the rest of the definitions, which is the two additions, the two subtractions and the loads from B[i+0], B[i+1], C[i+0], C[i+1] and D[i+0], D[i+1]. Similarly, Region 2 includes the stores to A[i+2], A[i+3], and the rest of the definitions, which is the two additions and the two subtractions, and the loads from B[i+2], B[i+3], C[i+2], C[i+3] and D[i+2], D[i+3].

SLP operates on each region independently, as there are no inter-region dependencies that would allow it to cross. SLP's code generation will first generate vector code for Region 1, and will then generate code for Region 2, as shown

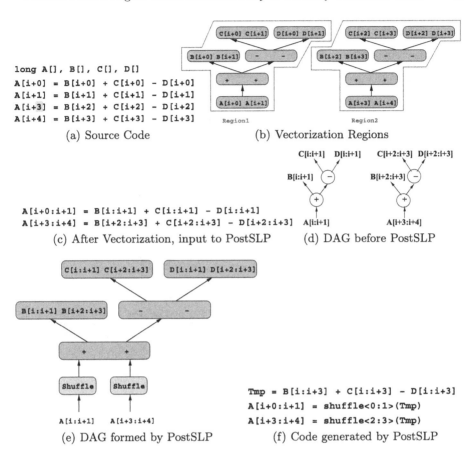

```
long A[], B[], C[], D[]
A[i+0] = B[i+0] + C[i+0] - D[i+0]
A[i+1] = B[i+1] + C[i+1] - D[i+1]
A[i+3] = B[i+2] + C[i+2] - D[i+2]
A[i+4] = B[i+3] + C[i+3] - D[i+3]
```

(a) Source Code

(b) Vectorization Regions

```
A[i+0:i+1] = B[i:i+1] + C[i:i+1] - D[i:i+1]
A[i+3:i+4] = B[i+2:i+3] + C[i+2:i+3] - D[i+2:i+3]
```

(c) After Vectorization, input to PostSLP

(d) DAG before PostSLP

(e) DAG formed by PostSLP

```
Tmp = B[i:i+3] + C[i:i+3] - D[i:i+3]
A[i+0:i+1] = shuffle<0:1>(Tmp)
A[i+3:i+4] = shuffle<2:3>(Tmp)
```

(f) Code generated by PostSLP

Fig. 4. PostSLP properly vectorizes sub-optimal regions.

in Fig. 4(c). The first two statements have been vectorized into one 2-wide vector statement, and the two last statements into a second vector statement.

PostSLP can do better than this. If we take a closer look into the code of Fig. 4(c), and its corresponding DAG of Fig. 4(d), we can see that there is opportunity for further vectorization by combining instructions across regions. The vector loads from B[i:i+1] and B[i+2:i+3] are accessing adjacent memory locations and can therefore be combined into a more efficient 4-wide vector load from B[i:i+3], as shown in Fig. 4(e). Similarly, the loads from C[i:i+1] and C[i+2:i+3], the loads from D[i:i+1], and D[i+2:i+3] and the 2-wide vector additions and subtractions can all be combined into 4-wide operations. Since the 2-wide vector values are still used by the 2-wide stores to array A, we need to add additional shuffle[1] instructions that extract the 2-wide subvectors. The resulting wider (partially 4-wide) optimized code is shown in Fig. 4(f).

---

[1] The shuffle instructions of these examples are similar to LLVM's shufflevector instructions.

3.2   Partially Vectorized Code

In the previous example of Sect. 3.1, we showed that the state-of-the-art algorithms can vectorize with smaller than the ideal vector width, because, by design, they operate on regions that restrict the instructions that get considered for vectorization.

In this example we show that the auto-vectorizer may partially vectorize some code, which is an opportunity for PostSLP to further vectorize the code, as shown in Fig. 5.

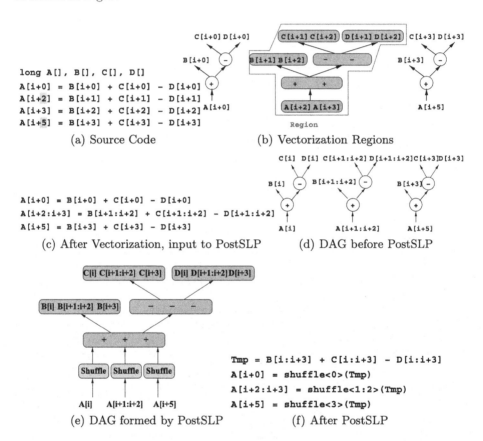

Fig. 5. PostSLP on partially vectorized code.

When the state-of-the-art SLP auto-vectorizer is given the code of Fig. 5(a), it will identify the two stores to A[i+2] and A[i+3] as stores to consecutive addresses and will form a seed group out of them. The stores to A[i] and A[i+5] are accessing memory locations that are not consecutive to the seed group, therefore they are not considered for vectorization. The vectorizer will then from a bottom-up vector region, as shown in Fig. 5(b), which includes the two additions, the two subtractions and the loads from B[i+1], B[i+2], C[i+1], C[i+2] and D[i+1],

D[i+2]. Since there are no more seeds available to the vectorizer, the rest of the code will remain scalar.

The code generator of the vectorization pass will widen each instruction in the region and will generate the code of Fig. 5(c). This code includes two scalar statements A[i+0]=B[i+0]+C[i+0]-D[i+0], A[i+5]=B[i+3]+C[i+3]-D[i+3], and the 2-wide: A[i+2:i+3]=B[i+1:i+2]+C[i+1:i+2]-D[i+1:i+2].

With the help of the PostSLP post-vectorization pass, we can do better. PostSLP figures out that the scalar loads from B[i+0], B[i+1:i+2] and B[i+3] are all consecutive in memory, and will optimize them into a single 4-wide load from B[i+0:i+3], as shown in Fig. 5(e). Similarly, the loads from C[i+0], C[i+1:i+2] and C[i+3] can be combined into a 4-wide load C[i:i+3], the loads from D[i+0], D[i+1:i+2] and D[i+3] are combined into D[i:i+3], and also the additions and subtractions can also be combined into 4-wide versions. The resulting code (Fig. 5(f)) also contains shuffle instructions that extract the scalars or sub-vector elements from the 4-wide vectors.

3.3 Vectorizing for the Widest Data Type

When a loop contains instructions of various bit-widths, for example f32 (float) and f64 (double), the vectorizer may try to vectorize based on the widest data type (in this case f64). This ensures that the widest vector type corresponds to a legal instruction on the target architecture.

Given the code of Fig. 6(a), LLVM's loop vectorizer will vectorize it 4-wide for a 256-bit target architecture, because we can only fit 4 instructions of the widest type. LLVM's vectorizer will also unroll the code 8 times, to help increase ILP, leading to the code of Fig. 6(b).

Now let's take a closer look into the vector widths generated by the loop vectorizer. Figure 6(c) highlights the vector width differences within the for loop code. Some code trees are 256-bit wide (A[...] = B[...] + C[...] + D[...]), while others are 128-bit wide (E[...] = F[...] + G[...] + H[...]), leaving the target vector hardware under-utilized. This is where the PostSLP can improve the computational throughput. By grouping together and re-vectorizing the consecutive 128-bit instructions, it can form wider 256-bit instructions, as shown in Fig. 6(d). All of the resulting code is 256-bit wide, with (A[...] = ...) being 4-wide and (D[...] = ...) being 8-wide. This code will obviously perform faster on the target hardware.

4 PostSLP

This section describes the PostSLP algorithm in detail. It is implemented as a separate compiler pass in LLVM's high level optimizer *opt*. It is placed right after the SLP Vectorizer, in order to post-process the code that has been vectorized by either vectorizer. The algorithm resembles the high level structure of the SLP algorithm, but there are several major differences:

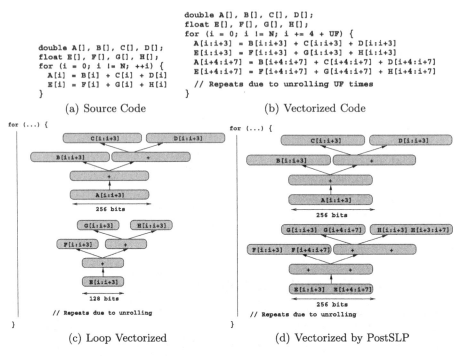

(a) Source Code   (b) Vectorized Code

(c) Loop Vectorized   (d) Vectorized by PostSLP

Fig. 6. PostSLP vectorizes wider than the loop vectorizer.

1. Its groups can contain both scalars and vectors,
2. It can cross vectorization regions horizontally by considering each widening point as a potential seed,
3. It can grow the graph towards either definitions or uses, similarly to [21],
4. Its code generator and scheduler can effectively generate code for any combination of scalars and vectors in the groups.

4.1   Mix of Scalar and Vector Seeds

The algorithm starts by looking for load and store instructions (either scalars or vectors) that are accessing consecutive memory addresses (Listing 1.1 line 6). All mixed groups of scalar and vector loads or stores that can be combined into wider vector loads or stores with vector sizes supported by the target architecture become the seed groups. For example, the two `<2 x i64>` loads from `B[i:i+1]` and `B[i+2:i+3]` of Fig. 4(c) become a valid load group, since a `<4 x i64>` instruction is supported by our target architecture. Similarly, the three loads from `B[i+0]`, `B[i+1:i+2]`, `B[i+3]` of Fig. 5(c) are `i64`, `<2 x i64>` and `i64` which can also be combined into a single `<4 x i64>` vector. Please note that unlike LLVM's SLP algorithm, we are not considering a group of scalar-only instructions as a seed, because we are only interested in groups of vectors or groups of scalars and vectors.

Listing 1.1. Main function of PostSLP.

```
1  // Entry point of the function pass.
2  PostSLP(F) {
3    // Go through all basic blocks.
4    for (BB : F) {
5      // Looks for seed instructions.
6      findConsecutiveLoadsAndStores()
7      // The main function of the pass.
8      buildTreesAndCodegen()
9    }
10 }
11
12 // The main body of the algorithm.
13 buildTreesAndCodegen() {
14   while(SeedGroup=getNextSeedGroup()){
15     if (canSchedule(seedGroup)) {
16       // Build tree.
17       growTree(SeedGroup)
18       // Evaluate cost.
19       Cost = getTreeCost(SeedGroup)
20       // Check profitability
21       if (Cost < Threshold) {
22         // Generate code only if
                profitable.
23         codeGenTree(SeedGroup)
24       }
25     }
26     // Remove seed from worklist
27     removeTreeSeeds(SeedGroup)
28   }
29 }
```

4.2 Tree Creation

Then next step is to build the trees for all seeds and generate code (Listing 1.1 line 8). The body of this function is listed in line 13.

The function keeps iterating until it has processed all seeds (line 14). It grabs a seed group and follows both the uses and definitions of each instruction in the group node, in an attempt to grow the tree with new nodes (line 17), similarly to [21]. The body of this function is listed in Listing 1.2 line 2. The candidates for new group node need to meet certain requirements, which are part of the isCandidate() function call of Listing 1.2 lines 40 and 19, otherwise they get discarded:

- They have to be of the same opcode, for example all additions, or all stores. Some mixing of opcodes could be allowed with minimal modifications (for example additions with subtractions), but it is currently not supported by our implementation.
- They need to have a single use. This requirement guarantees that we are building a tree, not a generic graph, which simplifies code generation. This constraint could also be removed in a future implementation.
- The type of the instructions (e.g., int8, <4 x float>, <2 x i64> etc.) should: (i) have compatible scalar types, and (ii) should be supported by the target architecture for the desired vector length. For example, a <5 x i64> is not supported by a 256-bit AVX2 target.
- The values must not repeat (each instruction is allowed once) and should not be empty.
- The vector size should remain the same across the whole tree. For example, you are not allowed to have both <4 x i32> and <8 x i32> nodes in the tree.
- The instruction's opcode should be one of the white-listed ones. For example, branches are not vectorized.
- The instruction should not be already part of the tree. If it is, then we don't need to extend the tree further, as these nodes have already been visited. In this case, the code generator will either re-use the vector value of the node, or emit a **shuffle** operation if needed.

In addition to these requirements, it must be legal for the candidates to be scheduled together back-to-back without violating any dependencies. Otherwise vectorizing the instructions would break the program semantics. This is done with the help of an instruction scheduler, being called in Listing 1.2 lines 26 and 26. This is a list-scheduler capable of operating on groups of scalars, vectors, or a mix of the two. It is designed to operate on a dependence DAG that gets built on-the-fly for the instructions within an instruction window that includes all the instructions in the tree so far, including the candidate group.

This whole process of (i) forming a group, (ii) checking its eligibility and legality, and (iii) attempting to grow the tree towards the definitions and uses, repeats until there are no more candidates to add to the tree.

Examples of these trees are shown in Sect. 3. Figures 4(e) and 5(e) show the group trees formed for the examples of Sects. 3.1 and 3.2 respectively. The green nodes represent the instructions that will be grouped together into 4-wide vectors, while the non-colored nodes at the root of the tree show the instructions that will not be modified by PostSLP. Each narrower (scalar or narrower vector) store instruction gets its input through the shuffle nodes (shown in yellow)[2]. These shuffle instructions create sub-vectors out of the larger input vectors. For example, the the left hand side shuffle of Fig. 4(e) reads a `<4 x i64>` input and generates a `<2 x i64>` output that feeds into the `A[i:i+1]` store.

4.3   Profitability

Now that the tree has been completed, we have to check whether vectorizing the tree is profitable (Listing 1.1 line 19) before we generate code. To this end we need to compare the initial cost of the code against the new one, after Post-SLP. The cost calculation is done by querying the TTI cost model of LLVM for each individual instruction and summing each individual cost. The profitability function we use considers the following: If the projected cost of the code after PostSLP is less than the original cost (line 21), then PostSLP is considered profitable and we proceed with code generation (line 23). Since PostSLP is capable of handling any mix of scalar and vector instructions, it is particularly important in our case to model the cost of the extraction and insertion from/to vectors or scalars correctly.

4.4   Code Generation (Scheduling and Widening)

The code generation step modifies the IR (Listing 1.1 line 23). It performs two distinct operations.

- The first one performs instruction scheduling on the tree, using the same algorithm as in the tree-building phase (as discussed in Sect. 4.2). This step will always succeed (i.e., we will not find grows that are illegal to schedule), since

---

[2] In LLVM, we use either the `shufflevector` instructions when the output is a vector instruction, or `extractelement` when the output is scalar.

we have already checked that each individual group node can be scheduled while building the tree itself (Listing 1.2 lines 26 and 47). This step makes sure that the instructions in each group node are scheduled back-to-back, and are placed in the same order as when the dependencies where checked during grow_tree().
- The second part is instruction widening, which replaces the individual instructions in each group node with their widened counterpart. This is performed in a reverse-post-order traversal of the tree (top-down). A vector instruction is generated with a bit-width equal to the sum of the individual instructions in the group node. For example, if the group contained two i32 instructions and one <2 x i32>, the resulting vector instruction will be of <4 x i32> type. The newly generated vector instruction is then emitted in the code and the corresponding group instructions are erased. This new instruction gets its operands from its immediate predecessors in the use-def chains, as they have already been widened by the algorithm, because of the top-down traversal. Finally, for the external uses and operands to the vectorized instructions, the appropriate vector extract/insert instructios get generated using either insertelement, extractelement, or shufflevector instructions.

Once widening is performed, the initial group and any other groups that belong in the group tree get removed from the worklist, as we are done working with it (line 27). Finally, the algorithm repeats until no more groups are left in the worklist (line 14).

5   Results

5.1   Experimental Setup

We implemented PostSLP in the development branch of LLVM 7 as a separate compiler pass. The pass executes after LLVM's SLP vectorizer pass. We compiled the workloads with the following configurations: *O3:* which corresponds to *-O3* which has all vectorizers enabled by default, and *O3+PostSLP:* which is *-O3* with the PostSLP pass also enabled.

All C/C++ workloads were compiled with clang/clang++ using *-O3 - march=skylake -mtune=skylake*. The target platform is a Linux-4.9.0, glibc-2.23 based system with an Intel® Core™ i5-6440HQ CPU and 8 GB RAM. We evaluated our approach on unmodified SPEC CPU2006. We also extracted unmodified kernels from SPEC CPU2006 to help focus on code that triggers PostSLP. For all results, we report the average of 10 executions, after skipping the first warm-up run. The error bars show the standard deviation. The profitability scores we report are based on LLVM's TTI costs (see Sect. 4).

5.2   Performance of Full Benchmarks

We measured the performance of full CPU2006 benchmarks and we report the results in Fig. 7(a). The results are normalized to O3. Please note that we are

Listing 1.2. PostSLP grow tree function

```
1  // Entry point for growTree function
2  growTree(SeedGroup) {
3    growTreeRec(SeedGroup)
4  }
5  // Recursion towards Defs and Uses
6  growTreeRec(Group) {
7    Group.Users = getUsers(Group)
8    if (Group.Users)
9      growTreeRec(Group.Users)
10   Group.Operands = getOperands(Group)
11   if (Group.Operands)
12     growTreeRec(Group.Operands)
13 }
14 // Appends users to Group if possible
15 getUsers(Group) {
16   for (Instr in Group.getInstrs()){
17     for (User in Instr.getUsers()) {
18       OperandIdx = getOperandIdx(User,
                                    Instr)
19       if (! isCandidate(User)) {
20         Group.setMustScatterUsers()
21         return
22       }
23     }
24     Users.push_back(User);
25     NewGroup = createNewGroup(Users)
26     if (! tryScheduleGroup(NewGroup)) {
27       delete NewGroup
28       Group.setMustScatterUsers()
29       return
30     }
31     Group.setUser(NewGroup)
32     NewGroup.setOperand(OperandIdx,
                          Group)
33   }
34 }
35 // Try append operands to Group
36 getOperands(Group) {
37   for (Instr in Group.getInstrs()) {
38     for (Oprnd in Instr.getOperands()){
39       OprndIdx = getOperandIdx(Instr,
                                  Oprnd)
40       if (! isCandidate(Oprnd)) {
41         Group.setMustGatherOperand(
                                  OprndIdx)
42         return
43       }
44       Operands.push_back(Oprnd)
45     }
46     NewGroup = createNewGroup(Operands)
47     if (! tryScheduleGroup(NewGroup)) {
48       delete NewGroup
49       Group.setMustGatherOperand(
                                  OprndIdx)
50       continue;
51     }
52     Group.setOperand(OprndIdx, NewGroup)
53     NewGroup.setUser(Group);
54   }
55 }
```

Table 1. Kernels used in our evaluation.

Kernel	Benchmark	Filename:Line
433-su3-rdot	433.milc	su3_rdot.c:10
433-realtrace-su3	433.milc	realtr.c:14
483-gs-compute-closest-cw	482.sphinx3	gs.c:214
482-vector-dist-maha	482.sphinx3	vector.c:266
482-vector-dist-eucl	482.sphinx3	vector.c:238
motiv-regions	Section 3.1	Figure 4(a)
motiv-scalars	Section 3.2	Figure 5(a)
motiv-widest	Section 3.3	Figure 6(a)

only showing the results for those workloads that triggered PostSLP, the rest of them perform identically to O3. There are three benchmarks that perform significantly better than O3, namely 444.namd (about 0.4%), 464.h264ref (about 2.5%), and 482.sphinx3 (about 1.1%).

These are very significant performance improvements given that our baseline is an industrial strength compiler, that has been optimized and tuned for SPEC benchmarks over several years. Moreover, our comparison is a fair one, as PostSLP is designed within the constraints of production compilers: i.e., strict constraints in space and time complexity.

For the remaining workloads, O3+PostSLP performs practically identical to O3, with the performance differences being within the noise margin.

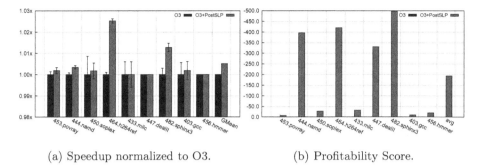

(a) Speedup normalized to O3.   (b) Profitability Score.

Fig. 7. Full benchmark results.

The profitability score is determined statically by the sum of $CostAfter - CostBefore$ for all trees formed by PostSLP. As mentioned in Sect. 4.3, non profitable trees are discarded by the algorithm and are not considered for code generation. Therefore, the profitability score for any workload is always greater or equal to zero. The more negative the score the better, as negative values correspond to cost savings. The profitability calculation makes use of LLVM's TTI cost modeling API for computing the costs, but as a rule of thumb, a simple fast instruction has a cost of 1.

Figure 7(b) reports the accumulated profitability score across each benchmark, as reported by the PostSLP pass. This is a static metric that reports how much more profitable PostSLP was compared to O3. All of the benchmarks that show a significant performance improvement, namely 444.namd, 464.h264ref and 482.sphinx3, also show a large improvement in profitability score. However, other benchmarks like 447.dealII, do not show similar overall speedups, even though their profitability score is quite considerable. This is not a surprising outcome, as the static profitability score does not necessarily correlate strongly with performance improvements. For example, it is possible that all of the profitability improvements correspond to code sections with very small execution time coverage.

5.3   Kernels

To help show that PostSLP has a wider applicability and can help improve real code regardless of its performance impact across a full benchmark, we extracted some functions from CPU 2006 where PostSLP triggered , as shown in Table 1. We reported the execution speedup normalized to O3 in Fig. 8(a). We also included the motivating examples of Sects. 3.1 and 3.2 for completeness.

Since these are whole unmodified functions, the performance improvements we are getting depend on the coverage of the code that got widened by Post-SLP compared to the rest of the code in the function. Therefore the performance improvements vary considerably across kernels. It is interesting to note that some of the kernels show some very high performance improvements (e.g., the 433.milc derived ones), while the full benchmark they got extracted from, shows no performance difference. This shows that PostSLP does have a wider applicability, regardless of its impact on full spec benchmarks.

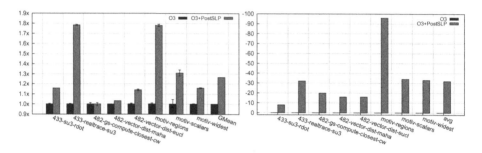

(a) Speedup Normalized to O3.   (b) Profitability Scores of Kernels.

Fig. 8. Kernel results.

Now, let's consider the profitability scores of Fig. 8(b). This plot does indeed show that PostSLP widening improves the profitability of the code, according to the compiler's cost model. However, if we contrast this plot against the results in Fig. 8(a), we can see that cost improvements do not necessarily result in actual performance improvements. For example, 482-gs-compute-closest-cw, barely shows any performance improvements, even though it has a healthy profitability score of −20. This is primarily because, in our experience, LLVM's TTI API is overly conservative in reporting costs and is rather oblivious of low-level optimizations which are possible in the back-end.

5.4   Compilation Time

Our PostSLP algorithm introduces a new compilation pass in the pipeline. This introduces a very small compilation time overhead in the general case when compiling large benchmarks. The worst case scenario is when the PostSLP pass gets activated for the main bulk of the workload being compiled. We measured a worst-case compilation-time increase of 14% in a couple of kernels, with a geomean increase of about 8%, as shown in Fig. 9. Please note that when compiling full benchmarks, the compilation time overhead is barely noticeable.

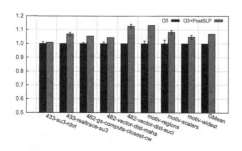

Fig. 9. Compilation time of Kernels.

6   Related Work

6.1   Loop Auto-vectorization

Auto-vectorization techniques have traditionally focused on vectorizing loops [32]. These loop-based algorithms work by fusing consecutive loop iterations into a single vectorized iteration in a strip-mining fashion, widening each scalar instruction in the loop body to work on vector elements. Early works of Allen and Kennedy on the Parallel Fortran Converter [1,2], the works of Kuck et al. [9], Wolfe [31], and Davies et al. [4] solve many of the fundamental problems of loop vectorizers. Since then, numerous other improvements have been proposed in the literature and implemented in production compilers, e.g. [3,17,27].

Whole function vectorization has been the focus of Karrenberg et al. [7]. Masten et al. [14] propose a loop vectorization-based technique for whole function vectorization.

6.2   SLP Auto-vectorization

SLP Vectorization was first proposed by Larsen and Amarasinghe [10]. It is a complementary technique to loop vectorization which focuses on vectorizing straight-line code instead of loops. Straight-line code vectorization algorithms have been implemented in compilers such as GCC [5] and LLVM, with bottom-up SLP (Rosen et al. [29]) being one that is widely adopted due to its low run-time overhead while still providing good vectorization coverage.

Since its conception, several improvements have been proposed for straight-line-code vectorization in general [6,12,15,20,30]. The widely used bottom-up SLP algorithm has also been improved in several ways [21–26]. Combining loop-vectorization and SLP has been explored by [29] and [34], while [33] enables SIMD widths that are not supported by the target hardware. Recently Rocha et al. [28] describe an SLP-aware loop-unrolling technique that improves the effectiveness of the vectorizer by force-unrolling the code when SLP can successfully vectorize it.

6.3   Re-vectorization

Re-vectorization has recently become the focus of research papers that attempt to improve the performance of legacy binaries [13], or legacy hand-vectorized source code [16]. Both approaches implement an SLP-style algorithm along with specific transformations for their domain, e.g., shuffle optimization, unrolling.

PostSLP, on the other hand, is designed to improve auto-vectorization in the common compilation flow of production compilers. To our knowledge, it is the first work that addresses the issues related to vectorization regions and partially vectorized code. PostSLP is a post-processing pass, placed after both vectorizers in the compilation pipeline. It optimizes the sub-optimally vectorized code, by operating across regions, combining both scalars and vectors, further widening instructions that were either completely missed or were sub-optimally vectorized by the production loop and SLP vectorizers.

7 Conclusion

We presented PostSLP, a novel post-processing cross-region vectorization pass that aims at improving the performance of code that has either been partially vectorized, or fully vectorized but with a sub-optimal vector width. It is capable of combining vector instructions, scalar instructions or any mix of the two, generated by either the loop or the SLP vectorization passes. As a result, Post-SLP can generate more efficient, wider vector instructions out of smaller vectors or scalars generated by the prior vectorization passes. We have implemented PostSLP in LLVM and have evaluated its effectiveness on SPEC CPU2006. The results show improved performance on real-world code with a minimal increase in compilation time.

References

1. Allen, J.R., Kennedy, K.: PFC: A program to convert Fortran to parallel form. Technical report 82-6, Rice University (1982)
2. Allen, J.R., Kennedy, K.: Automatic translation of Fortran programs to vector form. TOPLAS (1987)
3. Anderson, A., Malik, A., Gregg, D.: Automatic vectorization of interleaved data revisited. ACM TACO **12**, 1–25 (2015)
4. Davies, J., et al.: The KAP/S-1- an advanced source-to-source vectorizer for the S-1 Mark IIa supercomputer. In: ICPP (1986)
5. GCC: GNU compiler collection (2015). http://gcc.gnu.org
6. Huh, J., Tuck, J.: Improving the effectiveness of searching for isomorphic chains in superword level parallelism. In: MICRO (2017)
7. Karrenberg, R., Hack, S.: Whole-function vectorization. In: CGO (2011)
8. Kennedy, K., Allen, J.R.: Optimizing Compilers for Modern Architectures: A Dependence-Based Approach. Morgan Kaufmann Publishers Inc., Burlington (2001)
9. Kuck, D.J., et al.: Dependence graphs and compiler optimizations. In: POPL (1981)
10. Larsen, S., Amarasinghe, S.: Exploiting superword level parallelism with multimedia instruction sets. In: PLDI (2000)
11. Lattner, C., Adve, V.: LLVM: a compilation framework for lifelong program analysis transformation. In: CGO (2004)
12. Liu, J., Zhang, Y., Jang, O., Ding, W., Kandemir, M.: A compiler framework for extracting superword level parallelism. In: PLDI (2012)
13. Liu, Y.-P., et al.: Exploiting asymmetric SIMD register configurations in ARM-to-x86 dynamic binary translation. In: PACT (2017)
14. Masten, M., Tyurin, E., Mitropoulou, K., Saito, H., Garcia, E.: Function/Kernel vectorization via loop vectorizer. In: LLVM-HPC (2018)
15. Mendis, C., Amarasinghe, S.: goSLP: globally optimized superword level parallelism framework. In: OOPSLA (2018)
16. Mendis, C., Jain, A., Jain, P., Amarasinghe, S.: Revec: program rejuvenation through revectorization. In: CC (2019)
17. Nuzman, D., Rosen, I., Zaks, A.: Auto-vectorization of interleaved data for SIMD. In: PLDI (2006)
18. Nuzman, D., Zaks, A.: Outer-loop vectorization: revisited for short SIMD architectures. In: PACT (2008)

19. OpenMP Application Program Inteface. https://www.openmp.org/specifications/
20. Park, Y., Seo, S., Park, H., Cho, H., Mahlke, S.: SIMD defragmenter: efficient ILP realization on data-parallel architectures. In: ASPLOS (2012)
21. Porpodas, V.: SuperGraph-SLP auto-vectorization. In: PACT (2017)
22. Porpodas, V., Jones, T.M.: Throttling automatic vectorization: when less is more. In: PACT (2015)
23. Porpodas, V., et al.: PSLP: padded SLP automatic vectorization. In: CGO (2015)
24. Porpodas, V., Rocha, R.C., et al.: Super-node SLP: optimized vectorization for code sequences containing operators and their inverse elements. In: CGO (2019)
25. Porpodas, V., Rocha, R.C.O., Góes, L.F.W.: VW-SLP: auto-vectorization with adaptive vector width. In: PACT (2018)
26. Porpodas, V., Rocha, R.C.O., Góes, L.F.W.: Look-ahead SLP: auto-vectorization in the presence of commutative operations. In: CGO (2018)
27. Ren, G., et al.: Optimizing data permutations for SIMD devices. In: PLDI (2006)
28. Rocha, R.C.O., et al.: Vectorization-aware loop unrolling with seed forwarding. In: CC (2020)
29. Rosen, I., et al.: Loop-aware SLP in GCC. In: GCC Developers' Summit (2007)
30. Shin, J., Hall, M., Chame, J.: Superword-level parallelism in the presence of control flow. In: CGO (2005)
31. Wolfe, M.: Vector optimization vs. vectorization. In: Houstis, E.N., Papatheodorou, T.S., Polychronopoulos, C.D. (eds.) ICS 1987. LNCS, vol. 297, pp. 309–315. Springer, Heidelberg (1988). https://doi.org/10.1007/3-540-18991-2_18
32. Wolfe, M.J.: High Performance Compilers for Parallel Computing. Addison-Wesley, Boston (1995)
33. Zhou, H., Xue, J.: A compiler approach for exploiting partial SIMD parallelism. TACO **13**, 1–26 (2016)
34. Zhou, H., Xue, J.: Exploiting mixed SIMD parallelism by reducing data reorganization overhead. In: CGO (2016)

FLARE: Flexibly Sharing Commodity GPUs to Enforce QoS and Improve Utilization

Wei Han[1(✉)], Daniel Mawhirter[1], Bo Wu[1], Lin Ma[2], and Chen Tian[2]

[1] Colorado School of Mines, Golden, USA
{whan,dmawhirt}@mymail.mines.edu, bwu@mines.edu
[2] Huawei US R&D Center, Santa Clara, USA
{lin.ma,chen.tian}@huawei.com

Abstract. A modern GPU integrates tens of streaming multi-processors (SMs) on the chip. When used in data centers, the GPUs often suffer from under-utilization for exclusive access reservations, hence demanding multitasking (i.e., co-running applications) to reduce the total cost of ownership. However, latency-critical applications may experience too much interference to meet Quality-of-Service (QoS) targets. In this paper, we propose a software system, FLARE, to spatially share commodity GPUs between latency-critical applications and best-effort applications to enforce QoS as well as maximize overall throughput. By transforming the kernels of best-effort applications, FLARE enables both SM partitioning and thread block partitioning within an SM for co-running applications. It uses a microbenchmark guided static configuration search combined with online dynamic search to locate the optimal (near-optimal) strategy to partition resources. Evaluated on 11 benchmarks and 2 real-world applications, FLARE improves hardware utilization by an average of 1.39X compared to the preemption-based approach.

1 Introduction

Datacenters are gaining increasing popularity as they significantly reduce the computation and storage cost for clients. However, the tremendous up-front investment in servers accounts for 50–70% of the total cost of ownership [4]. The problem is exacerbated by the wide adoption of expensive high-end GPUs to leverage the massive parallelism to accelerate various types of workloads, such as deep neural networks and graph analytics [11,28]. Unfortunately, while CPU utilization in servers is already low (ranging from 10% to 70% [18]), GPU under-utilization is more severe due to the complex dynamic behaviors of GPU applications [8].

A fundamental cause of hardware under-utilization is the strict QoS requirements of latency-critical (LC) applications (e.g., web services and deep learning inference). To meet the QoS target, a conservative scheduler will reserve the entire server for the LC application. A promising solution is multitasking, which

W. Han and D. Mawhirter—Equal contribution.

© Springer Nature Switzerland AG 2021
S. Pande and V. Sarkar (Eds.): LCPC 2019, LNCS 11998, pp. 32–48, 2021.
https://doi.org/10.1007/978-3-030-72789-5_3

co-locates best-effort (BE) applications together with the LC application to share the same server and hence the GPUs. However, the BE application may interfere with the LC application, resulting in unacceptable performance degradation for LC requests. Notably, when both co-running applications heavily use the GPU, the slowdown of the LC requests could be over $10\times$ [31].

As far as we know, Baymax [8] and Laius [32] are the only software systems that enforce QoS for shared GPU systems. Baymax assumes that the GPU is a non-preemptable processor and hence a long-running kernel reserves the entire GPU. However, a high-end GPU has tens of streaming multi-processors (SMs), which cannot be fully utilized by a single kernel. As we show in Sect. 2, GPU kernels may scale poorly in terms of SMs or threads within an SM. Laius takes advantage of the hardware-based partitioning capability but is limited to SM-level partitioning, therefore failing to addressing the scalability issues within SMs.

In this paper, we aim at improving GPU utilization by flexibly partitioning the abundant computational resource between co-running BE and LC applications. We assume that the source code of BE is available and an BE application is constantly running on the GPU when the LC application arrives. Instead of only coordinating GPU kernel executions, we allow a BE application to yield just enough resource to meet the QoS target of the LC kernel. To achieve this goal, we face multiple challenges. First, while one only needs to consider a 1-D resource space for CPU core allocation [20], the GPU has many SMs and each SM concurrently runs several groups of threads (i.e., thread blocks), thus forming a 2-D resource space. Second, since the GPU by default runs the launched kernels in an FIFO manner, a kernel from the BE application may use up all SMs, thus blocking the kernel of the LC application. We need to design a software mechanism to enable the two kernels to run simultaneously on different parts of the GPU. Third, the co-running kernels interfere with each other on a variety of hardware resources, including shared interconnect, L1 cache, L2 cache, streaming cores, and device memory. Therefore, quantifying the performance degradation given a partitioning configuration is difficult. Finally, we try to enforce QoS and maximize utilization which are two conflicting goals. Specifically, by allocating more resources to the LC application, we have a better chance to meet the QoS goal. But it probably reduces the overall throughput at the same time.

To overcome the challenges and improve utilization of *commodity* GPUs, we design and implement a software system, FLARE, which enables flexible GPU sharing, meets QoS goals for LC applications, and maximizes throughput for BE applications. FLARE transforms the kernel of the BE application to be able to yield k ($1 \leq k \leq MaxBlksPerSM$) thread blocks on a subset of n SMs ($1 \leq n \leq MaxSMs$). The pair n_k is called a configuration. The threads of the LC kernel can then be scheduled to run on the released hardware resource. The key novelty of FLARE is its intelligent runtime to quickly figure out the optimal GPU resource partitioning strategy by avoiding pitfalls from two popular existing approaches as follows. The performance model-based approach uses offline training to predict the best configuration [8,33], but its accuracy may suffer from input sensitivity and complicated hardware contention. On the other hand, a pure dynamic approach (e.g., online profiling and adjusting [19,34]) may not be responsive enough. Worse, it may explore detrimental configurations that lead to hampered QoS or hardware under-utilization. FLARE employs a hybrid methodology. It uses microbenchmarks to characterize the co-run performance degradation space, so given two co-running kernels it quickly predicts an initial configuration to use. Then FLARE leverages the degradation space to dynamically search for the optimal configuration. We show in comprehensive experiments that FLARE outperforms the preemption-based approach while satisfying the QoS targets.

2   Background

Driven by the demand for high-throughput capabilities, the GPU has evolved to leverage massive parallelism with a many-core design to provide huge computational throughput and memory bandwidth. The cores of NVIDIA GPUs are called Streaming Multiprocessors, each of which can simultaneously host multiple active thread blocks (also known as Cooperative Thread Array) contexts. The number of active thread blocks that an SM can host depends on the hardware resource of the SM (i.e., register file size) and the resource requirement of the thread blocks. When a thread block runs on an SM, it is executed in a SIMD fashion with 32 threads (called a warp) at a time.

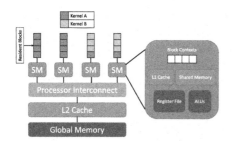

Fig. 1. Graphics Processing Unit (GPU)

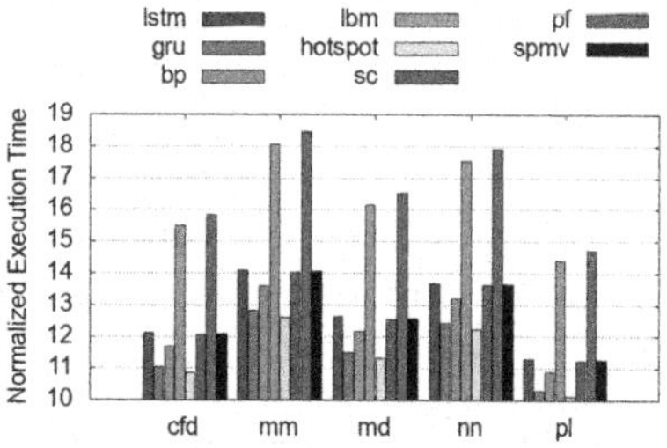

Fig. 2. QoS violation for co-runs when the GPU is unpreemptable.

Conceptually, all the thread blocks of the launched kernels wait in a queue. The hardware implements a FIFO thread block scheduler, which dispatches the waiting thread blocks to SMs as long as the available hardware resource can satisfy the resource demands. Hence, a kernel's thread blocks are guaranteed to be scheduled first before any other thread block of a later launched kernel.

Starting from the Fermi architecture, NVIDIA GPUs support concurrent kernel execution. Later, NVIDIA introduced the Multi-Process Service (MPS), which enables kernels from different applications to be executed simultaneously on the same GPU. However, due to significant context switch overhead, the GPU hardware does not support temporal core sharing. Consequently, the co-running kernels spatially share a GPU only when the earlier launched kernel cannot consume all the computational resources. Due to the organization of the hardware, Fig. 1 shows an interesting resource sharing scenario. The co-running thread blocks from both kernel A and B on the same SM compete to use the L1 cache and ALUs and all the currently running thread blocks contend for use of the interconnect, L2 cache and global memory bandwidth.

3   Motivation and Challenges

3.1   QoS Issues of Non-preemptable Kernels

To understand the detrimental effect of non-preemptable kernel execution on QoS violation, we run 40 pairs of kernels (details in Sect. 5) on an NVIDIA Volta GPU. Figure 2 shows the performance degradation of the LC kernels when they are immediately launched after the BE kernels shown on the X axis. Observe that QoS is violated for all the pairs even if the QoS target is as large as 10 times of the corresponding solo-run execution time when sharing is disabled. This is because the entire time the BE kernel is finishing normally, the LC kernel has to wait in queue, a clearly unacceptable solution.

3.2   Scalability Issues of Preemption-Based Solutions

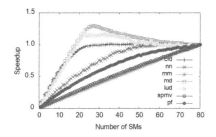

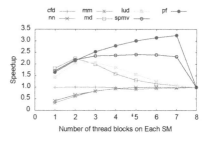

Fig. 3. Solo-run scalability with respect to the number of SMs

Fig. 4. Solo-run scalability with respect to the number of thread blocks on each SM

Recent work, such as FLEP [31] and Effisha [6], has proposed low-overhead software-based mechanisms to realize preemption on GPUs. With the capability of preemption, we can easily address the QoS issue by preempting the BE kernel whenever an LC arrives. However, the drawback of preemption is that LC kernels monopolize all the available resources regardless of how efficiently it will utilize them. We show the scalability of 7 benchmarks in Fig. 3 and Fig. 4 when we respectively increase the number of SMs and the number of thread blocks within each SM. Since the default scheduling uses up the SMs and thread blocks, the results show that less resource does not necessarily lead to worse performance. Moreover, different applications may have different scaling characteristics. For example, MM (matrix multiplication) prefers more computational resources, while MD's performance culminates with a small portion of the resources (i.e., 26 SMs or 2 thread blocks per SM). Therefore, we need an approach to appropriately partition the GPU to simultaneously corun kernels for the optimal utilization.

3.3   Spatial Co-running and Its Challenges

In order to run a pair of BE and LC application simultaneously, we need a mechanism for the BE application to be able to yield resources (entire SMs or thread block slots of SMs) to the LC application. Though the reduced resource availability and introduced contention cause slowdown for both kernels, we observe such a mechanism allows one to produce a better trade-off between QoS guarantees and overall GPU utilization.

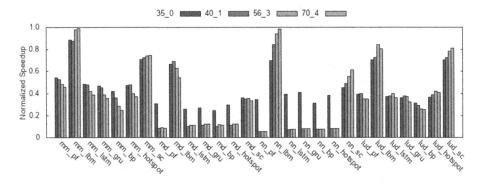

Fig. 5. LC kernel speedup with 280 thread blocks being allocated under different configurations

To understand the complexity of the interference due to co-running, we run 40 kernel pairs with 280 thread blocks allocated to each of the LC kernels. Figure 5 shows the performance degradation of the LC kernels with four different configurations. On the X axis, the notation A_B represents a BE kernel A co-running with a LC kernel B. Observe that the slowdown varies significantly across LC kernels or even the co-runs of the same LC kernel with different BE kernels. Figure 6 reports the overall throughput improvement (defined in Sect. 5) and demonstrates the difficulty of predicting the best configuration for the co-runs.

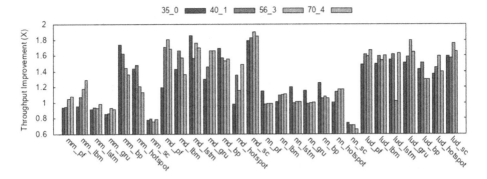

Fig. 6. Overall throughput improvement under different configurations

4 FLARE

4.1 System Overview

The goal of FLARE is to enable flexible sharing between LC and BE applications and optimize resource partitioning to enforce QoS as well as maximize overall throughput of co-run pairs. FLARE addresses the trade-off between latency and throughput based on offline and online dynamic search algorithms to quickly figure out an optimized co-running configuration. The system, as shown in Fig. 7, consists of the following three components:

Kernel Transformation. FLARE transforms the BE application to allow it to yield an arbitrary number of thread blocks on each SM. Note that we assume no access to the source code of the kernels of LC applications submitted by users, but the LC kernels can automatically use the yielded resources thanks to Nvidia's support of concurrent kernel executions.

Initial Configuration Selection. To address the problem of unavailable LC applications for offline profiling, FLARE co-runs pairs of diverse microbenchmarks with many resource sharing configurations to characterize the performance degradation space. Based on the characterization, when the LC application arrives, FLARE only profiles its kernel invocation once to quickly model the performance degradation for both the LC and BE applications. FLARE then selects an initial configuration to spatially co-run the applications.

Online Refinement. During the co-running, FLARE collects the performance degradation timing data as feedback to dynamically adapt the next configuration to use. By using the co-run degradation data of microbenchmarks, FLARE intelligently skips configurations and quickly reaches the optimal configuration to use for spatial co-running.

4.2   Kernel Transformation: Enabling Spatial Sharing

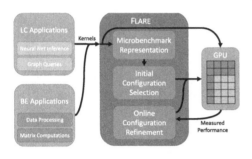

Kernel transformation enables the BE application to yield resources when a LC application is scheduled to the same GPU. The design, inspired by SM-centric transformation [30] and FLEP [31], runs just enough thread blocks to occupy the whole GPU. Specifically, given that a GPU has N SMs and each SM runs up to K thread blocks,

Fig. 7. The FLARE system

FLARE schedules $N \times K$ thread blocks, each running the algorithm described in Fig. 8a. Every thread block first invokes $get\_sm\_id()$ to obtain the ID of the host SM and then $atomic\_get\_blk\_id()$ to get its unique block ID on that SM, starting from 0. Each thread block stays in a while loop as long as there are tasks left to execute. At the beginning of each iteration, each thread block gets a unique ID. If a thread block ID is larger than the specified value $num\_blks[sm\_id]$, which is set by CPU, it means that the thread block needs to be yielded. To control the spinning overhead, we follow the approached proposed in [31] to control the granularity of the tasks. Once the resource of the yielded thread blocks is released, the kernel of the LC application can acquire the resource and start co-running. After the LC application is finished, the BE application is notified and launches the same number of thread blocks as yielded to fully occupy the GPU again.

Although the algorithm enables arbitrary ways to yield thread blocks, it requires the CPU and GPU to share the array num_blks, containing num_SMs elements, which may incur non-trivial communication overhead when num_SMs is large for high-end GPUs. To address this problem, FLARE uses the algorithm shown in Fig. 8b to sacrifice flexibility for reduced overhead. In this new design, FLARE asks the BE kernel to yield the same number of thread blocks (i.e., k) on a subset of SMs (i.e., n). Since thread blocks of a kernel have similar behaviors and the SMs are homogeneous, we expect this simplified design to perform as well as the more flexible one.

```
//Run by each thread block of BE kernel   //n: number of SMs to yield blocks
//Global array num_blks[num_SMs]          //k: number of blocks to yield
BE_Kernel(...) {                          BE_Kernel(...) {
    sm_id = get_sm_id();                      sm_id = get_sm_id();
    blk_id = atomic_get_blk_id();             blk_id = atomic_get_blk_id();
    while(task_queue is non-empty) {          while(task_queue is non-empty) {
        if( blk_id > num_blks[sm_id]) quit;       if( sm_id < n && blk_id > num_blks[sm_id]) quit;
        else {                                    else {
            task = pull_task();                       task = pull_task();
            execute(task);                            execute(task);
}}}                                       }}}
```

(a)   Arbitrary   thread   (b) Less flexible thread block yield-
block yielding.   ing to reduce overhead.

Fig. 8. Transformed BE kernels to allow spatial co-run.

4.3   Initial Configuration Selection: Microbenchmark Driven

Due to the large spectrum of LC applications, FLARE cannot exhaustively profile BE-LC co-run pairs to find the optimal configuration. Instead, FLARE estimates the performance of BE-LC co-runs using microbenchmarks. Each kernel is matched with microbenchmark configurations that best represent its solo-run profiling statistics. Designing microbenchmarks that represent real-world applications is not easy, because the performance of a kernel is affected by many factors and the importance of each factor varies for different kernels. But the relevant features should be those related to resources for which the kernels contend when co-running. Out of the 120 performance counters of NVIDIA's *nvprof* profiler, we select the following 7 metrics which reflect or affect resource contention: L1, L2 cache hit rate, DRAM, L2, and L1 bandwidth utilization, arithmetic intensity, and total number of instructions.

To produce microbenchmark programs (also called microbenchmark instances in this paper) with varied features, we design a parameterized kernel with two parts. Here a instance is a microbenchmark with unique values on the 7 metrics. The first part loads a 1-D array and the second part contains a loop that performs pure arithmetic operations on the loaded data in each iteration. The microbenchmarks use the following 4 parameters to sample the configuration space: *stride length* to specify the distance between memory accesses from adjacent threads and hence control spatial locality of each thread block, *overlap ratio* to specifying the overlap between working sets of adjacent warps, *iterations* to control arithmetic intensity by specifying the number of iterations of the loop and *the number of threads* to run in total.

With 9 different stride lengths from 0 to 128 elements (L2 cache line size), 5 different overlap ratios ranging from 0 to 0.2, iteration counts from 1 to 4, and a fixed number 160K of threads, there are 180 different configurations of the microbenchmark. We find that the range of these metrics covers most real world applications by tuning these parameters.

Running all pairs of these microbenchmarks on all possible co-run configurations gives a large input dataset for training models to get a sense of the patterns that arise. Given 180 different instances of the microbenchmark, we co-run each pair of them in all possible ways to spatially share the GPU, resulting in a total of 640×640 co-runs. Based on these results, FLARE has the following two methods to select the initial configuration.

Linear Regression. The linear model has 16 features: 14 profile features from two microbenchmark instances and the SM configuration (i.e., n and k in Fig. 8b). The linear regression maps that 16-element vector onto the 1-dimensional output space describing either estimated latency or throughput. FLARE builds the linear model with these 16 features and trains the model using all the data from the offline co-runs through the least squares method. FLARE profiles one iteration of a solo-run of the BE kernel and the LC kernel (when it becomes available) to obtain the 14 characterization features and combine them with the other two features to get the feature vector of co-run applications. Then FLARE uses the linear regression models to estimate the co-run performance degradation given each of the co-run configurations, and finally selects the one that satisfies QoS and maximizes throughput. Since the linear models are quite lightweight, the initial configuration-selection based on this method has a trivial overhead.

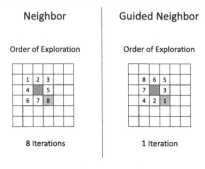

Fig. 9. Online search methods.

Nearest Neighbor. Like the linear regression method, the nearest neighbor method also profiles one iteration of the BE and LC kernels to obtain their characterization features. For each kernel, it then searches for a profiling characterization feature vector among the microbenchmarks that is the most similar to that kernel in Euclidean distance. Specifically, each value of the 7-element feature vectors is normalized to the range (0,1), and this method searches for the nearest microbenchmark feature vector b to the feature vector of the real benchmark m. The nearest neighbor method selects the microbenchmark for which the quantity $\|m - b\|_2$ is minimized. Each pair of representatives has offline-generated performance results on all of the co-run configurations available, so this gives another estimate of the performance degradation across the configuration space. Based on this, FLARE selects the configuration that satisfies QoS and maximizes throughput. This method requires no training and incurs negligible runtime overhead.

4.4   Online Refinement: Dynamic Reconfiguration

The final configuration we select should be one with the highest possible throughput while still satisfying QoS. The initial configurations produced by the previously discussed methods are unlikely to match the globally optimal result every time. Therefore, configurations will need further refinement based on real performance feedback as shown in Fig. 7. FLARE starts at the initial configuration and gradually explores the neighborhood to finally reach the optimal configuration. FLARE includes two approaches to performing the search as follows.

Neighbor Search. We demonstrate the idea of the first approach pictorially in Fig. 9 (left panel). The cells represent configurations. Towards the bottom left corner, the configurations give more resources to the LC kernel. The search process starts with an anchor cell (colored in blue), which should initially correspond to the configuration returned by the process described in Sect. 4.3. It then explores all the 8 neighbor cells (the numbers show the order of the exploration), and selects the best as the new anchor cell for the next round. Here the meaning of best is double-folded. When QoS is met, the best means that the overall throughput is optimal around neighbors. Otherwise, the best stands for the steepest decent of LC performance. This repeats until arriving at a cell where QoS is met and its throughput is the highest around its neighbors.

Guided Neighbor Search. While the previous approach explores its neighborhood exhaustively, this approach searches first in the direction suggested by the microbenchmark data. Each neighbor cell has corresponding microbenchmark data, and therefore estimated QoS and throughput values associated with it. This gives some order to the neighbors in terms of their expected configuration performance, and we can simply explore the one with the best estimated performance. For example, Fig. 9 (right panel) shows that according to the microbenchmark data, the bottom right neighbor configuration (labeled by 1) should produce the highest performance for the LC kernel. We then explore that configuration and select it as the anchor for the next round. By leveraging the microbenchmark data, we substantially decrease the number of steps required to converge. This process continues until it reaches a configuration where the QoS requirement of LC is satisfied and microbenchmark throughput is maximized.

5   Evaluation

5.1   Experimental Setup

We evaluate FLARE using an NVIDIA TITAN V GPU with 12 GB onboard memory hosted by a server with an Intel Xeon E3-1286 v3 CPU and 32 GB main memory. The system runs Ubuntu 16.04 with kernel version 4.4.0-141, NVIDIA driver 410.48, and CUDA 10.0. We focus our evaluation on eleven benchmarks and two real-world applications. The benchmarks are from three popular benchmark suites: Rodinia [5], SHOC [10], and NVIDIA's CUDA SDK. Two real applications, TC [1] and CN [23], represent deep learning inference workloads. TC uses an LSTM [12] model to classify documents and CN uses a GRU [9] model to predict the likely next character given an input string. Both of these inference applications heavily utilize the GPU, and are classified as LC applications. We also evaluate SPMV (SHOC), SC, PF, HOTSPOT, LBM and BP (Rodinia) as LC applications and MD (SHOC), MM (CUDA SDK), NN, LUD and CFD (Rodinia) as BE applications. Only the BE applications require adaptation to yield resources, while the LC applications can run unmodified.

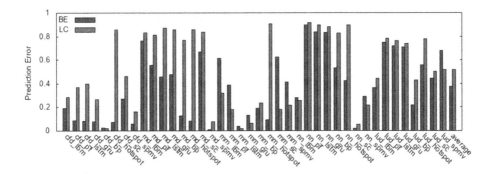

Fig. 10. Performance estimation error evaluation.

5.2   Evaluation Strategy

We evaluate the performance of our approaches under the following scenario. The BE application runs continuously and consumes the entire GPU when no LC application is present. When a LC application arrives, the BE application yields part or all of the computation resources on the GPU to the LC application and two applications start to run simultaneously on the device. The LC application has a QoS deadline, and if its execution time exceeds this deadline the QoS is violated. As soon as the LC kernel completes, the BE application launches a kernel to reclaims all of the yielded hardware resources and resumes running exclusively. For this scenario, we always launch the BE kernel first and then start the LC kernel in a different CUDA stream. In order to compare with CUDA Multi-Process Service (MPS), we observe that simple SM-based partitioning gives the same performance results as MPS, and consider it as a possible configuration. Note that unlike FLARE, MPS does not support dynamic resource allocation. Once the application is launched, its allocation of the GPU resource cannot be changed. Thus, the MPS results in this section represent the best possible results MPS can produce.

In this paper, throughput refers to the number of instructions executed per microsecond. We define the overall throughput of a co-run pair as,

$$P^c = \left(\text{INS}_{LC} + \text{INS}_{BE}^c\right)/T_{LC}^c \qquad (1)$$

where P^c is the overall throughput of co-run, INS_{LC} and INS_{BE}^c are the number of instructions of LC and BE applications during co-run, and T_{LC}^c is the performance of a co-run LC kernel. We are going to compare this overall throughput with the sequential throughput during T_{LC}^c. When a LC kernel arrives, the BE application will yield the GPU to the LC. Then the LC kernel starts to run and will be finished in T_{LC}^s. The BE resumes thereafter. But we only need to consider the number of BE instructions, INS_{BE}^{tw}, finished in time window $T_{LC}^c - T_{LC}^s$, because our interest is to see throughput improvement of co-run. Therefore, the sequential throughput is given by

$$P^s = \left(\text{INS}_{LC} + \text{INS}_{BE}^{tw}\right)/T_{LC}^c \qquad (2)$$

The ratio of P^c to the sequential throughput P^s gives us the throughput improvement.

We compare FLARE with the preemption-based approaches proposed in EffiSha [6] and FLEP [31]. Since the two approaches are similar, we only use FLEP as the baseline. FLARE proposes three ways to choose resource partitioning configurations: model-based, online search-based, and hybrid. The model-based approach incurs trivial runtime overhead but may choose a poor configuration where a QoS target could possibly be missed, while the online search-based approach may need to explore many configurations to find a desirable one. This evaluation will demonstrate that the flaws in these approaches prevent them from achieving the best performance. Section 3 notes that the performance of an application may not be linear in terms of allocated resource. Worse, the resource contention due to co-running makes it even more difficult to statically predict the optimal configuration. Since **NN** outperforms **Linear Regression** in all cases, we only show the results on the former. A hybrid approach uses the model-based approach to select an initial configuration followed by a online search approach to refine the configuration. FLARE supports two online search methods regardless of the initial configuration, namely neighbor search (**NS**) and guided neighbor search (**GNS**). It leads to two hybrid approaches: **NN_NS** and **NN_GNS**. Therefore, we evaluate 5 approaches included in FLARE: **NN**, **NS**, **GNS**, **NN_NS** and **NN_GNS**.

5.3 Results

Due to limited space, we only show the results for 1.5X QoS, that is, the co-run latency of a LC kernel cannot exceed 1.5X its solo-run time. Figure 11 shows throughput improvement of FLARE with the best performing approach, **NN_GNS**, and binary search-based SM allocation with MPS. Observe that FLARE increases the average throughput improvement by 38.8% compared with FLEP. FLEP runs the LC application first to guarantee QoS and then the BE application after the LC application, thus missing co-running opportunities to improve throughput. As the figure shows, if MPS supports dynamic resource allocation, its performance could be close to FLARE. But FLARE still produces higher throughput because it not only considers SM allocation but also enables thread block allocation. We also measure the overheads of these 4 approaches. Figure 12 shows the runtime overheads to find the configurations. The **NN** approach only needs to profile one iteration and then run a lightweight model. Hence it incurs negligible overheads. Observe that with the help of **NN** choosing an initial configuration, the hybrid approaches need substantially less time to find optimal configurations. The average iterations of the 4 algorithms are 48, 41, 28, and 24. With the guidance of microbenchmarks, the average overhead is about halved. For the co-run pair NN_SC, the overheads of **NS** and **GNS** are 49 (**NN**) and 31 (**GNS**) iterations. These numbers are reduced to 9 and 14 using the microbenchmark guidance. The reason is that the initial configuration chosen by **NN** is closer to the optimal configuration of these benchmarks. This fact also indicates that our microbenchmarks capture crucial features of these benchmarks. It is important to point out that final chosen configurations by dynamic searching satisfy QoS, although the QoS may be violated along the way of the search process.

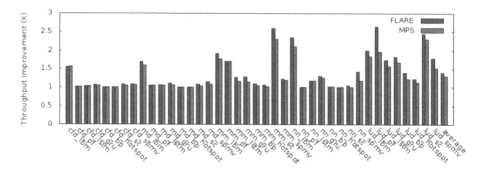

Fig. 11. Throughput Improvement at 1.5X QoS

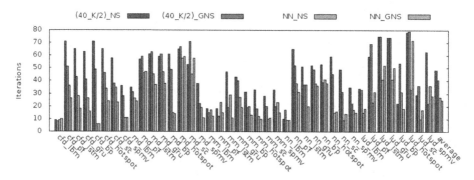

Fig. 12. Online searching overhead at 1.5X QoS

Micro-benchmark Prediction Error: Figure 10 shows the relative error of the performance degradation of LC applications and the relative error of overall throughput predicted by the **NN** method for each of the BE and LC kernels. The relative error is defined as $|D' - D|/max(D, D')$. The results demonstrate the inefficiency of model-based approaches to predict performance degradation. For NN_PF, the prediction error for throughput and the LC degradation is 89% and 92%, respectively. They are 39% and 18% for MM_PF. The reason is that the applications have dramatically different properties, such as memory access pattern and branch divergence, which are difficult to accurately characterize using microbenchmarks. Fortunately, the microbenchmarks still capture important features relevant to co-running for a number of benchmarks. For instance, the prediction errors are as low as 3% (overall throughput) and 1% (LC latency) for CFD_BP. On average, the **NN** method produces 37% prediction error for the throughput and 51% error for LC latency. Therefore, it is reasonable to use the **NN** method to choose an initial configuration for online search. The NN_PF pair is an exception in all the pairs. No matter how the resources are allocated to PF, the degradation is 15X, which is why the prediction errors are so large.

Real Applications: Figure 11 show the average throughput improvement across all the co-run pairs including real-world applications for different approaches. Figure 12 illustrates overheads to find resource configurations for real-world applications. The pair enclosed in parentheses indicates the initial configuration where MK is the number of maximum thread blocks an SM can host. Similar to the results on benchmarks, **NN** incurs minimum overhead. **NN** and **GNS** need a long search process evidenced by the substantial runtime overhead. **NN**, unfortunately, cannot find any configuration that satisfy QoS and hence results from the **NN** method are not included in these figures. Dynamic searching algorithms achieve the optimal overall throughput in all the 10 cases. The average throughput improvement of LSTM and GRU for 5 different pairs is 26% and 32%, respectively. The microbenchmark-based methods outperform **NN** and **GNS**. The overheads with microbenchmark guidance are about 60% of **NN** and **GNS**.

6   Related Work

Researchers have proposed architectural extensions to allow applications to co-run efficiently on the same GPU, with emphasis on cache sharing and bypassing [17], fine-grained sharing [29], preemption [21,26], dynamic resource management [22], and spatial multi-tasking [2,3]. The work [29] deals with spatial sharing through an enhanced scheduler (both thread block and warp level) to guarantee QoS. They use a quota to represent the QoS constraint. They assume that thread blocks are uniform in cost and the quota needs to reach zero at each epoch to satisfy QoS. To further improve the performance, they implement dynamic resource allocation by monitoring idle warps during each epoch. On the one hand, those techniques remain to be carefully evaluated for implementation in real GPUs. On the other hand, those studies do not systematically address reducing search overhead to find the best strategy for GPU sharing. Studies [16] have demonstrated that multi-tasking on GPUs can better utilize the hardware resource, but none of them predict performance degradation due to the co-running. Software systems, such as FLEP [31] and EffiSha [6], focus on lightweight preemption support but do not particularly study QoS enforcement. Baymax [8] and Prophet [7] predict GPU workload performance and use task re-ordering to handle QoS. Their approach to coordinate data transfers can be directly incorporated in FLARE to form a more general solution. Since they assume the GPUs are non-preemptable, they may use FLARE's methodology to further improve GPU utilization.

Another line of interesting work is practical GPU sharing in virtual environments, for which Hong et al. provide a comprehensive survey [14]. We briefly discuss several closely related studies. FairGV [13] achieves system-wide weighted fair sharing among GPU applications through collaborative scheduling and an accurate accounting mechanism. Gloop [25] proposes a new programming model to generate scheduling points in GPU kernels, which enables flexible suspending/resuming execution of GPU applications. Tian et al. propose a software system to virtualize Intel on-chip GPUs for graphics workloads [27]. None of these approaches have addressed fine-grained sharing or QoS of user-facing applications. To share the GPU memory GPUvm [24] partitions the GPU memory into regions and assign the regions to virtual machines. GPUswap [15] automatically coordinates GPU memory usage between applications even if the aggregate workload does not fit in GPU physical memory.

7   Conclusion

GPU sharing is a promising approach to improving hardware utilization, but resource contention may degrade the performance of the co-running latency-critical applications to violate QoS. In this paper, we demonstrated the complexities of partitioning GPU resources to enforce QoS and maximize throughput. To address the challenges, we proposed a software system named FLARE to enable and configure spatial GPU sharing between latency-critical and best-effort applications through kernel transformation, micro-benchmark guided partitioning and online configuration search. The experiment results showed 39% improvement on the overall throughput on 11 benchmarks and 2 real-world applications over existing systems. In the future, we plan to extend FLARE to address scenarios in which multiple latency-critical applications share the same GPU.

Acknowledgement. We would like to thank Akihiro Hayashi (our shepherd) and the anonymous reviewers for their constructive comments. This project was supported in part by NSF grant CCF-1823005 and an NSF CAREER Award (CNS-1750760).

References

1. Text classification in TensorFlow (2017). https://github.com/tensorflow/tensorflow/tree/master/tensorflow/examples/learn#text-classification
2. Adriaens, J., Compton, K., Kim, N.S., Schulte, M.J.: The case for GPGPU spatial multitasking. In: HPCA (2012)
3. Allen, T., Feng, X., Ge, R.: Slate: enabling workload-aware efficient multiprocessing for modern GPGPUs. In: IPDPS (2019)
4. Barroso, L.A., Clidaras, J., Hölzle, U.: The Datacenter as a Computer: An Introduction to the Design of Warehouse-Scale Machines, 2nd edn. Synthesis Lectures on Computer Architecture. Morgan & Claypool Publishers (2013)
5. Che, S., et al.: Rodinia: a benchmark suite for heterogeneous computing. In: IISWC (2009)
6. Chen, G., Zhao, Y., Shen, X., Zhou, H.: EffiSha: a software framework for enabling efficient preemptive scheduling of GPU. In: Sarkar, V., Rauchwerger, L. (eds.) PPoPP, pp. 3–16. ACM (2017)
7. Chen, Q., Yang, H., Guo, M., Kannan, R.S., Mars, J., Tang, L.: Prophet: precise QoS prediction on non-preemptive accelerators to improve utilization in warehouse-scale computers. In: ASPLOS (2017)
8. Chen, Q., Yang, H., Mars, J., Tang, L.: Baymax: QoS awareness and increased utilization of non-preemptive accelerators in warehouse scale computers. In: ASPLOS (2016)

9. Chung, J., Gülçehre, C., Cho, K., Bengio, Y.: Empirical evaluation of gated recurrent neural networks on sequence modeling. CoRR, abs/1412.3555 (2014)

10. Danalis, A., et al.: The scalable heterogeneous computing (SHOC) benchmark suite. In: GPGPU (2010)

11. Han, W., Mawhirter, D., Buland, M., Wu, B.: Graphie: large-scale asynchronous graph traversals on just a GPU. In: PACT 2017 (2017)

12. Hochreiter, S., Schmidhuber, J.: Long short-term memory. Neural Comput. **9**(8), 1735–1780 (1997)

13. Hong, C.-H., Spence, I.T.A., Nikolopoulos, D.S.: FairGV: fair and fast GPU virtualization. IEEE Trans. Parallel Distrib. Syst. **28**(12), 3472–3485 (2017)

14. Hong, C.-H., Spence, I.T.A., Nikolopoulos, D.S.: GPU virtualization and scheduling methods: a comprehensive survey. ACM Comput. Surv. **50**(3), 35:1–35:37 (2017)

15. Kehne, J., Metter, J., Bellosa, F.: GPUswap: enabling oversubscription of GPU memory through transparent swapping. In: VEE (2015)

16. Liang, Y., Huynh, H.P., Rupnow, K., Goh, R.S.M., Chen, D.: Efficient GPU spatial-temporal multitasking. IEEE Trans. Parallel Distrib. Syst. **26**(3), 748–760 (2015)

17. Liang, Y., Li, X., Xie, X.: Exploring cache bypassing and partitioning for multitasking on GPUs. In: ICCAD (2017)

18. Lo, D., Cheng, L., Govindaraju, R., Barroso, L.A., Kozyrakis, C.: Towards energy proportionality for large-scale latency-critical workloads. In: ISCA (2014)

19. Lo, D., Cheng, L., Govindaraju, R., Ranganathan, P., Kozyrakis, C.: Heracles: improving resource efficiency at scale. In: ISCA (2015)

20. Mars, J., Tang, L., Hundt, R., Skadron, K., Soffa, M.L.: Bubble-up: increasing utilization in modern warehouse scale computers via sensible co-locations. In: MICRO (2011)

21. Park, J.J.K., Park, Y., Mahlke, S.: Chimera: collaborative preemption for multitasking on a shared GPU. In: ASPLOS (2015)

22. Park, J.J.K., Park, Y., Mahlke, S.A.: Dynamic resource management for efficient utilization of multitasking GPUs. In: ASPLOS (2017)

23. Sutskever, I., Martens, J., Hinton, G.E.: Generating text with recurrent neural networks. In: ICML (2011)

24. Suzuki, Y., Kato, S., Yamada, H., Kono, K.: GPUvm: why not virtualizing GPUs at the hypervisor? In: USENIX ATC (2014)

25. Suzuki, Y., Yamada, H., Kato, S., Kono, K.: GLoop: an event-driven runtime for consolidating GPGPU applications. In: SoCC (2017)

26. Tanasic, I., Gelado, I., Cabezas, J., Ramirez, A., Navarro, N., Valero, M.: Enabling preemptive multiprogramming on GPUs. In: ISCA (2014)

27. Tian, K., Dong, Y., Cowperthwaite, D.: A full GPU virtualization solution with mediated pass-through. In: USENIX ATC (2014)

28. Wang, Y., Davidson, A., Pan, Y., Wu, Y., Riffel, A., Owens, J.D.: Gunrock: a high-performance graph processing library on the GPU. In: PPoPP (2015)

29. Wang, Z., Yang, J., Melhem, R., Childers, B., Zhang, Y., Guo, M.: Quality of service support for fine-grained sharing on GPUs. In: ISCA (2017)

30. Wu, B., Chen, G., Li, D., Shen, X., Vetter, J.S.: Enabling and exploiting flexible task assignment on GPU through SM-centric program transformations. In: ICS (2015)

31. Bo, W., Liu, X., Zhou, X., Jiang, C.: FLEP: enabling flexible and efficient preemption on GPUs. In: ASPLOS (2017)

32. Zhang, W., et al.: Laius: towards latency awareness and improved utilization of spatial multitasking accelerators in datacenters. In: ICS (2019)
33. Zhang, Y., Laurenzano, M.A., Mars, J., Tang, L.: SMiTe: precise QoS prediction on real-system SMT processors to improve utilization in warehouse scale computers. In: MICRO (2014)
34. Zhu, H., Erez, M.: Dirigent: enforcing QoS for latency-critical tasks on shared multicore systems. In: ASPLOS (2016)

Foundations of Consistency Types
for a Higher-Order Distributed Language

Xin Zhao[(⊠)] and Philipp Haller

KTH Royal Institute of Technology, Stockholm, Sweden
{xizhao,phaller}@kth.se

Abstract. Distributed systems address the increasing demand for fast access to resources and fault tolerance for data. However, due to scalability requirements, software developers need to trade consistency for performance. For certain data, consistency guarantees may be weakened if application correctness is unaffected. In contrast, data flow from data with weak consistency to data with strong consistency requirements is problematic, since application correctness may be broken.

In this paper, we propose LCD, a higher-order static consistency-typed language with replicated data types. The type system of LCD statically enforces noninterference between data types with weak consistency and data types with strong consistency. This means that updates of weakly-consistent data can never affect strongly-consistent data. Finally, our main theorem guarantees sequential consistency for so-called con operations in our language.

Keywords: Consistency types · Type system · Distributed programming

1 Introduction

Distributed systems are popular and applied to many areas. Different applications have different requirements of system consistency, e.g., a bank service needs to ensure that users get globally consistent information wherever they are, while a Twitter-like micro-blogging service just needs to ensure the causal sequence of messages ("tweets") among related users. In the same application, consistency requirements may vary in different scenarios, e.g., an online shopping service needs to provide the information for the user to browse as fast as possible, while when the user checks out for payment, the service needs to ensure a safe and consistent transaction.

A lot of consideration is required when a developer fixes bugs or makes optimizations for the current project. Unlike a local application, the verification work for a distributed program involves more expert experience and knowledge. Holt et al. [9] show a common programming mistake caused by the misuse of consistency. They point out that a type checking method can be provided in order to avoid similar errors. They introduce the so-called Inconsistent, Performance-bound, Approximate (IPA) storage system, which makes consistency properties explicit for distributed data and uses the type system to enforce consistency

© Springer Nature Switzerland AG 2021
S. Pande and V. Sarkar (Eds.): LCPC 2019, LNCS 11998, pp. 49–63, 2021.
https://doi.org/10.1007/978-3-030-72789-5_4

safety. However, their paper focused on providing a programming model and typed API; no formal account of the type system is provided.

In this paper, we focus on the theoretical part of designing a type system for consistency types and provide proofs of correctness properties such as type soundness. Importantly, we build on ideas from language-based information-flow security to enforce an essential noninterference property: in a well-typed program, weakly consistent data cannot flow into strongly consistent data.

This paper makes the following contributions:

- We introduce LCD, a higher-order static consistency-typed language with references. The language distinguishes different system behaviors between weak consistent and strongly consistent data.
- We prove type soundness for LCD. We also prove that the type system guarantees noninterference, enabling the safe use of both weakly and strongly consistent data within the same program. In addition, we discuss the consistency guarantees for LCD.

2   Overview

Many of the most widely-used applications are distributed systems with strong requirements regarding availability, latency, and throughput. It is important for such systems to tolerate network partitions. However, according to the CAP theorem [7], a fundamental result in distributed algorithms, such distributed applications must trade consistency for availability if network partitions must be tolerated. Here, we introduce a type system that enables a *provably safe use* of weakly consistent data and strongly consistent data within the same application.

Our type system provides two kinds of data types: (a) *consistent types* provide strong consistency; (b) *available types* provide availability, i.e., operations on available types never block. To achieve availability, operations on available types must weaken consistency. Specifically, in our language, available types provide *strong eventual consistency*, well-known from conflict-free replicated data types (CRDTs) [23]. CRDTs provide availability through asynchronous propagation of updates; the (eventual) convergence of replicas is ensured by commutativity properties of operations on their underlying data values. Consistent types are replicated data types which guarantee the consistency of replicas at all times. For this, a protocol for *distributed consensus*, such as Paxos [13] and Raft [21], is used to establish consistency upon each update of the data. As a result, operations applied to a consistent type behave as if the data was located and accessed on a single machine.

In some distributed systems, multiple levels of consistency coexist. For example, an online shop could store the order history and the recent-visit history associated with the same user account in different ways. While operations accessing the order history must be strongly consistent, the consistency of the recent-visit history could be weakened in order to increase availability for a better user (browsing) experience.

Inspired by techniques in information-flow security, which have been used to ensure confidentiality and integrity of information, we present a core language and type system, called LCD, which prevents data flows that could break consistency properties. LCD is based on a higher-order static security-typed language with references (SSL$_{Ref}$ [24]). In the following, we motivate our language design using a concrete example.

2.1 Motivating Example

A typical program error that a distributed application developer might make is to mix the usage of data from different consistency levels. In the following example, we show a possible error occurring in a simplified shopping platform.

In Fig. 1a, the productNumber function applies a fastRead operation to get the approximate number of the required product from a random available server. It is implemented in this way so that the realtimeDisplay function provides fast access for users to get a better surfing experience.

During the development of the platform, the productNumber function might be reused for implementing a checkOut function, as shown in Fig. 1b, which support price adjustment according to the stock. This does not cause any compilation errors; however, note that on line 5 of Fig. 1b, a weakly-consistent value returned from function productNumber is assigned to variable remaining, which is subsequently used for deciding the final payment price for the transaction (lines 6–7). As a result, the inconsistent remaining affects the final income of the company. This problem arises easily, because (1) there might be two different programmers responsible for implementing the display and check-out parts, so they might fail to notice the problem of data inconsistency in different functions, and (2) it is difficult to reproduce and debug this kind of bugs.

Analyzing the example in Fig. 1b, we note that there are two main issues when such an error happens. The first issue is the direct flow of data of different consistency, as on line 5, where variable remaining controls the consistent payment operation but is assigned a weakly-consistent value. The second issue is illegal implicit data flow, as on lines 6–7, where the comparison of weakly-consistent data affects the modification of the consistent state of the system (here, payment price).

2.2 Type System

Type Annotation. In LCD, programmers can annotate types with @loc, @con and @ava labels. Local types are the default, so only @con and @ava are made explicit. It is illegal to assign an available-typed value to a consistent-typed variable so that we prevent the direct flow of data from available to consistent variables. For example, in Fig. 1c lines 5–6, the assignment is illegal because function productNumber() returns an available Int that cannot be assigned to consistent variable remaining.

```
1  def productNumber(event: id): Int = {
2      fastRead(event + "product_num")
3  }
4  def realtimeDisplay(event: id) = {
5      display(productNumber(event))
6  }
```

(a) Original display implementation.

```
1  def productNumber(event: id): Int = {
2      fastRead(event + "product_num")
3  }
4  def checkOut(event: id) = {
5      val remaining = productNumber(event)
6      if (remaining >= event.bound)
7          val price = event.price * rebate
8      else val price = event.price
9      paymentProcess(price, event)
10 }
```

(b) Extended checkout implementation with error.

```
1  def productNumber(event: id): @ava Int = {
2      fastRead(event + "product_num")
3  }
4  def checkOut(event: id) = {
5      val remaining: @con Int =
6          productNumber(event)//illegal
7      if (remaining >= event.bound)
8          val price = event.price * rebate
9      else val price = event.price
10     paymentProcess(price, event)
11 }
```

(c) Option 1 for type checking (b) in LCD.

```
1  def productNumber(event: id): @ava Int = {
2      fastRead(event + "product_num")
3  }
4  def checkOut(event: id) = {
5      val remaining = productNumber(event)
6      val price: @con Int = event.price
7      if (remaining >= event.bound)
8          price = price * rebate//illegal
9      paymentProcess(price, event)
10 }
```

(d) Option 2 for type checking (b) in LCD.

Fig. 1. Shopping cart implementation.

Control Flow. In order to achieve the goal of having no information flow from available to consistent data, we also need to prevent *implicit flows*, which are caused by control flow. For example, in Fig. 1d the condition remaining >= event.bound has type available Boolean; thus, the modification for consistent data price depends on available variable remaining. LCD avoids this situation by checking the label of the condition. If the condition has label @ava, the type system disallows the then-branch to execute terms that might mutate the state of a reference with a lower label, which in LCD corresponds to a higher consistency level. In particular, @con $\preceq$ @ava, since the @con label indicates a higher consistency level.

3 Formal Semantics

In this section, we formally introduce our lattice-based calculus for distributed programming (LCD). We name it "lattice-based" since we consider an arbitrary but fixed lattice as one of the base types, and lattice types are commonly used for achieving eventual consistency for distributed systems (e.g., CRDTs [23]).

Our companion technical report [27] formalizes this language and proves type soundness as well as a noninterference property that prevents undesired information flow between available and consistent data.

3.1 Syntax

Figure 2 shows the syntax of our core language. Term language is essentially a typed functional language with Ocaml-style references. The additional feature of the language is that each value and type constructor is annotated with a label ℓ to distinguish different consistency levels. Labels ℓ form a partial order $\preceq$ where $\cdot$, con and ava refer to labels that are attached to local, consistent, and available data types, respectively. The relations among them are defined in Definition 1. Function abstraction and arrow types are carrying a latent effect [8], which restricts the consistency level of the values that might be written during the execution of the function. The highlighted term o is not part of the surface syntax but a reference location which only appears during the evaluation of a ref expression.

$$
\begin{array}{lll}
\ell & ::= \cdot \mid \mathsf{con} \mid \mathsf{ava} & \text{label} \\
t & ::= v \mid t \bigoplus t \mid t \text{ op } t \mid t\,t \mid \text{if } x \text{ then } \{\,s\,\} \text{ else } \{\,t\,\} & \\
& \quad \mid \mathsf{ref}_\ell\ t \mid\ !t \mid t := t & \text{terms} \\
r & ::= \mathsf{d} \mid \mathsf{true} \mid \mathsf{false} \mid (\lambda^\ell x : \tau.\ t) \mid \mathsf{unit} \mid \boxed{o} & \text{raw value} \\
v & ::= r_\ell \mid x & \text{labeled value} \\
\tau & ::= \mathsf{Bool}_\ell \mid \mathsf{Unit}_\ell \mid \mathsf{Lat}_\ell \mid \mathsf{Ref}_\ell\ \tau \mid \tau \xrightarrow{\ell}_\ell \tau & \text{types} \\
\bigoplus & ::= \vee \mid \wedge & \text{meet and join} \\
\mathsf{op} & ::= \preceq \mid \prec & \text{order operations}
\end{array}
$$

Fig. 2. Syntax of LCD core language

Definition 1 (Partial order on consistency types labels). *The partial order of consistency types label is:* $\cdot \preceq \mathsf{con} \qquad \mathsf{con} \preceq \mathsf{ava}$

Definition 2 (Subtyping relation $\preceq$ on types)

$$
\frac{T \in \{\mathsf{Bool}, \mathsf{Unit}, \mathsf{Lat}\} \qquad \ell \preceq \ell'}{T_\ell \preceq T_{\ell'}}
\qquad\qquad
\frac{\ell \preceq \ell'}{\mathsf{Ref}_\ell\ \tau \preceq \mathsf{Ref}_{\ell'}\ \tau}
$$

$$
\frac{\tau_1' \preceq \tau_1 \qquad \tau_2 \preceq \tau_2' \qquad \ell_1 \preceq \ell_1' \qquad \ell_2' \preceq \ell_2}{\tau_1 \xrightarrow{\ell_2}_{\ell_1} \tau_2 \preceq \tau_1' \xrightarrow{\ell_2'}_{\ell_1'} \tau_2'}
$$

3.2 Static Semantics

Figure 3 shows a few select typing rules. The typing judgement $\Gamma; \Sigma; \ell_c \vdash t : \tau$ says that term t has type τ under type environment Γ, store typing Σ and effect ℓ_c. The type environment Γ is a finite mapping from variables to their types. The store typing Σ maps reference locations o to the base type of the corresponding reference. For example, if $\Sigma(o) = \mathsf{Bool}_\ell$ then o has type $\mathsf{Ref}_\ell\ \mathsf{Bool}_\ell$. The consistency label ℓ_c denotes the current consistency effect of the evaluation context for the given term, which prevents low-consistency terms from mutating the state of high-consistency references.

$$\frac{\Gamma; \Sigma; \ell_c \vdash t_1 : \mathsf{Ref}_\ell\ \tau \quad \tau' \preceq \tau \quad \Gamma; \Sigma; \ell_c \vdash t_2 : \tau' \quad \ell_c \preceq \ell}{\Gamma; \Sigma; \ell_c \vdash t_1 := t_2 : \mathsf{Unit}_\ell} \ (\text{T-Assign})$$

Let us illustrate the above concepts using typing rule T-Assign. The T-Assign rule ensures that a term of type τ' is only assigned to a reference of type τ where τ' is a subtype of τ which means that the label of τ' must be lower than the label of τ. For example, it would be type-correct to assign a con value to an ava reference as long as their base types are equal.

The current consistency effect ℓ_c ensures that there are no illegal implicit flows. For example, $\Gamma; \Sigma; \mathsf{ava} \vdash t_{1\mathsf{con}} := t_{2\mathsf{con}}$ is illegal according to T-Assign, because $\mathsf{ava} \not\preceq \mathsf{con}$. Thus, when the current consistency effect is ava, we cannot mutate a con-labeled term.

In general, an LCD source program t is well-typed if $\cdot; \cdot; \cdot \vdash t : \tau$.

$$\frac{\Gamma; \Sigma; \ell_c \vdash t_i : \mathsf{Lat}_{\ell_i}}{\Gamma; \Sigma; \ell_c \vdash t_1\ \mathsf{op}\ t_2 : \mathsf{Bool}_{\ell_1 \curlyvee \ell_2}} \ (\text{T-RelOp})$$

$$\frac{\Gamma, x : \tau_1; \Sigma; \ell' \vdash t : \tau_2}{\Gamma; \Sigma; \ell_c \vdash (\lambda^{\ell'} x : \tau_1.\ t)_\ell : \tau_1 \xrightarrow{\ell'}_\ell \tau_2} \ (\text{T-Abs})$$

$$\frac{\Gamma; \Sigma; \ell_c \vdash t_1 : \tau_{11} \xrightarrow{\ell'}_\ell \tau_{12} \quad \tau_2 \preceq \tau_{11} \quad \Gamma; \Sigma; \ell_c \vdash t_2 : \tau_2 \quad \ell_c \curlyvee \ell \preceq \ell'}{\Gamma; \Sigma; \ell_c \vdash t_1\ t_2 : \tau_{12} \curlyvee \ell} \ (\text{T-App})$$

$$\frac{\Gamma; \Sigma; \ell_c \vdash t : \mathsf{Bool}_\ell \quad \Gamma; \Sigma; \ell_c \curlyvee \ell \vdash t_i : \tau_i \quad \tau = \tau_1 \curlyvee \tau_2 \curlyvee \ell}{\Gamma; \Sigma; \ell_c \vdash \mathbf{if}\ t\ \mathbf{then}\ t_1\ \mathbf{else}\ t_2 : \tau} \ (\text{T-If})$$

$$\frac{\begin{array}{c}\Gamma; \Sigma; \ell_c \vdash t : \tau' \quad \ell = \mathsf{ava} \implies \mathsf{raw}(\tau') = \mathsf{Lat} \quad \ell_c \preceq \ell \\ \mathsf{label}(\tau') \preceq \ell \quad \mathsf{label}(\tau) \prec \ell \implies \mathsf{refs}(t) = \emptyset \quad \tau = \tau \curlyvee \ell\end{array}}{\Gamma; \Sigma; \ell_c \vdash \mathsf{ref}_\ell\ t : \mathsf{Ref}_\ell\ \tau} \ (\text{T-Ref})$$

Fig. 3. Selected typing rules

T-RelOp types relational operations between two lattice values, yielding a boolean result after partial order comparison. $\curlyvee$ is a join operation to compute the least upper-bound for two labels. T-Abs type checks the function body with the latent label ℓ', and the arrow type has the same label as the function abstraction. T-App enforces consistency restrictions in a standard way. The latent label ℓ' upper-bound current consistency level and the operator label. The $\curlyvee$ between a type τ_{12} and a label ℓ is defined as an operation to join ℓ with the label of τ_{12}. The type of the entire term τ_{12} joins the label ℓ of the operator $\to$ to preserve the consistency level.

T-IF checks the current type of the predicate and propagate the label to the type checking of each branch statement. In this way, this rule prevents explicit information flow from higher labels to lower labels. The $\curlyvee$ between types is defined for types that have the same raw type and returns a type that has the joined label.

T-REF requires the reference body to be a lattice-type when the label is "ava". It checks that current consistency labels in the evaluation context, as well as the label of the reference body, are both lower than the label of the reference. The function $\mathsf{raw}(a)$ returns the raw value/type (without labels) for the value/type. The function $\mathsf{refs}(v)$ returns all the locations that are related with a term v. When the function returns an empty set, it means the term does not contain references.

The labels in LCD do record not only the consistency level of data but also reflect the actual distribution of data. For example, the term ref_{con} ref. 3 generates a consistent reference to a local location that does not exist on the server-side. Rule T-REF determines the term to be ill-typed.

Difference between LCD and SSL$_{\mathsf{Ref}}$ The following paragraph summarizes the main differences between LCD and SSL$_{\mathsf{Ref}}$.

– LCD uses labels to annotate different consistency levels for information flow tracking, while SSL$_{\mathsf{Ref}}$ uses annotations for security checks.
– LCD uses labels to notify the system on how to operate accordingly. (See dynamic semantics in Sect. 3.3 for more details.)

3.3 Dynamic Semantics

We formalize the dynamic semantics as a small-step operational semantics based on two judgements: $t_1 \mid \mu_1 \mid b_1 \overset{a}{\longrightarrow}^i t_2 \mid \mu_2 \mid b_2$ and $\{\langle t_1 \mid \mu_1 \mid b_1\rangle^i\} \cup P \mid M_1 \mid S_1 \overset{a}{\twoheadrightarrow} \{\langle t_2 \mid \mu_2 \mid b_2\rangle^i\} \cup P \mid M_2 \mid S_2$. The first judgement says that a term t_1, a local store μ_1, and a message buffer b_1 reduce to t_2, μ_2, and b_2, respectively, with an action a. The second judgement reduces the entire cloud state which contains a set of client programs P, a multiset of messages M, and a set of servers S. An action a is a pair which contains a current consistency label ℓ_c and an operation op which is either rd, wr, ref, or τ. op is used for analysing the consistency guarantees for LCD in Sect. 4.2, so we ignore it in this section.

Local Reduction. Figure 4 shows a few selected local reduction rules. The other rules are omitted and appear only in the companion technical report. Local operations follow the general reduction rules. b is a message sending buffer for modeling the network communication in eventually consistent systems.

E-RELOP is a simple rule that makes a reduction on terms without modifying store μ or buffers b. Some rules modify the store, for example, in E-LOCALREF, when a term $\mathsf{ref}^\tau\ v$ needs to be reduced, it first generates a location o that is not in the domain of the store μ ($o \notin dom(\mu)$). Then μ extends its mapping relation with a labeled v associate to o.

$$\frac{t_1 \mid \mu_1 \mid b_1 \overset{a}{\longrightarrow}{}^i t_2 \mid \mu_2 \mid b_2}{E[t_1] \mid \mu_1 \mid b_1 \overset{a}{\longrightarrow}{}^i E[t_2] \mid \mu_2 \mid b_2} \quad \text{(E-EVAL)}$$

$$\frac{d = d_1 \text{ op } d_2 \qquad \ell = \ell_1 \curlyvee \ell_2 \qquad a = (\ell_c, \tau)}{d_{1\ell_1} \text{ op } d_{2\ell_2} \mid \mu \mid b \overset{a}{\longrightarrow}{}^i d_\ell \mid \mu \mid b} \quad \text{(E-RELOP)}$$

$$\frac{o \notin dom(\mu) \qquad \mu' = \mu[o \mapsto v \curlyvee \ell_c] \qquad a = (\ell_c, \tau)}{\text{ref}_\cdot^\tau \; v \mid \mu \mid b \overset{a}{\longrightarrow}{}^i o. \mid \mu' \mid b} \quad \text{(E-LOCALREF)}$$

$$\frac{\begin{array}{c} i \in Ids \qquad o = (i, \iota) \text{ where } \iota \text{ fresh} \qquad \mu' = \mu[o \mapsto v \curlyvee \ell_c \curlyvee \text{ava}] \\ b' = b \cdot \text{update}[o, v, i, \emptyset, \mathtt{v}] \qquad \mathtt{v} \text{ fresh} \qquad a = (\ell_c, ref_{\text{ava}}^\mathtt{v}(o, v)) \end{array}}{\text{ref}_{\text{ava}}^\tau \; v \mid \mu \mid b \overset{a}{\longrightarrow}{}^i o_{\text{ava}} \mid \mu' \mid b'} \quad \text{(E-AVAREF)}$$

$$\frac{o \in dom(\mu) \qquad v = \mu(o) \qquad b' = b \cdot \text{req}[o, i] \qquad \mathtt{v} \text{ fresh} \qquad a = (\ell_c, rd_{\text{ava}}^\mathtt{v}(o, v, \mu))}{!o_{\text{ava}} \mid \mu \mid b \overset{a}{\longrightarrow}{}^i v \curlyvee \text{ava} \mid \mu \mid b'} \quad \text{(E-AVADEREF1)}$$

$$\frac{\begin{cases} \textbf{if } o \in dom(\mu) \textbf{ then } w = \mu(o), \mu' = \mu[o \mapsto (w \vee v) \curlyvee \ell_c \curlyvee \text{ava}] \\ \textbf{else } \mu' = \mu[o \mapsto v \curlyvee \ell_c \curlyvee \text{ava}] \end{cases} \\ b' = b \cdot \text{update}[o, v, i, \emptyset, \mathtt{v}] \qquad \mathtt{v} \text{ fresh} \qquad a = (\ell_c, wr_{\text{ava}}^\mathtt{v}(o, v))}{o_{\text{ava}} := v \mid \mu \mid b \overset{a}{\longrightarrow}{}^i \text{unit}_{\text{ava}} \mid \mu' \mid b'} \quad \text{(E-AVAASSIGN)}$$

Fig. 4. LCD: local reduction.

E-AVAREF creates an available reference. In contrast to E-LOCALREF, the generated location has a decentralized identifier which are defined as (i, ι) where i is the client ID and ι is freshly generated. The value stored in the location is stamped with label ava, and since it requires communication but not instant creation on the server-side, a message of the form $\text{update}[o, v, i, \emptyset, \mathtt{v}]$ is stored in the buffer for subsequent, asynchronous processing. Available data types are only weakly consistent; thus, it is sufficient for E-AVADEREF1 to obtain the value directly from the local store if the location is in the domain of the local storage. Meanwhile, a message of the form $\text{req}[o, i]$ is stored in the buffer for requesting a newer state from an available server. (For the condition where the location is not in the domain of the local store, see E-AVADEREF2 in Fig. 5.) E-AVAASSIGN first updates the local store depends on whether the location is locally buffered or not, and then puts a message of the form $\text{update}[o, v, i, \emptyset, \mathtt{v}]$ into the buffer for message propagation.

E-EVAL defines the form of local reduction relations. We use evaluation contexts here. Each evaluation context is a term with a hole ($[]$) somewhere inside it. We write $E[t]$ for the term obtained by replacing the hole in E with t. Evaluation contexts are defined as follows:

$$E \quad ::= [] \mid E \oplus t \mid v \oplus E \mid E \text{ op } t \mid v \text{ op } E \mid E \; t \mid v \; E \\ \mid \textbf{if } E \textbf{ then } t \textbf{ else } t \mid !E \mid E := t \mid v := E \mid \text{ref}_\ell E$$

All expressions propagate the current program label ℓ_c to subterms, and there is no additional runtime checking for types and effects required.

Distributed Reduction. Figure 5 shows the distributed reduction rules. Each client consists of a tuple $\langle t \mid \mu \mid b \rangle$, and each server has a structure similar to a local store μ. E-LOCAL reveals the relationship between reduction relations $\rightarrow^i$ and $\twoheadrightarrow^i$. E-AVADEREF2 shows the behavior of the system when the local store does not contain the required location o, which is a result returned from an available server. E-CONREF creates a consistent reference, and the generated location is stamped with a label con. Creating a consistent reference requires a totally-ordered update of all servers. This is expressed by simultaneously changing the state of all servers, in one step. A practical implementation would require an algorithm for distributed consensus. However, our semantics is designed for reasoning about source programs, on a high level, instead of the implementation of the underlying distributed algorithms. Therefore, we abstract from the underlying distributed consensus algorithm. E-CONDEREF returns a value from a random server, and the value is still consistent because all the write operations are strongly synchronized. Similarly, for E-CONASSIGN, we update the remote side in one step to express the fact that to get a consistent result from the server-side or to assign a consistent data type, all the servers need to synchronize and reach a consistent state before completing the consistent operation.

$$\frac{t \mid \mu \mid b \xrightarrow{a}^i t' \mid \mu' \mid b'}{\{\langle t \mid \mu \mid b \rangle^i\} \cup P \mid M \mid S \xtwoheadrightarrow{a} \{\langle t' \mid \mu' \mid b' \rangle^i\} \cup P \mid M \mid S} \quad \text{(E-LOCAL)}$$

$$\frac{o \notin dom(\mu) \qquad \exists S_r \in S. \; S_r(o) = v \qquad \mu' = \mu[o \mapsto v]}{\text{v fresh} \qquad a = (\ell_c, rd_{\mathsf{ava}}^{\mathsf{v}}(o, v, S_r))}{\{\langle !o_{\mathsf{ava}} \mid \mu \mid b \rangle^i\} \cup P \mid M \mid S \xtwoheadrightarrow{a} \{\langle v \curlyvee \mathsf{ava} \mid \mu' \mid b \rangle^i\} \cup P \mid M \mid S} \quad \text{(E-AVADEREF2)}$$

$$\frac{i \in Ids \qquad o = (i, \iota) \text{ where } \iota \text{ fresh} \qquad o \notin dom(\mu) \qquad \text{v fresh}}{a = (\ell_c, ref_{\mathsf{con}}^{\mathsf{v}}(o, v)) \qquad v' = v \curlyvee \ell_c \curlyvee \mathsf{con} \qquad \mu' = \mu[o \mapsto v']}{S' = \bigcup S_r' \text{ where } \forall S_r \in S, S_r' = (S_r.s[o \mapsto v'], \text{v} \cdot S_r.seq)}{\{\langle \mathsf{ref}_{\mathsf{con}}^{\tau} \; v \mid \mu \mid b \rangle^i\} \cup P \mid M \mid S \xtwoheadrightarrow{a} \{\langle o_{\mathsf{con}} \mid \mu' \mid b \rangle^i\} \cup P \mid M \mid S'} \quad \text{(E-CONREF)}$$

$$\frac{\exists S_r \in S. \; S_r(o) = v \qquad \mu' = \mu[o \mapsto v]}{\text{v fresh} \qquad a = (\ell_c, rd_{\mathsf{con}}^{\mathsf{v}}(o, v, S_r))}{\{\langle !o_{\mathsf{con}} \mid \mu \mid b \rangle^i\} \cup P \mid M \mid S \xtwoheadrightarrow{a} \{\langle v \curlyvee \mathsf{con} \mid \mu \mid b \rangle^i\} \cup P \mid M \mid S} \quad \text{(E-CONDEREF)}$$

$$\frac{v' = v \curlyvee \ell_c \curlyvee \mathsf{con} \qquad \mu' = \mu[o \mapsto v'] \qquad \text{v fresh} \qquad a = (\ell_c, wr_{\mathsf{con}}^{\mathsf{v}}(o, v))}{S' = \bigcup S_r' \text{ where } \forall S_r \in S, S_r' = (S_r.s[o \mapsto v'], \text{v} \cdot S_r.seq)}{\{\langle o_{\mathsf{con}} := v \mid \mu \mid b \rangle^i\} \cup P \mid M \mid S \xtwoheadrightarrow{a} \{\langle \mathsf{unit}_{\mathsf{con}} \mid \mu' \mid b \rangle^i\} \cup P \mid M \mid S'}$$
$$\text{(E-CONASSIGN)}$$

Fig. 5. LCD: Distributed reduction.

$$\frac{b = m \cdot b' \qquad M' = m \cup M \qquad a = (\ell_c, \tau)}{\{\langle t \mid \mu \mid b)^i\} \cup P \mid M \mid S \xrightarrow{a} \{\langle t \mid \mu \mid b')^i\} \cup P \mid M' \mid S} \quad \text{(E-SEND)}$$

$$\frac{M = \{\text{update}[o, v, i, R, \mathrm{v}]\} \uplus M' \qquad R = ids(S) \qquad a = (\ell_c, \tau)}{P \mid M \mid S \xrightarrow{a} P \mid M' \mid S} \quad \text{(E-GC)}$$

$$\frac{M = \{\text{req}[o, i]\} \cup M' \qquad \exists S_r \in S.S_r(o) = v \qquad \mu' = \mu[o \mapsto v \curlyvee \ell_c] \qquad a = (\ell_c, \tau)}{\{\langle t \mid \mu \mid b)^i\} \cup P \mid M \mid S \xrightarrow{a} \{\langle t \mid \mu' \mid b)^i\} \cup P \mid M' \mid S}$$
$$\text{(E-PROCESS-REQUEST)}$$

$$\frac{\begin{array}{c} M = \{\text{update}[o, v, i, R, \mathrm{v}]\} \cup M'' \qquad S = \{S_r\} \uplus S'' \qquad r \notin R \\ \begin{cases} \text{if } o \notin S_r \text{ then } S_r' = (S_r.s[o \mapsto v \curlyvee \ell_c], \mathrm{v} \cdot S_r.seq) \\ \text{else } S_r' = (S_r.s[o \mapsto v \vee S_r.s(o) \curlyvee \ell_c], \mathrm{v} \cdot S_r.seq) \end{cases} \qquad S' = \{S_r'\} \cup S'' \\ M' = \{\text{update}[o, v, i, R \cup \{r\}, \mathrm{v}]\} \cup M'' \qquad a = (\ell_c, \tau) \end{array}}{P \mid M \mid S \xrightarrow{a} P \mid M' \mid S'}$$
$$\text{(E-PROCESS-UPDATE)}$$

Fig. 6. LCD: message processing.

Figure 6 shows the message processing of LCD. E-SEND moves a message from buffer b to message set M. E-GC removes a message that has already been received by all servers. E-PROCESSUPDATE processes a message update$[o, v, i, R, \mathrm{v}]$ which contains the update information (o, v, i), a set of receivers R that already received the message and the event id v. It updates a server that does not belong to R and adds a new message for further propagation. If the message contains a location o that does not exist on the server, then the server creates a new mapping; otherwise, the value at the same location is updated. E-PROCESSREQUEST processes a message req$[o, i]$. It pushes the state of location o in one of the replicas back to client i, updating its local state.

Well-Formed Configurations. Figure 7 shows a few selected well-formed configurations. These rules are essential for establishing subject reduction (Sect. 4.1). WF-STORE defines the well typeness of the store with respcet to a typing context Γ and a store typing Σ.

$$\frac{dom(\mu) \in dom(\Sigma) \qquad \forall o \in dom(\mu) \; \exists \ell_c. \; \Sigma; \ell_c \vdash \mu(o) : \tau \wedge \tau = \Sigma(o)}{\Sigma \vdash \mu} \quad \text{(WF-STORE2)}$$

$$\frac{\Sigma \vdash \mu \quad \Sigma \vdash b}{\exists \Gamma, \ell_c. \; \Gamma; \Sigma; \ell_c \vdash t : \tau} \qquad \frac{\Sigma \vdash \langle t \mid \mu \mid b)^i \quad \Sigma \vdash P}{\Sigma \vdash \{\langle t \mid \mu \mid b)^i\} \cup P} \qquad \frac{\Sigma \vdash P \quad \Sigma \vdash M}{\Sigma \vdash S}$$
$$\frac{}{\Sigma \vdash \langle t \mid \mu \mid b)^i} \qquad \qquad \qquad \qquad \qquad \frac{}{\Sigma \vdash P \mid M \mid S}$$
$$\text{(WF-PROGRAMCONFIG)} \qquad \qquad \text{(WF-PROGRAM)} \qquad \qquad \text{(WF-CONFIG)}$$

Fig. 7. Selected well-formedness rules.

4 Properties of LCD

4.1 Correctness Properties

We prove two properties of LCD: type soundness and noninterference. The full proofs are in our companion technical report [27].

Type soundness is an essential property of a type system, and it guarantees that well-typed terms do not "go wrong". The proof consists of two parts: preservation and progress. The preservation theorem states that for a well-typed program and corresponding static and runtime environment, the reduction keeps the well-formedness of the environment. Moreover, the progress theorem states that for any well-typed program, it either is a value or can be evaluated.

The preservation theorem for LCD considers local reduction and distributed reduction respectively so that we could cover all the possible reduction relations. The proof is done by induction on a derivation of $t \mid \mu \mid b \xrightarrow{a}^i t' \mid \mu' \mid b'$ and $P \mid M \mid S \xrightarrow{a} P' \mid M' \mid S'$.

The proof of progress theorem for LCD is done by first considering the normalization on a single client where the term is either a value or reducible, then analyzing the message processing rules for the system to prove that all the messages in the buffer can be eventually delivered to the required server. Combining the local client progress with distributed server progress, we get the conclusion for the system progress.

The noninterference property of LCD shows that the type system prevents the data flow from available computations to consistent computations. That is, any values that are labeled with ava will not influence the mutation of locations that are labeled with con. Due to this property, LCD can be safely used to solve the problem in Fig. 1b.

We can prove noninterference by proving that related substitutions preserve logical equivalences [25]. This concept introduces a model of observers that will observe the possible information from a certain consistency level. If two terms are logical equivalent, an observer cannot distinguish the difference between two terms. So the noninterference theorem, in other words, states that an arbitrary observer cannot distinguish values higher in the lattice.

4.2 Consistency Properties

In this section, we use abstract executions [1] to formalize consistency properties of LCD.

Definition 3 (Abstract executions). *Let $L = P \mid M \mid S$ be a well-formed configuration, i.e., $\Sigma \vdash P \mid M \mid S$ for some Σ. An* abstract execution *for con operations is a tuple $\mathbb{A} = \langle L, \mathrm{OP}, \mathrm{RB}, \mathrm{RVAL}, \mathrm{SP}, \mathrm{VIS}, \mathrm{AR} \rangle$ where:*

- *$\mathrm{OP} : \mathbb{V} \to \{op_\ell^\mathsf{v}(o, v)\}$ maps events to operations.*
- *$\mathrm{RVAL} : \mathbb{V} \times \mathsf{Values} \cup \{\triangledown\}$ describes the value returned by the operation, or the special symbol $\triangledown$ ($\triangledown \notin \mathsf{Values}$ which means there is no return value for the operation).*

- $\mathrm{RB} \subseteq \mathbb{V} \times \mathbb{V}$ *records the returns-before order.*
- $\mathrm{SP} : Ids \to \mathbb{V}$ *maps client ids to events.*
- $\mathrm{VIS} \subseteq \mathbb{V} \times \mathbb{V}$ *records whether the effects of an operation are visible to another operation on the server side. An event u is visible to an event v if the update performed by u has been delivered to the replica performing v before v is issued.*
- $\mathrm{AR} \subseteq \mathbb{V} \times \mathbb{V}$ *records the arbitration order which is a total order of operations across all programs.*

The well-formedness of abstraction execution can be found in our technical report [27]. Rules in Fig. 8 provides an operational way to associate abstract executions with LCD. Here we use the information from action a as we mentioned in Sect. 3.3. a contains a label ℓ and an operation field op. The The remaining transitions of the system are considered as internal changes that do not affect history and are handled by rule (A-Internal).

$$
\frac{
\begin{array}{c}
L \xrightarrow{(\ell_c, rd_\ell^{\mathsf{v}}(o,v,R))} L' \quad \mathsf{v} \notin dom(\mathrm{OP}) \quad \mathrm{OP}' = \mathrm{OP}[\mathsf{v} \mapsto \mathsf{op}_{\mathsf{con}}^{\mathsf{v}}(o,v)] \\
\mathrm{RB}' = \mathrm{RB} \cup (\{\mathsf{w} \in R.seq\} \cup \{\mathbb{k} \mid \mathbb{k} \in \mathrm{SP}(i) \wedge \mathrm{OP}(\mathbb{k}) \neq wr_{\mathsf{ava}}^{\mathsf{v}}(o,v')\} \times \{\mathsf{v}\}) \\
\mathrm{SP}' = \mathrm{SP}[i \mapsto \mathrm{SP}(i) \cup \{\mathsf{v}\}] \quad \mathrm{VIS}' = \begin{cases} \mathrm{VIS} \cup (\{\mathsf{w} \mid \mathsf{w} \in R\}) \text{ if } R \neq \mu \\ \mathrm{VIS} \cup (\{\mathrm{SP}(i)\} \times \{\mathsf{v}\}) \textbf{otherwise} \end{cases} \\
\mathrm{RVAL}' = \mathrm{RVAL}[\mathsf{v} \mapsto v]
\end{array}
}{
\langle L, \mathrm{OP}, \mathrm{RB}, \mathrm{RVAL}, \mathrm{SP}, \mathrm{VIS}, \mathrm{AR} \rangle \xrightarrow{(\ell_c, rd_\ell^{\mathsf{v}}(o,v,R))}_i \langle L', \mathrm{OP}', \mathrm{RB}', \mathrm{RVAL}', \mathrm{SP}', \mathrm{VIS}', \mathrm{AR} \rangle
}
$$
(A-Read)

$$
\frac{
\begin{array}{c}
L \xrightarrow{(\ell_c, \mathsf{op}_\ell^{\mathsf{v}}(o,v))} L' \quad \mathsf{v} \notin dom(\mathrm{OP}) \quad \mathrm{OP}' = \mathrm{OP}[\mathsf{v} \mapsto \mathsf{op}_\ell^{\mathsf{v}}(o,v)] \\
\mathrm{RB}' = \mathrm{RB} \cup (\{\mathsf{w} \in S.seq\} \cup \{\mathbb{k} \mid \mathbb{k} \in \mathrm{SP}(i) \wedge \mathrm{OP}(\mathbb{k}) \neq wr_{\mathsf{ava}}^{\mathsf{v}}(o,v')\} \times \{\mathsf{v}\}) \\
\mathrm{SP}' = \mathrm{SP}[i \mapsto \mathrm{SP}(i) \cup \{\mathsf{v}\}] \quad \mathrm{AR}' = \mathrm{AR} \cup (\{\mathsf{w} \mid \forall S_r \in S.\mathsf{w} \in S_r.seq\} \times \{\mathsf{v}\}) \\
\mathsf{op} \in \{\mathsf{wr}, \mathsf{ref}\} \quad \mathrm{RVAL}' = \begin{cases} \mathrm{RVAL}[\mathsf{v} \mapsto o] \text{ if } \mathsf{op} = ref \\ \mathrm{RVAL}[\mathsf{v} \mapsto unit] \text{ if } \mathsf{op} = wr \end{cases}
\end{array}
}{
\langle L, \mathrm{OP}, \mathrm{RB}, \mathrm{RVAL}, \mathrm{SP}, \mathrm{VIS}, \mathrm{AR} \rangle \xrightarrow{(\ell_c, \mathsf{op}_\ell^{\mathsf{v}}(o,v))}_i \langle L', \mathrm{OP}', \mathrm{RB}', \mathrm{RVAL}', \mathrm{SP}', \mathrm{VIS}, \mathrm{AR}' \rangle
}
$$
(A-Write)

$$
\frac{
\begin{array}{c}
P \mid M \mid S \xrightarrow{a} P \mid M' \mid S' \quad S = S_r \cup S_{rs} \quad S' = \mathsf{v} \cdot S_r \cup S'_{rs} \\
a = (\ell_c, \tau) \quad \mathrm{AR}' = \mathrm{AR} \cup (\{\mathsf{w} \mid \forall S_r \in S.\mathsf{w} \in S_r.seq\} \times \{\mathsf{v}\})
\end{array}
}{
\langle P \mid M \mid S, \mathrm{OP}, \mathrm{RB}, \mathrm{RVAL}, \mathrm{SP}, \mathrm{VIS}, \mathrm{AR} \rangle \xrightarrow{a}_i \langle P \mid M \mid S', \mathrm{OP}, \mathrm{RVAL}, \mathrm{RB}, \mathrm{SP}, \mathrm{VIS}, \mathrm{AR}' \rangle
}
$$
(A-MsgProcess)

$$
\frac{
P \mid M \mid S \xrightarrow{a} P' \mid M' \mid S \quad a = (\ell_c, \tau)
}{
\langle P \mid M \mid S, \mathrm{OP}, \mathrm{RB}, \mathrm{RVAL}, \mathrm{SP}, \mathrm{VIS}, \mathrm{AR} \rangle \xrightarrow{a}_i \langle P' \mid M' \mid S, \mathrm{OP}, \mathrm{RVAL}, \mathrm{RB}, \mathrm{SP}, \mathrm{VIS}, \mathrm{AR} \rangle
}
$$
(A-Internal)

Fig. 8. Abstraction computation for LCD.

The following example shows that the LCD system exhibits a non-monotonic write anomaly if we consider all the operations in history.

Example (Non-monotonic write anomaly)**.** *Consider the following system consisting of two programs.*

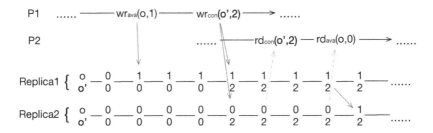

Due to the slow propagation of the ava operation $\mathsf{wr}_{ava}(o,1)$, *the visible order for a program's writes is not preserved anymore. The possible execution order violates sequential consistency.*

However, if we separate the analysis for ava and con operations, we can find more interesting properties. Due to the noninterference property, there is no information flows from ava operations to con operations, which means ava operations do not affect con operations. Then we can analyze the consistency guarantees for con operations and ava operations separately. Based on the collection of execution histories (see Fig. 8), we state that *for well-formed LCD programs,* con *operations provide sequential consistency.*

5   Related Work

Consistency Models. According to the CAP theorem [7], consistency, availability and fault tolerance cannot be achieved at the same time for any distributed system. Therefore, there exist multiple consistency models, such as eventual consistency [3], causal consistency [11], read-after-write consistency [16], and sequential consistency [12]. They define different contracts between the system and the user. It is also common that a system provides mixed levels of consistency, such as fork consistency [15,19], lazy replication [10], and red-blue consistency [14].

Consistency Types. The concept of consistency types first appears in paper [9]. They design an IPA storage system to provide consistency safety and error-bounded consistency. Our work instead uses language-based information flow tracking techniques to guarantee noninterference, and we provide a formal semantics and type system. ConSysT [18] is another programming language that supports heterogeneous consistency specifications at the type level. However, the work is under development and only presents the syntax of a core calculus without references, as well as subtyping rules. Neither dynamic semantics nor correctness properties are given. MixT [20] develops a domain-specific language for transactions with mixed consistency levels, and CScript [5] develops an object-oriented programming language for supporting mixed-consistency applications.Conflict-free replicated data types (CRDTs) [23] are designed to permit monotonic updates, and they are suitable for achieving eventual consistency. Cloud types [2] are more general compared with CRDTs. They preserve availability by "read my own writes" and achieve eventual consistency using a global sequence protocol [4] whenever the network is available.

Information Flow Control. Information flow control tracks how information propagates within a program to guarantee a specific property. It is a popular method in the security fields. The research on information flow security has lasted for over 40 years. Our work is inspired by [24], which provides a higher-order static security-typed language with references. We transfer the concept of security levels into consistency levels and obtain a noninterference property. LJGS [6] is another security type system for object-oriented languages. EnerJ [22] considers the isolation of two program parts under an energy-accuracy trade-off scenario. Recently, there are also some works on studying information flow security with different memory models. Vaughan and Millstein [26] first studied noninterference on total store order, [17] then extended the studies to four different memory models. These works provide a better insight into the impact of weak memory models on information flow security.

6   Conclusion

In order to meet increasing demands for scalability, availability, and fault tolerance, distributed system developers, need to trade consistency for availability. However, mixing strongly consistent and weakly consistent data within the same application can give rise to bugs that are difficult to find and fix. In this paper, we presented a type system that enables the safe use of both kinds of data within the same program. The proof of a noninterference theorem guarantees that updates of weakly-consistent data can never affect strongly-consistent data. Finally, the main theorem states that sequential consistency is guaranteed for so-called "con" operations in our language. We believe this result is an important step towards programming languages that enable the safe use of weakly consistent data alongside strongly consistent data in order to increase the scalability, availability, and fault tolerance of future distributed systems.

Acknowledgments. This work is supported by the China Scholarship Council 201600160040, and by the Tianhe Supercomputer Project 2018YFB0204301.

References

1. Burckhardt, S.: Principles of eventual consistency. Found. Trends Program. Lang. 1(1–2), 1–150 (2014)
2. Burckhardt, S., Fähndrich, M., Leijen, D., Wood, B.P.: Cloud types for eventual consistency. In: Noble, J. (ed.) ECOOP 2012. LNCS, vol. 7313, pp. 283–307. Springer, Heidelberg (2012). https://doi.org/10.1007/978-3-642-31057-7_14
3. Burckhardt, S., Gotsman, A., Yang, H.: Understanding eventual consistency. Technical report MSR-TR-2013-39, Microsoft Research (2013)
4. Burckhardt, S., Leijen, D., Protzenko, J., Fähndrich, M.: Global sequence protocol: a robust abstraction for replicated shared state. In: ECOOP, pp. 568–590 (2015)
5. De Porre, K., Myter, F., Scholliers, C., Boix, E.G.: CScript: a distributed programming language for building mixed-consistency applications. J. Parallel Distrib. Comput. **144**, 109–123 (2020)

6. Fennell, L., Thiemann, P.: LJGS: gradual security types for object-oriented languages. In: ECOOP, pp. 9:1–9:26 (2016)
7. Gilbert, S., Lynch, N.A.: Brewer's conjecture and the feasibility of consistent, available, partition-tolerant web services. SIGACT News **33**(2), 51–59 (2002)
8. Heintze, N., Riecke, J.G.: The SLam calculus: Programming with secrecy and integrity. In: POPL,pp. 365–377 (1998)
9. Holt, B., Bornholt, J., Zhang, I., Ports, D.R.K., Oskin, M., Ceze, L.: Disciplined inconsistency with consistency types. In: SoCC, pp. 279–293 (2016)
10. Ladin, R., Liskov, B., Ghemawat, S.: Providing high availability using lazy replication. ACM Trans. Comput. Syst. **10**(4), 360–391 (1992)
11. Lamport, L.: Time, clocks, and the ordering of events in a distributed system. Commun. ACM **21**(7), 558–565 (1978)
12. Lamport, L.: How to make a multiprocessor computer that correctly executes multiprocess programs. IEEE Trans. Comput. C **28**(9), 690 (1979)
13. Lamport, L.: The part-time parliament. ACM Trans. Comput. Syst **16**(2), 133–169 (1998)
14. Li, C., Porto, D., Clement, A., Gehrke, J., Preguiça, N.M., Rodrigues, R.: Making geo-replicated systems fast as possible, consistent when necessary. In: OSDI. pp. 265–278 (2012)
15. Li, J., Krohn, M.N., Mazieres, D., Shasha, D.: Secure untrusted data repository (SUNDR). In: OSDI, pp. 121–136, December 2004
16. Lu, H., et al.: Existential consistency: measuring and understanding consistency at Facebook. In: SOSP, pp. 295–310 (2015)
17. Mantel, H., Perner, M., Sauer, J.: Noninterference under weak memory models. In: CSF, pp. 80–94 (2014)
18. Margara, A., Salvaneschi, G.: Consistency types for safe and efficient distributed programming. In: FTfJP, pp. 8:1–8:2 (2017)
19. Mazieres, S.: Building secure file systems out of byzantine storage. In: PODC, pp. 108–117 (2002)
20. Milano, M., Myers, A.C.: MixT: a language for mixing consistency in geodistributed transactions. In: Proceedings of the 39th ACM SIGPLAN Conference on Programming Language Design and Implementation, PLDI 2018, Philadelphia, PA, USA, 18–22 June 2018, pp. 226–241. ACM (2018)
21. Ongaro, D., Ousterhout, J.K.: In search of an understandable consensus algorithm. In: USENIX ATC, pp. 305–319 (2014)
22. Sampson, A., Dietl, W., Fortuna, E., Gnanapragasam, D., Ceze, L., Grossman, D.: EnerJ: approximate data types for safe and general low-power computation. In: PLDI, pp. 164–174 (2011)
23. Shapiro, M., Preguiça, N., Baquero, C., Zawirski, M.: Conflict-free replicated data types. In: Défago, X., Petit, F., Villain, V. (eds.) SSS 2011. LNCS, vol. 6976, pp. 386–400. Springer, Heidelberg (2011). https://doi.org/10.1007/978-3-642-24550-3_29
24. Toro, M., Garcia, R., Tanter, É.: Type-driven gradual security with references. ACM Trans. Program. Lang. Syst **40**(4), 161–1655 (2018)
25. Tse, S., Zdancewic, S.: A design for a security-typed language with certificate-based declassification. In: Sagiv, M. (ed.) ESOP 2005. LNCS, vol. 3444, pp. 279–294. Springer, Heidelberg (2005). https://doi.org/10.1007/978-3-540-31987-0_20
26. Vaughan, J.A., Millstein, T.D.: Secure information flow for concurrent programs under total store order. In: CSF, pp. 19–29 (2012)
27. Zhao, X., Haller, P.: On consistency types for lattice-based distributed programming languages. CoRR abs/1907.00822 (2019). http://arxiv.org/abs/1907.00822

Common Subexpression Convergence: A New Code Optimization for SIMT Processors

Sana Damani[(✉)] and Vivek Sarkar[(✉)]

Georgia Institute of Technology, Atlanta, GA, USA
{sdamani,vsarkar}@gatech.edu

Abstract. On SIMT processors, when threads in a warp diverge at a branch, the hardware scheduler serializes their execution, thereby resulting in reduced SIMT efficiency. We propose a new compiler optimization, Common Subexpression Convergence (CSC), that uses cross-block scheduling to ensure that expression trees that are common across diverged paths are moved to convergent regions and executed by more/all threads in parallel, thereby improving SIMT efficiency and execution time. Our optimization framework is based on a dynamic programming algorithm for finding maximally profitable common expression subgraphs. We also introduce a general approach to test the legality of our optimization based on the program dependence graph, and a heuristic-based cost model to decide when the optimization should be applied. We demonstrate the potential benefits of our approach through a preliminary hand-optimized evaluation using synthetic benchmarks and a BitonicSort example program.

Keywords: SIMT processors · Thread divergence · Compiler optimizations · GPUs

1 Introduction

On Single Instruction Multiple Thread (SIMT) processors, such as a GPU, all threads in a warp execute the same instruction at the same program counter location in parallel on different data. However, when a branch instruction is encountered such that the branch condition evaluates to *taken* for some threads and *not taken* for others, then the threads in the warp are said to have *diverged*. To handle this situation, the hardware scheduler in a SIMT processor serializes the execution of threads within the divergent region, and the warp no longer issues instructions in parallel across threads in a warp, which results in reduced SIMT efficiency and thereby hurts overall execution time [6].

We propose a code motion optimization, called Common Subexpression Convergence (CSC), that helps reduce the cost of thread divergence in programs where *taken* and *not taken* paths of a divergent branch contain common operations. Our optimization moves such operations to a convergent region of execution where more/all threads can execute them in parallel.

For the remainder of this paper, we use Nvidia's thread and warp terminology and profile metrics [8], without loss of generality. To maximize SIMT efficiency, a

© Springer Nature Switzerland AG 2021
S. Pande and V. Sarkar (Eds.): LCPC 2019, LNCS 11998, pp. 64–73, 2021.
https://doi.org/10.1007/978-3-030-72789-5_5

measure of the proportion of time threads in a warp execute in parallel, we must minimize the number of instructions executed by threads in divergent regions.

The main contributions of this paper include:

- A dynamic programming based algorithm to find profitable common expression subgraphs across divergent branches.
- An approach to testi the legality of CSC based on the Program Dependence Graph (PDG).
- A cost model to decide when CSC is profitable.
- A preliminary hand-optimized evaluation of CSC on synthetic benchmarks and a BitonicSort example program.

We emphasize that this is a work in progress and that the main direction for future work is to build a complete automatic compiler implementation of the CSC optimization, and evaluate it on a large set of GPU benchmark programs.

2 Overview of Approach

In this section, we summarize the three code motion transformations used in our framework for optimizing common subexpression convergence. All three transformations are guaranteed to result in a SIMT efficiency that is greater than or equal to the prior SIMT efficiency. However, it is possible to sometimes see performance degradation due to increases in variable live ranges, introduction of pipeline stalls, or changes in cache behavior.

Hoist. This transformation moves common code to the nearest convergent control flow point before threads diverge at the branch, as illustrated in Listings 1.1 and 1.2. This is only legal if all incoming definitions are located at or before the branch, or can also be hoisted.

Listing 1.1. Before Hoist	**Listing 1.2.** After Hoist

```
1  b = ...;
2  c = ...;
3  if (threadId % 2)  {
4      a = b * c;
5      use a;
6  } else {
7      a = b * c;
8  }
```

```
1  b = ...;
2  c = ...;
3  a = b * c;
4  if (threadId % 2)  {
5      use a;
6  } else {
7      ...
8  }
```

Sink. This transformation moves common code to the nearest convergent control flow point after threads reconverge at the postdominator, as illustrated in Listings 1.3 and 1.4. This is only legal if all uses of the instruction and redefinitions of its operands can also be moved to the join point.

Listing 1.3. Before Sink

```
1   c = ...;
2   if (threadId % 2)  {
3       b = 10;
4       a = b * c;
5   } else {
6       a = b * c;
7   }
8   use a;
```

Listing 1.4. After Sink

```
1   c = ...;
2   if (threadId % 2)  {
3       b = 10;
4       ...
5   } else {
6       ...
7   }
8   a = b * c;
9   use a;
```

Split. To handle operations that can neither be hoisted nor sunk to a convergent region, we introduce an intermediate temporary reconvergence point within the divergent region, as illustrated in Listings 1.5 and 1.6. The common code can be moved to this region before threads diverge once again. As with Hoist and Sink, this transformation is guaranteed to result in a SIMT efficiency that is greater than or equal to the prior SIMT efficiency. However, Split can sometimes introduce more overhead compared to the Hoist and Sink transformations due to branch duplication and extra synchronization instructions.

Listing 1.5. Before Split

```
1    b = ...;
2    c = ...;
3    if (threadId % 2)  {
4        a = b * c;
5        use a;
6    } else {
7        b = 10;
8        a = b * c;
9    }
10   use a;
```

Listing 1.6. After Split

```
1    b = ...;
2    c = ...;
3    if (threadId % 2)  {
4        ...
5    } else {
6        b = 10;
7    }
8    a = b * c;
9    if (threadId % 2)  {
10       use a;
11   } else {
12       ...
13   }
14   use a;
```

Extension with Operand Renaming. Statements 2 and 5 in Listing 1.7 can be executed in parallel by different threads because they have the same opcode, even though their source and result operands do not match. This is legal because by virtue of the SIMT execution model, each thread performs the same operation *on different data*.

To optimize this code pattern, we can insert MOV instructions and rename operands so that statements (1) and (2) can be issued as a single instruction as seen in Listing 1.8. However, extra care is needed when performing the code convergence optimization with operand renaming, to account for the extra cost of MOV instructions.

Listing 1.7. Before Renaming	**Listing 1.8.** After Renaming

```
1  if (threadId % 2)  {          1  if (threadId % 2)  {
2      a = b * c;                2      x = b;
3      ...                       3  } else {
4  } else {                      4      x = d;
5      a = d * c;                5  }
6      ...                       6  a = x * c;
7  }                             7  use a;
8  use a;
```

Problem Statement: *Given a GPU program, identify the best combination of hoist, sink and split optimizations to move common operations to a convergent region such that no dependences are violated.*

Legality: A reordering transformation that preserves every dependence preserves the meaning of the program. As described above, Hoist and Sink are only performed if the transformation preserves all data dependences and Split does not alter the order of statements in the program. CSC is therefore a legal reordering optimization.

3   Algorithmic Details

At a high level, our algorithm finds common expression sub-graphs that are control dependent [2] on the same divergent branch and computes the profitability and legality of code motion. We first describe a dynamic programming solution for optimal sub-graph matching given two computation graphs. Next, we describe a region-based graph traversal approach that incrementally discovers and optimizes divergent branches.

3.1   Common Sub-expression Detection

Given two expression DAGs that are control dependent on the same divergent branch, our goal is to detect the maximally profitable matching subgraph. We shall use Listing 1.9 as our running example to explain this algorithm.

Listing 1.9. Dynamic Programming: Code Example

```
1  if (condition) { a = b * c;    d = a + c;    e = d * d; }
2  else           { a = b * c;    f = a / c;    e = f * f; }
```

To support operand re-use, we use expression DAGs rather than trees as shown in Fig. 1a. As in other work, we formally define the expression DAG to be a directed graph G such that leaves represent variables, interior nodes represent operators, and an edge from a to b indicates that b is an input to a. We assume an SSA representation so that each variable is defined only once. Our goal is to find a subgraph matching that maximizes (Benefit - Cost), where Cost and Benefit are defined as follows:

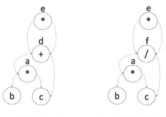

	b	c	a=b*c	d=a+b	e=d*d
b	0	-Cost(copy)	-Cost(copy)	-Cost(copy)	-Cost(copy)
c	-Cost(copy)	0	-Cost(copy)	-Cost(copy)	-Cost(copy)
a=b*c	-Cost(copy)	-Cost(copy)	Benefit(*) + T(b,b) + T(c,c)	-Cost(copy)	Benefit(*) + T(b,d) + T(c,d),
f=a/b	-Cost(copy)	-Cost(copy)	-Cost(copy)	-Cost(copy)	-Cost(copy)
e=f*f	-Cost(copy)	-Cost(copy)	Benefit(*) + T(f,b) + T(f,c)	-Cost(copy)	Benefit(*) + T(f,d) + T(f,d)

Expression DAG for Taken Path   Expression DAG for Not Taken Path

(a) Expression graph for Listing 1.9

(b) Dynamic Programming for Listing 1.9

Fig. 1. Dynamic programming

- Cost = Increase in number of copy instructions needed to handle operand renaming.
- Benefit = Decrease in number of divergently executed instructions. The benefit of moving a function call or loop into common code path may be much greater than the benefit of moving an arithmetic instruction, and we therefore introduce a weighted model for benefit computation, biased towards convergent execution of more expensive instructions.

Our dynamic programming solution, while optimal for the given cost model, may not always generate optimal code due to the limitations of the heuristic-based cost mode. In particular, we do not take into consideration the impact of code motion on scheduling and register pressure in Hoist and Sink transforms, or the cost of additional branch and synchronization instructions in the Split transform. Furthermore, Split may result in suboptimal application of compiler optimizations due to smaller basic blocks. We leave the exploration of these additional heuristics to future work and focus only on copy instructions in our cost model.

Table entries: Let $T(i, j)$ be the cost of matching node i and node j.

Initialization: $T(i, i)$ where i is a leaf node is trivially matched as having 0 cost while $T(i, j)$ where both i and j are leaf nodes is matched as having $+1$ cost required for the copy instruction.

Recurrence: We then define the recurrence to compute the profit of matching interior nodes, $T(i, j)$ as:
$T(i, j) = $ cost of copy insertion, if i and j have an operator mismatch
$T(i, j) = $ benefit of matching operator $+ \text{sum}(\max(\text{match subgraph}, \text{insert copy}))$
where, i and j belong to different expression DAGs.

Figure 1b shows the application of our dynamic programming approach on the program described in Listing 1.9.

3.2   Code Motion

We begin by building a program structure tree (PST) which is a hierarchical representation of single-entry single-exit regions of a control flow graph as described in [5]. We traverse this PST from leaves to the root, thereby ensuring that the innermost regions are handled first. This helps optimize programs with nested conditionals and loops.

At each region, we build a program dependence graph, a directed graph where nodes represent instructions in the region and edges between nodes represent control or data dependence between instructions. We use the control dependence edges to find operations that are control dependent on true and false edges of the same divergent branch, and data dependence edges to generate expression graphs and determine legality of code motion. Figures 2a and 2b represent the PDGs for Listing 1.1 and Listing 1.2 respectively.

> **Input** : Program P, threshold
> **Output:** Optimized Program P'
> **Function** *CommonSubexpressionConvergence(P)*

```
1    BuildPST();
2    for each region R in the PST in bottom up order do
3        BuildPDG(R);
4        if BranchIsDivergent(R.root) then
5            for each instruction I1 backwards in R.child0 do
6                for each instruction I2 backwards in R.child1 do
7                    D1 = BuildDAG(I1);
8                    D2 = BuildDAG(I2);
9                    Profit = MatchProfit(D1, D2);
10                   if Profit < threshold then
11                       continue;
12                   if LegalToHoist(D1, D2) then
13                       Hoist(D1, D2, R);
14                   else if LegalToSink(D1, D2) then
15                       Sink(D1, D2, R);
16                   else
17                       Split(D1, D2, R);
18       FlattenBranches();
```

Algorithm 1: Overall Algorithm for Common Subexpression Convergence

Next, we determine if the branch condition is divergent by checking if the branch depends on a thread-varying value using the method described in [1]. Finally, after each region is processed, we flatten the branches within the region to handle common sub-regions nested within outer regions. Branch flattening or predication eliminates branches in the region and converts control dependences to data dependences. Our algorithm treats these flattened branches as regular expression trees when handling the parent region. See Listing 1.11 for an example where branch flattening enabled additional optimization.

Branch flattening is insufficient for loops nested within regions which require special handling. When comparing two sub-regions within a region, we compare the loop bodies and iteration domains to detect common code and opportunity for optimization. If the loop iteration domains are non-identical, we may use loop peeling or index-set splitting to generate identical loops that can be hoisted. If the loop bodies are only partially common, we use loop distribution to separate out the common operations before performing code motion.

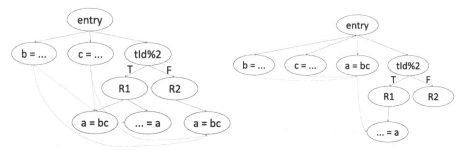

(a) PDG for Listing 1.1 before Hoisting.   (b) PDG for Listing 1.2 after Hoisting.

Fig. 2. PDGs before and after Hoist (solid and dashed edges correspond to control and data dependences respectively)

Listing 1.10. Nested Common Code

```
1  if (threadId % 2)  {
2      // common code
3      a = b * c;
4      use a;
5  } else {
6      if (threadId % 3) {
7          // common code
8          a = b * c;
9      }
10 }
```

Listing 1.11. Branch Flattening

```
1  if (threadId % 2)  {
2      p = true
3  } else {
4      p = threadId % 3;
5  }
6  // flattened common code
7  (p) a = b * c;
8  if (threadId % 2)  {
9      use a;
10 }
```

3.3   Time Complexity Analysis

We present an approximate solution to optimal expression DAG matching using a heuristic-based dynamic programming approach. The 2-dimensional table *Profit* takes $O(n^2)$ time to build, where n is the number of instructions within an expression DAG. This procedure is repeated for each instruction within the divergent branch. Hence, for each region R, the algorithm takes $O(n^2)$ time in the worst case because the *Profit* table caches matching data, thereby ensuring that each pair of instructions within the divergent branch is only compared once. If the number of regions is m, the overall optimization takes $O(mn^2)$ time.

4   Preliminary Results

We evaluated our algorithm by hand transformations on microbenchmarks designed to provide optimization opportunities for the (1) hoist, (2) sink, and (3) split transformations, as well as for the use of (4) a multi-way switch statement. Figure 3 shows increased SIMT efficiency, fewer memory operations and improved runtimes. In particular, moving code to convergent paths reduced the number of DRAM reads by up to 26×. We validated these results by created an automated implementation in the LLVM compiler for the Hoist transformation, which delivered comparable performance to our hand-coded implementation. For BitonicSort, our results show variability in execution times, with improvements in Max times and no degradation in Min and Average times with CSC. Listing 1.12 shows the relevant step of bitonic sort which has common code across divergent branches for a swap operation. We use branch flattening and sinking to move the common code to a convergent path and test our optimization using the GPU implementation of bitonic sort available on GitHub at [3].

Listing 1.12. Bitonic Sort

```
1   bitonic_sort(ascending)
2   {
3       if (ascending) {
4           // sort in ascending order
5           if (array[i]>array[j]) {
6               swap(array[i],array[j]);
    // common across diverged paths
7           }
8       }
9       else {
10          // sort in descending order
11          if (array[i]<array[j]) {
12              swap(array[i],array[j]);
    // common across diverged paths
13          }
14      }
15  }
```

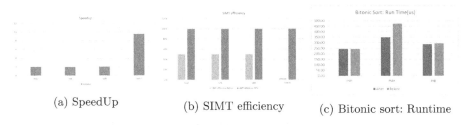

(a) SpeedUp   (b) SIMT efficiency   (c) Bitonic sort: Runtime

Fig. 3. Benchmark results

5   Related Work

Branch Fusion. Coutinho et al. describe branch fusion, a divergence optimization that uses a variation of sequence alignment, called instruction alignment, to identify common code across diverged paths [1] and merge divergent code using the *Split* transformation. They do not consider the use of code hoisting or sinking as a means to avoid the introduction of additional branch instructions. Further, their instruction alignment algorithm is restricted to common code discovered in a specific order, a limitation overcome by our graph-based approach.

Branch Distribution. Han and Abdelrahman propose branch distribution [4], an optimization to reduce branch divergence by factoring out structurally similar code from diverged paths thereby reducing the total number of dynamic instructions executed in the divergent region. They do not however provide an algorithm to detect and move common code in divergent branches; also, it is unclear whether their approach extends to loops and nested conditionals.

Partial Redundancy Elimination. CSC is similar to PRE in that they both aim at eliminating redundant execution of instructions in conditional code regions using code motion. However, while PRE eliminates redundant recomputation of a scalar value in single-threaded execution [7], CSC eliminates redundant re-execution of a vector operation by preventing temporal misalignment of an instruction across threads in a warp.

6   Conclusion and Future Work

In conclusion, we find that significant opportunity exists to improve SIMT efficiency in parallel programs with divergent branches. We have described a new $O(mn^2)$ time code motion optimization called Common Subexpression Convergence (CSC), which is designed to improve SIMT efficiency by moving common code from divergent to convergent paths of execution.

We believe that further opportunities for CSC may be found when targeting multicore CPU code (written using OpenCL or OpenMP, for example) to run on GPUs. Unlike hand-written CUDA code that is optimized for execution on the GPU, automatically generated GPU code from multicore CPU code may be suboptimal since divergence does not pose a performance penalty on multicore CPUs. Whereas common code across conditional branches is not redundant in CPU execution, the same code may perform poorly on SIMT architectures without the application of CSC. Additionally, the optimization can further be extended to interprocedural common subexpression convergence using analysis across function calls.

References

1. Coutinho, B., Sampaio, D., Pereira, F.M.Q., Meira Jr., W.: Divergence analysis and optimizations. In: 2011 International Conference on Parallel Architectures and Compilation Techniques (2011)

2. Cytron, R., Ferrante, J., Sarkar, V.: Compact representations for control dependence. In: Proceedings of the ACM SIGPLAN 1990 Conference on Programming Language Design and Implementation (1990)
3. Endler, M.: Bitonic Sort on CUDA
4. Han, T.D., Abdelrahman, T.S.: Reducing branch divergence in GPU programs. In: Proceedings of the Fourth Workshop on General Purpose Processing on Graphics Processing Units (2011)
5. Johnson, R., Pearson, D., Pingali, K.: The program structure tree: computing control regions in linear time. In: Proceedings of the ACM SIGPLAN 1994 Conference on Programming Language Design and Implementation (1994)
6. Lindholm, E., Nickolls, J., Oberman, S., Montrym, J.: Nvidia tesla: a unified graphics and computing architecture. IEEE Micro 28(2), 39–55 (2008)
7. Morel, E., Renvoise, C.: Global optimization by suppression of partial redundancies. ACM Commun. 22(2), 96–103 (1979)
8. NVIDIA. SIMT Efficiency

Using Performance Event Profiles
to Deduce an Execution Model of
MATLAB with Just-In-Time Compilation

Patryk Kiepas[1]([✉]) [ID], Corinne Ancourt[1] [ID], Claude Tadonki[1] [ID],
and Jarosław Koźlak[2] [ID]

[1] MINES ParisTech/PSL University, Paris, France
`{patryk.kiepas,corinne.ancourt,claude.tadonki}@mines-paristech.fr`
[2] AGH University of Science and Technology, Kraków, Poland
`kozlak@agh.edu.pl`

Abstract. The knowledge about how an interpreter executes programs allows writing faster code and creating powerful source-to-source compilers. However, many languages and environments either lack a specification of the execution semantics, or the semantics frequently changes with new releases. In this article, we present (1) *performance event profiles* with *execution regions*, inventive use of event-based sampling on processors where we correlate profiles of many performance events to find regions with desired properties. Furthermore, we use the *performance event profiles* to deduce (2) a static, tree-based *execution model* of MATLAB with the Just-In-Time (JIT) compilation. The environment of MATLAB is closed-source, which makes it a perfect testbed for our approach. With the new model and better understanding of how MATLAB executes programs, we propose a new code transformation, (3) *repacking of array slices*, which can increase the amount of JIT-compiled code in MATLAB programs.

Keywords: Hardware performance counters · Event-based sampling · Performance event profile · MATLAB · Just-In-Time compilation · Execution model · Repacking of array slices

1 Introduction

Listing 1.1 depicts how MATLAB programmers express element-wise computations as loops or array operations (with or without array slicing). All three codes perform the same computation producing the same result. However, they use a different type of floating-point operations, execute different number and kind of CPU instructions, and, more importantly, have vastly different performance.

S. Pande and V. Sarkar (Eds.): LCPC 2019, LNCS 11998, pp. 74–88, 2021.
https://doi.org/10.1007/978-3-030-72789-5_6

Listing 1.1. Three versions of the *striad* kernel (the Schönauer Vector Triad). In MATLAB, it is common to express loops as array operations (loop vectorisation).

```
% Scalar loop code (loop)
for k = 1:N
    a(k) = b(k) + c(k) .* d(k);
end
```

```
% Vector code with array slicing (vec)
a(1:N) = b(1:N) + c(1:N) .* d(1:N);
% Vector code on whole arrays (vec_01)
a = b + c .* d;
```

To find out about what kind of instruction codes from Listing 1.1 execute, we could use dynamic binary instrumentation with tools, e.g. DynamoRIO [2] or Intel PIN [11]. However, MATLAB is a closed-source environment with no linking symbols available. This closed nature of MATLAB makes even the task of matching machine code to a specific language component (e.g. garbage collector, JIT compiler, external libraries) hard. Moreover, the machine code of the MATLAB environment is mixed up with the dynamically generated code created by the JIT compiler.

Instead, we could analyse how codes from Listing 1.1 execute using popular metrics and performance model. For example: the Roofline Model by Williams et al. [20] which graphically shows if the code is memory or compute-bound; the Top-Down μ-architecture Analysis Method (TMAM) by Yasin [21] which indicates which part of the processor pipeline is the execution bottleneck with a detailed 4-level hierarchy of 33 metrics; or to use metrics like cache miss ratio or cycles per instructions (CPI) [10]. However, at the core, metrics and models mentioned above do not consider how the program execution changes over time, which is the key to successful analysis of MATLAB programs.

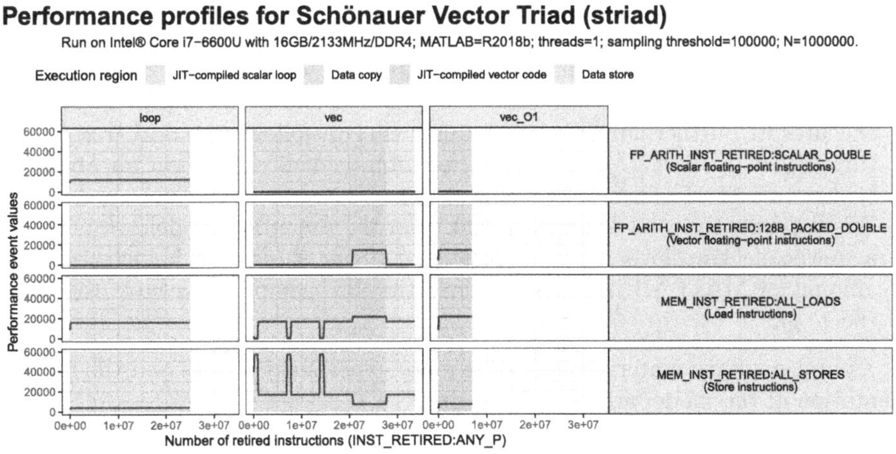

Fig. 1. Performance profiles of three versions of the *striad* kernel: loop computation (`loop`); vectorised operations with array slicing (`vec`); vectorised operations on all data (`vec_01`). The figure depicts four distinctive regions: JIT-compiled scalar loop, data copy, JIT-compiled vector code, and data store.

Figure 1 shows how the program execution of the three codes changes as more instructions on the processor retire. The graph depicts several *performance event profiles* built with the Event-Based Profiling (EBS) [16] of four performance events: scalar and vector floating-point operations, load and store instructions (from top to bottom). By aligning the profiles together, we find *execution regions* with particular properties, e.g. data copy or computation. Moreover, we can draw several observations from Fig. 1: (1) loops perform scalar arithmetic instructions; (2) array operations perform vector arithmetic instructions (e.g. with Intel SSE, AVX extensions); (3) array slicing requires a copy of the data; (4) loop and vector codes without array slices are perfectly regular.

Throughout this paper, we use the two concepts of *performance event profiles* and *execution regions* to discover rules of program execution in the MATLAB environment. We analyse built-in and user-defined functions, common arithmetic operators, array referencing and slicing, and the impact of the JIT compilation. Finally, we build a simple execution model of MATLAB programs from which we can derive promising code transformations.

In the paper, we make the following contributions:

- We describe *performance event profiles* built using hardware event-based sampling on processors (Sect. 2). The profiles consist of values of several performance events sampled over time. With a notion of *execution regions* in the profiles, we can find parts of programs with desired properties, e.g. data copy or floating-point computation.
- We briefly present our open-source tool `mPAPI`[1], which gives access to hardware performance counters from the MATLAB/Octave programs (Sect. 2). The tool uses the `PAPI` library [18] and supports two measurements modes: *counting* and *sampling*.
- Using *performance event profiles*, we deduce and build an *execution model* for MATLAB expressions in the presence of JIT compilation (Sect. 3). The proposed model takes source-code of expression and predicts how MATLAB executes it. Furthermore, the model uses easy-to-follow graphical tree structure, called *(minimal) instruction tree*, obtained directly from an abstract syntax tree (AST) form of this expression.
- Finally, with the knowledge obtained from the execution model, we propose a new code transformation, *repacking of array slices*, which increases the amount of MATLAB instructions that the JIT compiler executes together (Sect. 4).

Complementary materials including more experiment results and the implementation of the model are available online[2].

2   Performance Event Profiles

Performance event profiles describe the change in performance events measured over time. Fortunately, hardware performance counters in modern CPUs work

---

in two modes: (1) *counting mode* where the values of a performance event accumulate in a single register; and more importantly (2) *sampling mode* where a program interruption occurs and a measurement is taken every time a sampling event used as "time" reaches a specified *sampling threshold*. Therefore, the capabilities of building performance profiles are already built-in inside modern CPUs with mechanisms of *counter overflow*, Event-Based Sampling (EBS), and recently Precise Event-Based Sampling (PEBS) on Intel processors [4, 16].

2.1 Concept Definitions

Performance Event Profile. We define a performance profile as $P = (T, M)$ where $T = (t_1, t_2, \ldots, t_l)$ and $M = (m_1, m_2, \ldots, m_l)$ are sequences of the sampling event and measurement values such that $t_i, m_i \in \mathbb{N}$, and the sampling event values are strictly increasing $\forall i < j : t_i < t_j$. Both T and M have the same length l, and the length of the profile is denoted by $|P| = l$. Moreover, T and M have their *event domain* $\mathcal{E}$, which states what performance event the sequence represents. The universe of event domain $\mathcal{E}$ contains any performance event available on the CPU. For example, a sequence M of *L1 cache misses* measurements has the event domain as follows $\mathcal{E}(M) = $ L1D:REPLACEMENT. The event domain of the performance profile $\mathcal{E}(P) = (\mathcal{E}(T), \mathcal{E}(M))$ with sequences T and M creates a full description of the profile. Event domains specify the profile content, where M holds the measurements and T stores values of the sampling event.

Profiles Group. Building only one performance profile at a time would result in poor resource management, as the rest of hardware performance registers are unused. Therefore, it is beneficial to measure several performance profiles at once, creating a *group* $G = \{P_1, P_2, \ldots, P_g\}$ of g profiles. In a machine with N hardware performance registers, we can create only $g = N - 1$ profiles, because the last register measures the sampling event. Moreover, profiles in a group are *aligned* because they are measured together; thus, we can simplify the group definition to $G = (T, \{M_1, M_2, \ldots, M_g\})$, where the profiles and their measurements share the sampling event from T. As in the case of performance profiles, groups have their event domain $\mathcal{E}(G) = (\mathcal{E}(T), \{\mathcal{E}(M_1), \mathcal{E}(M_2), \ldots, \mathcal{E}(M_g)\})$.

Execution Region. A section of the program execution with particular properties is an *execution region* expressed as a binary predicate $\varphi : T \rightarrow \{0, 1\}$. The predicate marks the desired region in the domain of the sampling event. Thus, the predicate indicates when the region starts and ends during the program execution. Moreover, the data copy region indicates either the occurrence of array slicing or at least where program execution has properties similar to the data copy. In the construction of the predicate φ, we use only aligned measurements coming from the same profiles group. Otherwise, ambiguities can appear, e.g. when two performance profiles P_1 and P_2 have different length $|P_1| \neq |P_2|$. Nevertheless, it is possible to use performance profiles from two or more groups after aligning them using, e.g. dynamic time warping (DTW) [7].

2.2   Performance Profiles with mPAPI

Apart from manually programming hardware performance counters, several libraries give easy access to both modes of measurement: counting and sampling. In our work, we have focused on the PAPI [18], because it is a comprehensive, open-source, up-to-date, actively maintained library with a C API which makes it possible to integrate with MATLAB through C MEX API[3]. In order to access performance event directly from MATLAB source-code and to mitigate the possible imprecisions and overheads of measuring hardware performance counters [19,22], we have built mPAPI, an open-source tool for MATLAB. mPAPI supports counting and sampling modes of collecting performance events, along with multiplexed and per-thread measurements.

3   Execution Model for JIT Compilation in MATLAB

Without a Just-In-Time (JIT) compiler, MATLAB would be an interpreter which executes (interprets) instructions step by step. The interpreter fetches, decodes, and executes each instruction in isolation without any knowledge about future instructions. However, with the JIT compiler, MATLAB can defer execution of the instruction as long as possible (in the APL interpreter, this concept is known as *drag-along* [1]). This delay often creates new optimisation opportunities for the JIT compiler, because the compiler carries information about future instructions. The opportunity leads to better instruction scheduling, register allocation and code optimisations, especially involving the execution of two or more instructions which can execute together. In this section, we prepare a model describing when the JIT compiler optimises code regions consisting of many instructions.

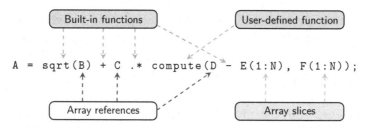

Fig. 2. Common components of expressions with array operations in MATLAB.

Scope of the Model. We focus on expressions consisting of four components depicted in Fig. 2: (1) built-in functions; (2) user-defined functions; (3) array references; and (4) array slices. Our model aims at expressing these components and their order of execution.

---

[3] https://www.mathworks.com/help/matlab/call-mex-files-1.html.

Instruction Block. Instead of compiling only single instructions, the JIT compiler can compile whole blocks of instructions, thus, benefiting from new optimisation opportunities. We define the *instruction block* Γ as a program segment containing one or more instructions $\Gamma.inst = \{\gamma_1, \gamma_2, \ldots\}$. Each instruction γ_i indicates a call to the MATLAB built-in or user-defined function. Array slicing is expressed separately, because it always performs the same operation, a data copy. Furthermore, a single block can contain multiple calls to the same function (thus, $\Gamma.inst$ is a multiset).

All instructions from the block are scheduled together for the execution by the JIT compiler. Therefore, we say they are *JIT-compiled*, which means, the JIT compiler is responsible for fetching, decoding, optimising, and scheduling them together for the execution. However, we are not concerned about their order, because in many cases, the original execution order would be hard to deduce and highly dependent on the compiler, compilation heuristics, and the target machine.

Detecting Instruction Blocks. The result of the JIT compilation of an instruction block is a machine code stored in the instruction cache on the processor. Before the execution, the processor fetches and decodes this machine code into microoperations (μops), executable by the processor. The fetch-decode phase results in several observable performance events on the processor, such as instruction cache miss (`L2_RQSTS:CODE_RD_MISS`) and hit (`L2_RQSTS:ALL_CODE_RD`). Therefore, an activity of the performance events related to the fetch-decode phase could indicate the beginning and end of the instruction block execution.

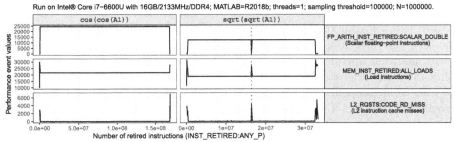

Detection of instruction blocks

Fig. 3. Code examples generating one and two instruction blocks. In this example, `cos` is a combinable function.

Figure 3 presents how the activity of the L2 instruction cache misses indicates boundaries of instruction blocks. The first code `cos(cos(A1))` is JIT-compiled and executed as one instruction block because we observe the activity of the cache misses only at the beginning and end of the computation. The second code `sqrt(sqrt(A1))` is also JIT-compiled; however, the code is divided into two instruction blocks marked by the spike of cache misses in the middle of the computation. The existence of two instruction blocks indicates here that the sqrt function is not *combinable* with itself and requires one instruction block for each call. In the next paragraph, we use the concept of *combinable function* to find which functions can coexist with others in the same instruction block. The execution of fewer instruction blocks resulting from the use of combinable functions can improve program efficiency.

Combinable Functions. Instruction blocks can potentially contain any combination of functions which make it infeasible to test them all. Therefore, we propose to use three simple detection patterns in Table 1, to assess if a given function is *combinable*, meaning, it can coexist with other functions in the same instruction block. Every pattern in Table 1 is a composition of at least two functions because only then we can observe if the JIT compiler creates two instruction blocks for one expression and if the function is combinable.

Table 1. Three detection patterns used for finding dynamic (JIT) compilation of MATLAB functions. The presented patterns use built-in functions, cos and atan2.

Detection pattern	Unary	Binary
Self-composition	cos(cos(A1))	atan2(atan2(A1, A2), A3)
Composition plus:+	cos(A1)+cos(A2)	atan2(A1, A2)+atan2(A3, A4)
Arguments plus:+	cos(A1+A2)	atan2(A1+A2, A3+A4)

Table 1 presents code patterns which we use to detect if given built-in functions (unary and binary) can be a part of a multi-instruction block. The first pattern is a self-composition f(f(A)), which is the simplest way for one function to create a complex expression. The next two patterns compose function f with addition operator +/plus, which is JIT-compiled (we have verified this using the same approach as described). The second pattern f(A)+f(B) tests if the plus composes well with functions f as its arguments. Finally, the third pattern f(A+B) validates if the function f executes with a complex expression as its argument inside a single instruction block.

Using these three patterns from Table 1, we have executed various built-in functions to find out several *combinable functions*: abs, ceil, cos, exp, floor, ldivide=.\, minus=-, plus=+, rdivide=./, round, sin, tan, times=.*, transpose, and others. The list of non-*combinable functions* includes acos, cumsum, diff, fft, log, mtimes=*, power, prod, sqrt, sum, and much more. Furthermore, although not shown in the paper, the user-defined functions are never *combinable*, and they evaluate just like non-combinable built-in functions do.

3.1   The Minimal Instruction Tree Model

The knowledge about (non-)combinable functions and the content of particular instruction blocks lack the information about the execution order of these blocks. Furthermore, because instruction blocks do not express array slicing, we would also like to track when the slicing appears. For this task, this section introduces instruction trees.

Instruction Tree. Similar to the abstract syntax tree (AST), the *instruction tree* represents instructions and usages of variables. However, unlike in the AST, a single inter-node in the instruction tree can represent several instructions enclosed inside an instruction block. Steps 1 and 2 in Fig. 4 visualise the difference between the AST and the corresponding instruction tree. The initial translation from the AST to the instruction tree is straightforward, as it only requires a one-to-one mapping of each instruction to ● *instruction block* node; each array reference to □ *array reference* leaf; and each array slice to ■ *array slice* leaf. For simplicity, and because it does not generate any execution regions, we remove the leaf of the reference A3 and instead, we store it in the corresponding instruction block (grey set in step 3 in Fig. 4).

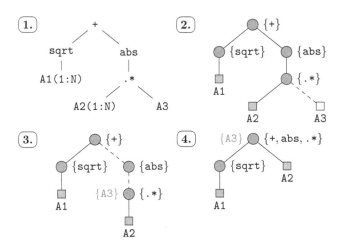

Fig. 4. Steps required for obtaining the minimal instruction tree: (1) conversion to the AST; (2) one-to-one translation of the AST to the instruction tree with the removal of array references; (3) application of Algorithm 1; (4) the result minimal form of the instruction tree.

Minimal Instruction Tree. At this point, our instruction tree is in the maximal form, because each instruction has its block. However, the JIT compilation in MATLAB can combine such blocks. Algorithm 1 expresses this merging as a repetitive process which combines pairs of instruction blocks as long as there exists any pair of combinable blocks left. Therefore, the result of Algorithm 1 is a *minimal instruction tree* consisting of a minimum possible number of instruction blocks, such as the tree from step 4 in Fig. 4. The resulting tree indicates the order of execution regions occurring during the execution of MATLAB expressions.

Algorithm 1. Building of a minimal instruction tree by the repetitive merging of instruction blocks inside an instruction tree.

Input: the root node of the initial instruction tree
Output: minimal instruction tree

```
 1: function CANMERGE(node)
 2:     correctInst ← node.inst ⊆ combinableFunctions
 3:     return ISINSTRUCTIONBLOCK(node)∧correctInst

 4: function BUILDMINIMALTREE(node)
 5:     revChildren ← REVERSELIST(node.children)        ▷ Visit from right-to-left
 6:     for child in revChildren do
 7:         BUILDMINIMALTREE(child)                      ▷ Recursive visit of the tree
 8:     if CANMERGE(node)∧CANMERGE(node.parent) then
 9:         if ¬HASRIGHTSIBLING(node) then
10:             node.parent.inst ← node.inst ⊎ node.parent.inst
11:             ATTACH(node.children, node.parent)
12:             REMOVEFROMPARENT(node)
```

Obtaining the Minimal Instruction Tree. The main function BUILDMINIMAL-TREE from Algorithm 1 is a recursive method which traverses the input instruction tree and finds candidates of instruction blocks for merging. The routine traverses the tree in a post-order, but with children visited right-to-left (lines 5–7). The reason for the reversed visit of children is the evaluation order of arguments in MATLAB, which is left-to-right. Hence, MATLAB evaluates expression e1 + e2 starting with arguments e1, e2 and finishing with the + operator which creates an evaluation sequence: e1, e2, +. With the standard post-order traversal and left-to-right visiting of children, we would never merge e1 with + (even if possible), because the second expression e2 stands on the way—e2 evaluates in between e1 and +. However, if we visit children right-to-left, then we could merge e2 with + and give to e1 an opportunity to combine with a newly created block of instructions {e2,+}. Therefore, the merge of a node with its parent is possible only when the node has none of the right siblings (line 9).

The presented perspective on merging nodes (instruction blocks) is related to the structure of the instruction tree, which encodes the evaluation order of MATLAB operations. However, the lack of right siblings node is not the only condition required for merging instruction blocks. The other condition, even more important, is if both instruction blocks contain only *combinable functions* which can be merged. The function CANMERGE from Algorithm 1 encapsulates the condition, and it is used in line 8. Moreover, the CANMERGE can work only on instruction blocks; hence, the use of the ISINSTRUCTIONBLOCK predicate. Finally, we merge two nodes by adding together the instructions from both merged blocks (line 10). The operation ⊎ is a *multiset sum*, which not only performs a union between two multisets, but it also adds repeated elements multiple times inside the result multiset. The subsequent operations rebuild the structure of the instruction tree by connecting child nodes (line 11) and removing one of the merged nodes (line 12).

Instruction Chain. Finally, we flatten the minimal instruction tree (step 4 from Fig. 4) by traversing it in the post-order manner (left branch, right branch, root). The result is an *instruction chain* which represents the order of execution regions during the program run presented in Fig. 5.

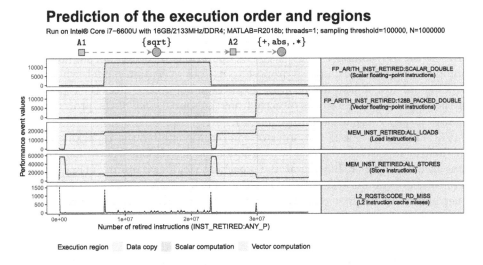

Fig. 5. Prediction of execution order and regions from the instruction chain.

4 Repacking of Array Slices

Array slicing affects the performance of MATLAB programs in two ways: (1) it creates a copy of the requested subset of an array; and (2) it sometimes prevents the JIT compiler from merging two or more operations into one instruction block. Usually, array slicing is necessary for programs, and we need to perform the copy at some point. However, it is possible to move the copying before the computation. Therefore, the computation uses only references to the already copied array slices, which allows the JIT compiler to merge and execute operations together. In this section, we show how to extract array slices and better schedule computations by repacking array slices into new variables.

Listing 1.2. Repacking of array slices on `crni3` loop from the LCPC16 suite [3].

```
1  % Original code
2  X(1:(N-1)) = (B(1:(N-1)) - C(1:(N-1)) .* X(2:N)) ./ D(1:(N-1));
3  % After repacking of array slices
4  tmp_b = B(1:(N-1));
5  tmp_c = C(1:(N-1));
6  tmp_x = X(2:N);
7  tmp_d = D(1:(N-1));
8  X(1:(N-1)) = (tmp_b - tmp_c .* tmp_x) ./ tmp_d;
```

Transformation. Listing 1.2 presents the simple idea behind the repacking of array slices. The transformation replaces every indexed read reference (array slice) in the right-hand side of the assignment (line 2) by a reference to a tempo-rary variable `tmp_*` which holds the array slice (line 8). The code on lines from 4 to 7 depicts how array slices are repacked into new temporary variables `tmp_*`.

Application. The transformation is especially useful in cases where array slicing prevents the JIT compiler from executing operations together. For finding good candidates of the repacking, we propose to use our execution model, which pre-dicts the order of computations in the expression before and after the repacking. Furthermore, the model works directly from the source code of the program and requires no prior execution (static model).

The knowledge about the order of computations after the repacking shows whether the repacking creates new instruction blocks, regions where many opera-tions execute together. In general, the repacking yields two results: (1) no change to the order of computations; or (2) creation of new instruction blocks by merging other blocks. In the first case, the repacking does not improve program perfor-mance. However, the sole existence of new instruction blocks (2) is not sufficient to guarantee the performance improvement.

Results. Figure 6 presents the relative increase of the performance after the repacking of array slices measured on three kernels: `crni3` loop from LCPC16 [3], `state_fragment` (kernel 7) from Livermore[4], and `s211` from TSVC [12] benchmark suites.

One occurring pattern in the data from Fig. 6 is a better performance of the repacking obtained on the newer version of MATLAB R2018b. A possible explanation of this is the improved JIT compiler. In that case, the repacking reveals a massive opportunity for the JIT compilation, which the results show.

The repacking for `TSVC:s211` kernel decreases the performance for the major-ity of tests. However, the execution model can predict this outcome. The result is the same instruction chain of the code before and after the repacking. In other words, the repacking is not profitable because it does not decrease the number of instruction blocks required for the execution.

---

[4] https://www.netlib.org/benchmark/livermore.

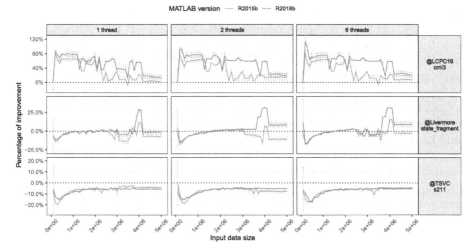

Fig. 6. Result of applying repacking of array slices. Not every computation benefits from the transformation (TSVC/s211).

Other two loops LCLP16:crni3 and Livermore:state_kernel are perfect examples of how the performance gain from the repacking depends on the size of input data, the number of threads, the MATLAB version, and the code itself. In the current form, the execution model is insufficient to answer if the repacking increases the performance. Thus, the repacking should be considered with the code profiling to find out if the transformation is beneficial in the given context.

5   Related Works

In our work, we have utilised and combined various concepts, such as: analysing large-scale and time-varying behaviours, characterising programs with performance counters or vertical profiling. Nevertheless, we have not found works similar to ours. We suspect that the main reason for the lack of similar works is because the bulk of research work analysing programs behaviour deals only with open-source, freely available solutions. Therefore, the problems which we deal with in this paper are unnoticed, as the source code is provided.

Time-Varying Behaviour. One of the first studies of program properties changing through the program execution was a study of large-scale patterns in the SPEC95 benchmark suite by Sherwood and Calder [14]. The work looked for patterns in performance profiles of, e.g. instructions per cycles (IPC), cache miss rate or branch prediction miss rate, in terms of committed instructions. A new result of the study was finding *cyclic behaviours* in benchmarks which specify how long we should run the benchmarks to obtain representative results.

Subsequent studies by Sherwood et al. improved the idea of time-varying, large-scale patterns by either creating an automatic machine-independent technique for finding large-scale pattern [15] or proposing a hardware (and software) tracking and prediction method for reoccurring phase behaviours [13]. Although our work deals with small scale time-varying changes and lacks phase behaviour, the work of Sherwood et al. is an early example of the detailed analysis of performance profiles. In another interesting study, Duesterwald et al. [5] argued that time-varying behaviours are essential and should be incorporated into adaptive systems to improve program performance and energy consumption. The results show that programs present time-varying behaviour at even small scale which could be used, e.g. to predict the value of one metrics based on another.

Characterising Programs with Performance Counters. The study by Eeckhout et al. [6] used hardware performance counters to analyse interactions between various Java Virtual Machines (JVM), processors, and programs. The results show that differences between JVMs implementations are more significant than differences from running various benchmarks on the same implementation. Similarly, to our study, Eeckhout et al. looked directly into the performance events to see how interpreted programs perform on processors. The use of traces with performance events (similar to traces from mPAPI tool) was visible in the study by Sweeney et al. [17] which described a methodology to analyse the performance of Jikes RVM, research virtual machine. The traces allow understanding better the interactions between various components of Java program execution: the application, virtual machine, operating system, and the μ-architecture. However, the authors noted that traces of performance counters are not enough to explain certain performance phenomena. Therefore, the work was just a prequel to *vertical profiling*.

Vertical Profiling. Across three papers, Hauswirth et al. [7–9] explored the idea of vertical profiling, a methodology for understanding and correlating performance data over time from multiple levels of abstractions: server, hardware, virtual machine (VM), operating system (OS), application. At the core, in correlating performance from multiple levels of abstraction lies the same idea as in our use of performance event profiles, however, in our case, we correlate multiple performance events coming from the same abstraction—a processor. In the second paper, authors evaluated several techniques for automated trace alignment coming from different measurements [7]. So far, in our work, we have used only a small amount of performance events which are measured at once. Nevertheless, in the future, we plan to consider trace alignment as well.

6   Conclusion

In the paper, we have described two concepts of *performance event profile* and *execution region* which originated from the need for describing program execution of the closed-source MATLAB environment (Sect. 2). The combination of *performance event profiles* with *execution regions* captures the time-varying behaviour of programs by tracking their execution directly on CPU. Moreover, we have presented our open-source tool `mPAPI` for accessing hardware performance counters in MATLAB/Octave programs and building performance profiles.

Furthermore, we have used *performance event profiles* and *execution regions* to build a tree-based execution model for expressions in the vectorised MATLAB programs (Sect. 3). The model predicts execution regions and their order for a given MATLAB expression. Moreover, the model highlights functions scheduled for the combined execution, by the JIT compiler (as *instruction blocks*).

Finally, with the knowledge about program execution in MATLAB, we have introduced a simple, yet powerful code transformation *repacking of array slices* (up to 80% of performance increase on benchmark `LCPC16:crni3`; but when misused, the repacking decreases performance up to -20%). However, for now, the transformation should be considered in the context of Profile-Guided Optimisations (PGO), until we further develop the execution model to predict the performance gain of the repacking.

The work presented in this paper is the first step to obtain an entirely usable execution model for MATLAB programs. The future work includes: (1) consideration of vector instructions; (2) prediction of parallel execution; (3) extending the model with control-flow; (4) quantifying the precision of the model and accuracy of measurements of performance events. Moreover, we plan to test the approach on other interpreters with JIT compilers: PyPy for Python[5] and Julia[6]. However, we do not plan to go beyond the domain of scientific computing.

References

1. Aycock, J.: A brief history of just-in-time. ACM Comput. Surv. **35**(2), 97–113 (2003). https://doi.org/10.1145/857076.857077
2. Bruening, D., Garnett, T., Amarasinghe, S.: An infrastructure for adaptive dynamic optimization. In: International Symposium on Code Generation and Optimization, CGO, vol. 2003, pp. 265–275 (2003). https://doi.org/10.1109/CGO.2003.1191551
3. Chen, H., Krolik, A., Lavoie, E., Hendren, L.: Automatic vectorization for MATLAB. In: Ding, C., Criswell, J., Wu, P. (eds.) LCPC 2016. LNCS, vol. 10136, pp. 171–187. Springer, Cham (2017). https://doi.org/10.1007/978-3-319-52709-3_14
4. Doweck, J., et al.: Inside 6th-generation intel core: new microarchitecture code-named skylake. IEEE Micro **37**(2), 52–62 (2017). https://doi.org/10.1109/MM.2017.38
5. Duesterwald, E., Cascaval, C., Dwarkadas, S.: Characterizing and predicting program behavior and its variability. In: Parallel Architectures and Compilation Techniques, PACT, vol. 2003, pp. 220–231 (2003). https://doi.org/10.1109/PACT.2003.1238018
6. Eeckhout, L., Georges, A., De Bosschere, K.: How java programs interact with virtual machines at the microarchitectural level. In: ACM SIGPLAN Notices, vol. 38, no. 11, p. 169 (2003). https://doi.org/10.1145/949343.949321

---

[5] https://pypy.org/.

[6] https://julialang.org/.

7. Hauswirth, M., Diwan, A., Sweeney, P.F., Mozer, M.C.: Automating vertical profiling. In: ACM SIGPLAN Notices, vol. 40, no. 10, p. 281 (2006). https://doi.org/10.1145/1103845.1094834
8. Hauswirth, M., Sweeney, P.F., Diwan, A.: Temporal vertical profiling. Softw. Pract. Experience **40**(8), 627–654 (2010). https://doi.org/10.1002/spe.972
9. Hauswirth, M., Sweeney, P.F., Diwan, A., Hind, M.: Vertical profiling: understanding the behavior of object-oriented applications. In: Object-Oriented Programming, Systems, Languages, and Applications, OOPSLA 2004, vol. 39, p. 251 (2004). https://doi.org/10.1145/1028976.1028998
10. Hennessy, J.L., Patterson, D.: Computer Architecture: A Quantitive Approach. Morgan Kaufmann, United States (2017)
11. Luk, C.K., et al.: Pin: building customized program analysis tools with dynamic instrumentation. In: Programming Language Design and Implementation, PLDI 2005, p. 190. ACM Press (2005). https://doi.org/10.1145/1065010.1065034
12. Maleki, S., Gao, Y., Garzarán, M.J., Wong, T., Padua, D.A.: An evaluation of vectorizing compilers. In: Parallel Architectures and Compilation Techniques, PACT, vol. 2011, no. 7, pp. 372–382 (2011). https://doi.org/10.1109/PACT.2011.68
13. Sherwood, T., Perelman, E., Hamerly, G., Sair, S., Calder, B.: Discovering and exploiting program phases. IEEE Micro **23**(6), 84–93 (2003). https://doi.org/10.1109/MM.2003.1261391
14. Sherwood, T., Calder, B.: Time Varying Behavior of Programs. Technical report (1999). https://cseweb.ucsd.edu/~calder/papers/UCSD-CS99-630.pdf
15. Sherwood, T., Perelman, E., Hamerly, G., Calder, B.: Automatically characterizing large scale program behavior. In: Architectural Support for Programming Languages and Operating Systems, ASPLOS 2002, vol. 36, p. 45 (2002). https://doi.org/10.1145/605397.605403
16. Sprunt, B.: The basics of performance-monitoring hardware. IEEE Micro **22**(4), 64–71 (2002). https://doi.org/10.1109/MM.2002.1028477
17. Sweeney, P.F., et al.: Using hardware performance monitors to understand the behavior of java applications. In: Virtual Machine Research And Technology Symposium, VM, vol. 2004, p. 5 (2004)
18. Terpstra, D., Jagode, H., You, H., Dongarra, J.: Collecting performance data with PAPI-C. In: Müller, M., Resch, M., Schulz, A., Nagel, W. (eds.) Tools for High Performance Computing, vol. 2009, pp. 157–173 (2010). https://doi.org/10.1007/978-3-642-11261-4_11
19. Weaver, V.M., McKee, S.A.: Can hardware performance counters be trusted? In: International Symposium on Workload Characterization, IISWC, vol. 2008, pp. 141–150 (2008). https://doi.org/10.1109/IISWC.2008.4636099
20. Williams, S., Waterman, A., Patterson, D.: Roofline: an insightful visual performance model for multicore architectures. Commun. ACM **52**(4), 65 (2009). https://doi.org/10.1145/1498765.1498785
21. Yasin, A.: A top-down method for performance analysis and counters architecture. In: International Symposium on Performance Analysis of Systems and Software, ISPASS, vol. 2014, pp. 35–44 (2014). https://doi.org/10.1109/ISPASS.2014.6844459
22. Zaparanuks, D., Jovic, M., Hauswirth, M.: Accuracy of performance counter measurements. In: International Symposium on Performance Analysis of Systems and Software, ISPASS, vol. 2009, pp. 23–32 (2009). https://doi.org/10.1109/ISPASS.2009.4919635

CLAM: Compiler Leasing of Accelerator Memory

Dong Chen[1($\boxtimes$)], Chen Ding[2], and Dorin Patru[3]

[1] Department of Computer Science, National University of Defense Technology,
Changsha, China
[2] Department of Computer Science, University of Rochester, Rochester, NY, USA
cding@cs.rochester.edu
[3] Department of Electrical Engineering, Rochester Institute of Technology,
Rochester, NY, USA
dxpeee@rit.edu

Abstract. With Moore's Law ending and general-purpose processor speed platcauing, there are increasing interests and adoption of accelerators designed and built with FPGAs or SOCs. It is challenging to program the local memory of an accelerator. Past solutions are either based on scratchpad memory, which is entirely compiler managed, or on cache, which admits no direct program control.

This paper proposes a new approach similar to memory allocation where a program treats local memory as a heap and controls its allocation, while the hardware manages the remaining operations, e.g. data fetch and placement. The position paper describes this collaborative solution, discusses open research questions, and presents some preliminary results.

1 Introduction

Modern accelerators such as FPGAs and SoCs have tremendous advantage in power efficiency and performance over general purpose processors. The paradigms are called reconfigurable computing or spatial computing to symbolize the massive parallelism and extreme specialization. Programming is difficult for accelerators. Part of the difficulty is programming the local memory on the FPGA or on SoC.

Existing solutions to control the memory hierarchy are largely bi-polar: they are either completely programmatic, requiring program data and accesses known at compile time, as is the case for shared memory on GPUs, or completely automatic, as in the case of modern caches (which may be implemented in either hardware or software). Collaborative caching, a term coined by Wang et al. [11], uses cache hints and provides a "middle path" where program knowledge is passed to the cache as hints. However, caching is assisted but not controlled by a program.

For many applications, especially those that run on accelerators, a compiler can effectively analyze and optimize program locality, for example through the

© Springer Nature Switzerland AG 2021
S. Pande and V. Sarkar (Eds.): LCPC 2019, LNCS 11998, pp. 89–97, 2021.
https://doi.org/10.1007/978-3-030-72789-5_7

polyhedral compilation framework [2] and static sampling [4]. Caching is too restrictive since it does not utilize program knowledge. Fully software controlled, however, is difficult to implement, and the resulting programs are difficult to port, e.g. when local memory changes in size.

This paper presents a new collaborative solution based on program control of the allocation of local memory. We assume that all other functions of the local memory, e.g. data placement and lookup, are automatic as in a cache. We call this approach *Compiler Leasing of Accelerator Memory (CLAM)*. CLAM targets all programming models using static or dynamic allocated arrays. With CLAM, the program is in charge of allocating the cache space and leaves the rest to the cache implementation. While a similar idea may be used for general-purpose CPUs, although programming support is likely more complex, if possible at all. In this work, we focus on accelerators and loop based kernel code.

2   Compiler Leasing of Accelerator Memory

2.1   Background: Cache Allocation Using Leases

A *lease cache* is a new type of cache interface, where a program specifies a length of time called the lease at each data access. The lease cache stores the data block in the cache for the duration of the lease. Lease cache enables a program to allocate the cache space by controlling the lease. Cache allocation in this fashion is analogous to memory allocation—a lease is the lifetime of a data block in the cache.

If the access is a miss, it is loaded into the lease cache and given the lease. If the access is a hit, the lease of the data block is renewed. In either case, a lease is given at *every* data access. The lease is measured by the number of accesses rather than the physical time. A lease of 1000 means that the lease cache keeps the data block until 1000 accesses later. The lease is renewed if the data block is accessed before the end of the lease; otherwise, the block is evicted from the cache.

It helps to draw an analogy with an automatic water faucet. When a faucet detects a user's hand, it discharges water for a period of time. This time can be viewed as a lease. If a hand is detected again, the lease is renewed. If not, the lease eventually expires and the water valve is closed. If a lease is too short, water stops while a user is still washing, but if it is too long, it wastes water. By controlling the lease, a program controls the cache allocation.

2.2   CLAM System Design

Using the lease cache, the software and hardware can collaborate in managing the local memory, where software communicates program knowledge to hardware through leases. Table 1 shows the novel aspects of this collaborative design compared to the two traditional solutions.

As Denning characterized, local memory management includes three problems: fetch, placement, and replacement [5]. Table 1 shows that, if the local

Table 1. Comparison between three techniques of local memory management: program management, hardware caching, and the proposed collaborative solution.

		Local memory management		
		Scratchpad (programmed)	Cache (automatic by hardware)	Lease cache (compiler-hw collaboartion)
Design	fetch	programmed	auto	auto
	placement	programmed	auto	auto
	replacement (eviction)	programmed	auto	programmed
	actual occupancy	varied	monotone / bounded	varied
Performance	data transfer	bulk	on-demand (incremental)	on-demand (incremental)
	clairvoyance	program based	history based	program based
Correctness / safety	free from accidental overwrite	no guarantee	guaranteed	guarateed
	lifetime	guaranteed	no guarantee	guaranteed
Costs	data lookup	no	yes	yes
	runtime management overhead	no (prog managed)	yes (hardware managed)	yes (hardware managed)

memory is implemented as a scratchpad, all three problems must be solved by the programmer. If the local memory is made into a conventional cache, all three problems are solved automatically by the hardware. If we use the lease cache, the program solves only the replacement problem, while the hardware solves the other two problems. Since the allocation is under program control, a program may choose to use all or a part of the local memory, just as it can with the scratchpad memory.

The rest of Table 1 shows three other categories of concerns: performance, correctness, and costs. We consider two performance issues. The first is bulk vs incremental data transfer. If the local memory is implemented as a scratchpad, it needs explicit memory transfer by operations known as copy-in and copy-out. The data transfer is often in bulk to reduce program complexity. In comparison, the lease cache loads data on-demand when it is a miss and writes back gradually when modified data is evicted.

The other issue is optimization. A cache uses history based prediction and does not have full program knowledge. In the lease cache, a compiler can encode program knowledge using leases by a technique called CARL, describe next in Sect. 2.3.

We then consider correctness. With the scratchpad, a program may accidentally double allocate the same memory location. In the lease cache, the hardware controls the data placement, so a memory location is never leased to two data items simultaneously, and hence such error is impossible. The other issue is the lifetime. In the lease cache, the lifetime is guaranteed by the lease, so a program "knows" whether a data block is in the cache or not. Such knowledge can be precise and complete, enabling deterministic timing as needed by real-time systems such as network routing and automatic flying or driving. It also avoids side-channel attacks, where an attacker may infer the memory content by tricking the cache into evicting a resident data block.

2.3   Compiler Assigned Reference Leasing (CARL)

Recently Li et al. developed statistical caching called Optimal Steadystate Lease (OSL), where the reuse interval (RI), i.e. the number of accesses between consecutive accesses to the same memory location, is collected into a distribution, and the lease is assigned based on the RI distribution [9]. OSL is parameterized by the average cache size, and it is optimal in that no other lease assignment can yield a lower miss ratio for the same average cache size. For scientific code, Chen et al. have shown that a compiler can use static sampling to collect the RI distribution, especially at cache block granularity [4]. By combining static sampling and OSL, a compiler can assign optimal lease at each reference of a program, for any given cache size. Note that per-reference RI distributions collected by tracing [7] can also be fed into the compiler directly. The compiler consumes distributions and derives leases.

We call the technique *Compiler Assigned Reference Leasing (CARL)*[1]. We next consider several open issues and possible solutions.

2.4   Open Problems for Compiler Research

The first is encoding the lease. A lease is given at each memory load and store instruction. We envision an ISA change where a set of lease registers are used. Similar to data registers, we need enough to cover the number of memory references in a typical innermost loop. The second is portability. For a different size of local memory, a new lease is generated by CARL for each reference. This can be updated without recompiling a program. A similar solution is used to handle different program inputs without recompilation.

Another problem is how to deal with "overflow". CARL assigns leases to achieve a given average cache size. The dynamic demand may exceed the size of local memory. We will study hardware solutions, e.g. evicting cache blocks with the longest remaining lease, and software solutions, e.g. assigning leases to maintain a bounded cache size. In general it may be difficult to bound the largest occupancy. However, compiler analysis may provide a solution for regular loop nests [1,3,6,8,12]. In the past, tile size selection techniques have developed ways to estimate the size of the working set.

---

[1] The exact algorithm of CARL, its optimality in assigning leases, and a set of results (more on this later) were described in a different document under submission. Here we address the remaining problems of CARL.

Program optimization for CLAM raises new problems not addressed by the past work for LRU caches. Consider the overflow problem. The CLAM compiler can reorganize a program to provide not just maximal-size control but to balance the cache demand throughout the execution. If a loop nest has a large working set, it is beneficial to reduce the size. If the next loop nest has a small working set, it may be possible to defer part of the work from the first loop to the second. Optimization is still needed for the temporal cache demand, even when the average cache demand is already optimized.

Locality optimization for LRU cache is often based on minimizing the reuse distance. For the lease cache, the cache usage is directly determined by the lease, and the lease is determined by the reuse interval. The goal of the optimization is therefore to minimize the reuse interval. On the other hand, there is the issue of the maximal cache size. It is possible that by reducing the reuse interval, we may increase the imbalance of cache demand. Locality optimization is to minimize the average cache demand while maintaining a constant temporal cache demand.

2.5   Prototyping and Implementation on FPGAs

Large Field Programmable Gate Arrays (FPGAs) are organized today as Systems on a Chip (SoCs), as shown in Fig. 1. These contain a software based processing system, comprised of a one, two, or four-core processor, a programmable logic array, which is usually used to implement accelerators, and an application specific assortment of input/output peripherals (I/O-Ps). In turn, accelerators are generally implemented as either systolic arrays or vector processors. Either way, these accelerators process large amounts of data, whose on-time availability is paramount in meeting performance goals.

Local memory is organized as either a monolithic embedded memory, or as a cache for a higher capacity, external memory. Most SoCs have *hard* memory controllers. However, the availability of the programmable logic array offers a unique opportunity to implement a *soft* lease cache and its associated controller. Specifically, dynamic (i.e. at run-time) reconfiguration of a part of the programmable logic, a feature present in all high performance FPGAs, makes the implementation of a variable occupancy cache with variable block sizes possible, which are necessary lease cache characteristics described in the previous section. In effect, the availability of the programmable logic array allows the lease cache to adapt to the needs of the application as prescribed by the compiler through the lease values.

To evaluate the performance of a FPGA based lease cache, we envision two complementary approaches. First, the implementation of a RISCV processor and associated lease cache, and second, the implementation of an image processing accelerator and associated lease cache. The key to design a practical lease cache is to find an efficient way to do lease tracking during execution. We have not finished a prototype, so we use trace simulation in the next section.

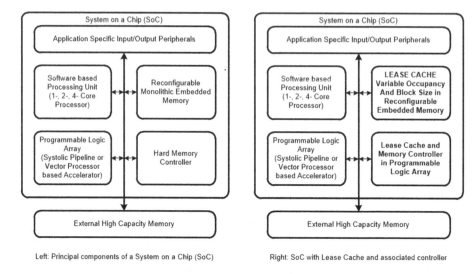

Left: Principal components of a System on a Chip (SoC)   Right: SoC with Lease Cache and associated controller

Fig. 1. System on a Chip (SoC) without (left) and with Lease Cache (right).

3   Preliminary Simulation Results

The cost of caching includes data lookup and management, and this cost can be reduced if we use large cache blocks. We envision cache blocks as large as half or even multiple kilobytes. Through preliminary results, we examine whether we can use large cache blocks. Depending on the design, it may be possible to use two or more cache block sizes, and let a compiler choose the right granularity.

By holding more data, a large cache block allows a program to amortize the cost. However, a danger is low cache utilization, when not all data (or in the extreme case all but one element) are used by the program before the block is evicted. We quantify this "danger" by the amount of extra data transfer between the cache and the memory. In particular, we compare the memory traffic with different size cache blocks. In this study we consider only memory reads (which causes a program to wait either due to the memory latency and/or the contention for memory bandwidth) and only those due to capacity misses (i.e. no cold-start misses). We consider only the fully-associative cache. In this setting, the traffic drops to zero with the complete cache reuse.

Figure 2 shows the amount of data transfer from memory to cache, i.e. data reads, for PolyBench [10][2]. The amount of data transfer is derived by the profiled miss ratio curve as one miss requires transferring one data block. For this experiment, we measure the cache with two policies: LRU and CARL. For each

---

[2] Due to page limit, we only show 6 representative benchmarks instead of all 30 benchmarks (*adi, cholesky, covariance, gemm, jacobi_1d, symm*). These 6 are selected based on the shape of the curves. The other 24 have similar curves to one of the showed benchmarks. The calculation for cache space cost of CARL assumes the assigned lease for each reference only apply to its data blocks have reuses.

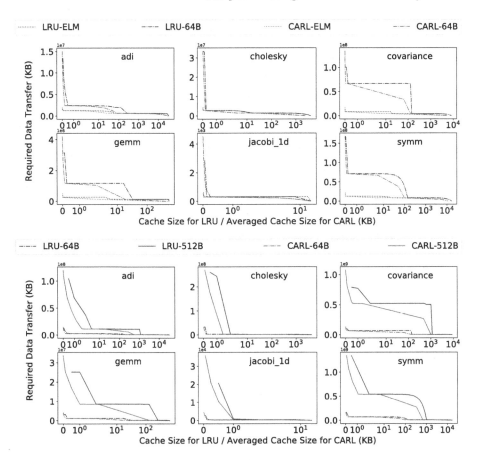

Fig. 2. Memory reads (KB) for PolyBench by two policies, LRU and CARL, each with element (ELM) and cache line granularity (64B, 512B)

policy, we measure three cache-block sizes: the element granularity ELM (8 bytes for double precision numbers), 64B (64 bytes, 8 elements) and 512B (512 bytes, 64 elements). The results are shown in Fig. 2, with ELM and 512B separated into two plots (with different y-axis limits) and 64B replicated in both.

Scientific computing is memory intensive. The y-axis is measured at scales at least a hundred mega-bytes (10^5 KBs) except *jacobi_1d*. Larger granularity will lead to larger read traffic at small cache sizes.

Comparing LRU-ELM and LRU-64B curves, we see a general pattern that at cache sizes less than 100 KB, the block granularity incurs much more memory transfer than the element granularity. At larger cache sizes, however, the difference becomes much smaller. This is the case for *adi, gemm, covariance, symm*. The granularity has little or no effect for *cholesky, jacobi_1d*. Comparing LRU-512B and LRU-64B, the difference happens in every test, and it is much greater than that between LRU-ELM and LRU-64B. The two curves converge at a cache size greater than those of LRU-ELM and LRU-64B do.

Interestingly, the coarser granularity can perform better, although this happens only in *jacobi_1d*, where there are a few cache sizes where LRU-64B incurs lower traffic than the element granularity. This can be explained by the effect of granularity on reuse distance. Let's measure the reuse distance in bytes. If the reuse happens between the same pair of accesses, the reuse distance can only increase with granularity. However, it is possible that a pair of reuses in element granularity is "interrupted" in block granularity by an intervening access to the same block due to spatial reuse. In the context of multi-threading, Wu and Yeung used two terms, *dilation* and *intercept*, to denote the effect that increases or decreases the concurrent reuse distance [13]. A coarser granularity has both effects of dilating reuses and intercepting them.

For the collaborative policy CARL, the granularity causes less a problem in every case compared to LRU. If we look at the two highest curves in each graph (the larger granularity), we see CARL incurs less memory traffic than LRU. As a result, the increase from CARL-ELM to CARL-64B is much less than the increase from LRU-ELM to LRU-64B. The difference is greater between CARL and LRU when the granularity increases from 64B to 512B. In addition, for the same policy, the two curves converge at a cache size almost always earlier for CARL than they do for LRU. The only exceptions are *co-variance* from ELM to 64B and *jacob 1d* from 64B to 512B.

The reason is that the compiler knowledge allows the cache to store data blocks with good reuses, so the block with extremely poor utilization are evicted by CARL more than by LRU, and the effect of poor spatial locality (due to larger granularity) is ameliorated. This improvement has two effects. First, CARL causes less memory traffic than LRU does when spatial locality is low. Second, CARL obtains full spatial reuse at a cache size smaller than LRU does.

Therefore, CLAM costs less than LRU when using larger cache blocks to reduce the caching overhead. The increase in the amount of memory transfer is smaller from poor spatial locality, as a result of the compiler knowledge used to improve cache reuse. The benefit adds to the better cache utilization by CARL over LRU with the same cache-block granularity, also shown in Fig. 2.

4   Summary

We have presented a design of CLAM based on CARL, discussed its advantages, open problems, and targeted accelerator platforms, and shown simulation results that the compiler knowledge allows the cache to use larger blocks with much less cost than LRU.

Acknowledgments. The authors wish to thank Dr. Sreepathi Pai and Shawn Maag for the initial participation, the anonymous reviewers of LCPC and the workshop participants for the feedback. The financial support was provided in part by the National Science Foundation (Contract No. CNS-1909099, CCF-1717877).

References

1. Beyls, K., D'Hollander, E.H.: Generating cache hints for improved program efficiency. J. Syst. Archit. **51**(4), 223–250 (2005)
2. Bondhugula, U., Hartono, A., Ramanujam, J., Sadayappan, P.: A practical automatic polyhedral parallelizer and locality optimizer. In: Proceedings of the ACM SIGPLAN Conference on Programming Language Design and Implementation, pp. 101–113 (2008)
3. Cascaval, C., Padua, D.A.: Estimating cache misses and locality using stack distances. In: Proceedings of the International Conference on Supercomputing, pp. 150–159 (2003)
4. Chen, D., Liu, F., Ding, C., Pai, S.: Locality analysis through static parallel sampling. In: Proceedings of the ACM SIGPLAN Conference on Programming Language Design and Implementation. pp. 557–570 (2018), http://doi.acm.org/10.1145/3192366.3192402
5. Denning, P.J.: Virtual memory. ACM Comput. Surv. **2**(3), 153–189 (1970). https://doi.acm.org/10.1145/356571.356573
6. Ghosh, S., Martonosi, M., Malik, S.: Cache miss equations: an analytical representation of cache misses. In: Proceedings of the 11th International Conference on Supercomputing, pp. 317–324. ACM (1997)
7. Hu, X., Wang, X., Zhou, L., Luo, Y., Ding, C., Wang, Z.: Kinetic modeling of data eviction in cache. In: Proceedings of USENIX Annual Technical Conference, pp. 351–364 (2016). https://www.usenix.org/conference/atc16/technical-sessions/presentation/hu
8. Kennedy, K., McKinley, K.S.: Optimizing for parallelism and data locality. In: ACM International Conference on Supercomputing 25th Anniversary Volume, pp. 151–162. ACM (1992)
9. Li, P., Pronovost, C., Wilson, W., Tait, B., Zhou, J., Ding, C., Criswell, J.: Beating OPT with statistical clairvoyance and variable size caching. In: Proceedings of the International Conference on Architectural Support for Programming Languages and Operating Systems, pp. 243–256 (2019). https://doi.org/10.1145/3297858.3304067
10. Pouchet, L.N., Yuki, T.: Polybench/c 4.2.1. https://sourceforge.net/projects/polybench/files/ (2016)
11. Wang, Z., McKinley, K.S., L.Rosenberg, A., Weems, C.C.: Using the compiler to improve cache replacement decisions. In: Proceedings of the International Conference on Parallel Architecture and Compilation Techniques, Charlottesville, Virginia (2002)
12. Wolf, M.E., Lam, M.S.: A data locality optimizing algorithm. In: Proceedings of the ACM SIGPLAN Conference on Programming Language Design and Implementation, pp. 30–44 (1991)
13. Wu, M., Yeung, D.: Efficient reuse distance analysis of multicore scaling for loop-based parallel programs. ACM Trans. Comput. Syst. **31**(1), 1 (2013). http://doi.acm.org/10.1145/2427631.2427632

Abstractions for Polyhedral Topology-Aware Tasking [Position Paper]

Martin Kong[(✉)]

The University of Oklahoma, Norman, OK 73019, USA
mkong@ou.edu

Abstract. Traditional polyhedral compilation techniques rely on Integer Linear Programming (ILP) and lexicographic optimization to compute optimal transformations. Although, these techniques excel at exposing and leveraging data and pipeline parallelism as well as exploiting (hidden) available locality, they are not the best suited when tackling problems such as the Manhattan distance in a grid.

In this short paper we propose techniques to sort and rank the various orderings of tasks mapped onto a network, while considering 3 different network topologies. We introduce new abstractions and develop a new compiler analysis to determine an optimal order of tasks w.r.t to the user-provided execution location. We propose a closed form for encoding in a single set all the possible orderings of tasks. In a nutshell, the encoding represents the topological orderings of nodes in a task graph. Once the closed form is built, we proceed to iteratively evaluate the total cost of each point in the set (an execution order). This involves computing the cost between every pair of adjacent tasks, and aggregating them to obtain the total cost. Finally, an optimal ordering is obtained by applying lexicographic minimization over all the points in the set.

Keywords: Polyhedral model · Topology-aware tasking · Affine modeling

1 Introduction and Motivation

Polyhedral compiler transformations such as the Pluto tiling hyperplane method [3] have proven to be quite successful in practice. These types of methods minimize the dependence distance between pairs of statement instances by creating a bounding parameterized function. In the context of high-level loop transformations this technique makes sense, since loops are inherently multi-dimensional and the problem perfectly matches the principles of lexicographic minimization, where every dimension i has a higher priority in the objective function than subsequent dimensions, i + 1, i + 2, etc. Such type of bounding function has also been used previously to determine minimum latency schedules [8,9].

Prior works in the area of automatic parallelization for distributed memory execution [1,2,6,7,10–14] assumed that all program tasks had the same

© Springer Nature Switzerland AG 2021
S. Pande and V. Sarkar (Eds.): LCPC 2019, LNCS 11998, pp. 98–107, 2021.
https://doi.org/10.1007/978-3-030-72789-5_8

latency, considered latencies as second or third optimization criteria, or ignored this problem altogether. Latency is a metric normally associated to the routing capabilities of a network, and has high relevance in applications where the unit of computation and communication are relatively small. Arguably, MPI collectives are the best examples of efficient algorithms that are both latency- and topology-aware. The techniques proposed in this work are a step forward to make compiler transformations aware of the underlying network topologies and of the largely variable network latencies that affect application performance.

The Need for Network Abstractions. We briefly motivate the need for network abstractions that depart from typical dependence minimization schemes. Practically all runtimes used in distributed computing provide a mechanism for pinning tasks to specific locations in a cluster. In addition, several task parallel runtimes (e.g. Parsec [4], Concurrent Collections [5]) provide one or more ways to dynamically create tasks and to schedule them. These actions involve some level of communication with very low transfer volume and long latencies. In Fig. 1 we show 4 synchronization free task instances, A, B, C and D, with their locations assigned manually by the end-user or by the underlying cluster in a 4×4 mesh; each subfigure represents a different communication scenario with varying tasks orderings. These can result from dynamically creating tasks, or from satisfying (small) data/control dependences that will deem the task instance ready for execution. For simplicity, we only present 4 possible cases. The four scenarios considered induce total latencies of 8 (center-left), 12 (center), 7 (center-right) and 15 (right). Our objective is to determine which of these orderings is the best.

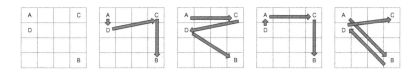

Fig. 1. Ordering alternatives of 4 tasks

The rest of this paper is organized as follows. Section 2 introduces the novel abstractions used to compute distances among task instances mapped in a network; Sect. 3 describes how to build the exploration space of task orderings; Sect. 4 presents a new algorithm to compute the best task ordering. Lastly, we make some concluding remarks in Sect. 5.

2   Network Abstractions

We rely on user-provided task affinity mappings, i.e. mappings of task instances to logical network coordinates, e.g. an MPI process rank. For the moment, we assume that these are provided as program annotations or automatically generated by a distributed tasking compiler such as PIPES [11]. We introduce suitable network abstractions (Sect. 2) to enable computing, in a direct fashion, the distance between any pair of network coordinates. The goal is to then leverage the information of task placement to compute *some cost* between pairs of tasks. Once these abstractions are properly in place, we use them in an iterative algorithm (Sect. 4) exploring a candidate space (Sect. 3). The points in this space represent total ordering among tasks in the graph. The algorithm computes a cost for each potential ordering, accumulates them in a map, and applies lexicographic minimization to determine the best task ordering.

We now introduce network abstractions that allow to evaluate point-to-point synchronization costs among tasks. We model 3 different networks with their respective abstractions: multi-dimensional meshes, fat-trees and multi-dimensional tori (meshes plus wrap-around links). We will first discuss the abstractions necessary to model meshes of arbitrary dimensions, followed by suitable extensions to model torus topologies, and ending this section by describing the approach to model distances in fat-tree networks.

2.1 Preliminaries

We assume that each *lexical task* has an iteration domain and an *affinity map* associated to it. The latter is akin to an *access function* [10], with the difference that the image of the function represents physical locations in the network (e.g. a compute-node in the cluster). We typically denote lexical tasks by letters R and S, and their affinity maps by A^R (resp. A^S). Each lexical task can consist of multiple instances, and hence their association to an iteration domain. $D^{R \to S}$ represents the set of dependence instances between lexical tasks R and S. Independently of the topology or network geometry, the set of compute locations is represented by a multi-dimensional set G.

For all three types of networks we assume that the affinity maps of all tasks are always provided. As we will see, topologies such as meshes and torus share structural similarities, and thus can share several of the proposed abstractions. However, a topology such as a fat-tree requires a different approach. While the former types can rely on several abstractions which can be composed layer by layer in order to compute the final distance metric between any pair of network coordinates, the latter requires a more direct approach.

2.2 Multi-dimensional Meshes

Multi-dimensional meshes are the simplest type of network topology that we model. Their regularity and overall structure allow for creating parameterized networks of arbitrary dimensions. We explain the role of each abstraction step by step. Given two tasks $R(\boldsymbol{x})$ and $S(\boldsymbol{y})$, with affinity maps A^R and A^S, and a dependence relation $D^{R \to S}$, the first step is to translate the *statement dependences* into *processor dependences*, $G^{R \to S}$. We achieve this by plugging the affinity maps $(A^R)^{-1}$ and A^S onto both sides of $D^{R \to S}$. This results in a map where both the domain and range are processor coordinates, $(A^R)^{-1} \circ D^{R \to S} \circ (A^S)$. The following step is to compute the difference between the domain and range of this dependence. This is easily done by using the ISL [15] function *deltas_map*. The range of this map will be a set consisting of the points representing *vector directions* (a signed magnitude along each dimension). However, since we need a single positive magnitude, and to avoid constructing a single complex map, we use two abstractions: the *positive direction map* and the *multiplex add map*. Intuitively, the former translate all the components of a point in the set to its non-negative value, whilst the latter sums up all the values of all dimensions into a single one. The application of these abstractions are illustrated in Fig. 2, with 4 lexical task instances *A, B, C and D* (each with a single instance), mapped onto a 4 × 4 two-dimensional mesh.

1. Affinity map coordinates (given):
   A=G[0,0];   B=G[3,3];
   C=G[0,3];   D=G[1,0]
2. Task/statement dependences (given):
   A→B;   B→C;   C→D;
3. Compute processor dependences:
   $G^{A \to B}$ = G[3,3] - G[0,0] = [3,3];
   $G^{B \to C}$ = G[0,3] - G[3,3] = [-3,0];
   $G^{C \to D}$ = G[1,0] - G[0,3] = [1,-3];
4. Compute "positive directions" from processor dependences:
   $+\mathrm{Dir}(G^{A \to B})$ = [3,3]; $+\mathrm{Dir}(G^{B \to C})$ = [3,0]; $+\mathrm{Dir}(G^{C \to D})$ = [1,3];
5. Compute task-to-task topology distance:
   Dist(A,B) = MultiplexAddMap([3,3]) = 6;
   Dist(B,C) = MultiplexAddMap([3,0]) = 3;
   Dist(C,D) = MultiplexAddMap([1,3]) = 4;

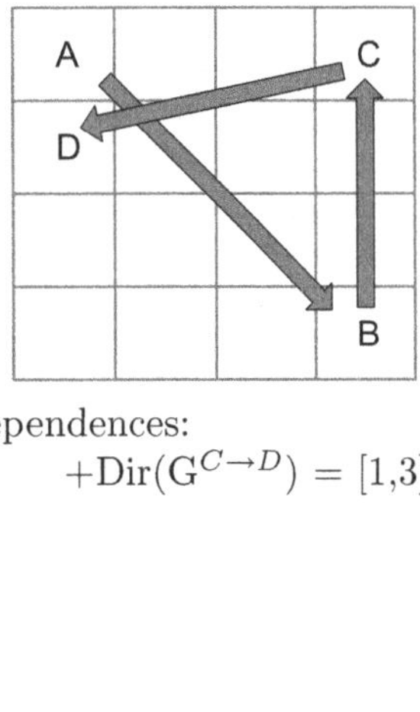

Fig. 2. 2D-mesh example: 4 × 4, 4 tasks (A, B, C, D)

2.3   Modeling Multi-dimensional Torus

Structurally, a D-dimensional torus with geometry $P_1 \times P_2 \times \cdots P_D$ is not too different from its mesh counterpart. The difference consists on having an additional link which connects the first and last element along each dimension. The main obstacle with representing a torus is the fact that the distance between two multi-dimensional points depends on whether the positive or negative direction is taken along each dimension. On a 1-dimensional torus (i.e. a ring), there are only two options; on a two-dimensional torus, we would have 4 and so on. This means that for an arbitrary D-dimensional torus, for every pair of points x and y, 2^D choices are possible. To compute the point-to-point distance between two vectors on a torus space, we require one more abstraction, the *selector map*. This map is constructed as follows. Both the input and output tuples will have, naturally, the same dimensionality. Assume the prototype of the *selector map* is

$\{[i_1, i_2, ...i_D] \rightarrow [o_1, o_2, ..., o_D]\}$. Next, we connect each dimension k of the output tuple with a constraint of the type $o_k = min(i_k, P_k - i_k)$, and build a conjunction from all the dimensions, so as to produce a map such as $\{[i_1, i_2, ...i_D] \rightarrow [o_1, o_2, ..., o_D] : o_1 = min(i_1, P_1 - i_1) \wedge o_2 = min(i_2, P_2 - i_2) \wedge ... \wedge o_D = min(i_D, P_D - i_D)\}$. Then, to complete the assembly of the *processor distance map* we insert this new map between the *positive direction map* and the *multiplex add map*.

2.4 Modeling Fat-Tree Networks

The structure of a fat-tree network is substantially different from that of a mesh or a torus. First, the distance from a location P_i to any other location P_j does not follow a linear or affine relation. Moreover, the coordinate space is always one dimensional, so all task tuples must be "flattened" prior to computing their separating distance. This step is assumed to be performed by a suitable user-provided affinity map. Figure 3 (left) shows a fat-tree network with 8 locations. In the right side of the same figure, we depict an 8×8 matrix defining the distance between any pair of locations. (Note: for convenience, in this example we use "fake distances" which are power of 2, and not the number of hops between any two locations). As one can see, this matrix exhibits some regularity. The observation here is that for a fixed number of locations P, $P^2/2$ entries in the matrix will have distance $2 \times log_2 P$, $P^2/4$ will have distance $2 \times (log_2 P - 1)$ and so on. Furthermore, this distance matrix is symmetric. To model this matrix we construct a relation with the prototype of the form $\{[[p_i] \rightarrow [p_j]] \rightarrow [k]\}$, where k is the distance. The reader can notice here the nested relation in the domain, consisting of the pair of locations p_i and p_j. Next, we partition the domain of this relation according to the values of $p_i, p_j \in \{0, ..., P-1\}$, maintaining the structure as in the example. Thus, given a fixed network size P, we generate $log_2(P) + 1$ types of partitions, where each partition can be identified by a distance $k \in \{0..log_2(P)+1\}$, or a similar function providing the distances among locations in these partitions. Clearly, the nature of this topology type does not require the abstractions presented on the previous sections, since there is no notion of direction. However, the structure itself requires explicit enumeration of all tree coordinates, which is only possible when P (the number of locations) is a fixed, non-parametric, value.

3 Building the Candidate Space

We now proceed to explain how to construct the closed form of the exploration space. This form is a set where each member point represents a complete ordering of lexical tasks, but not at the level of tasks instances. We introduce a simplifying assumption which is that instances of different tasks do not overlap. Having this premise permits us to model tasks at a coarser granularity, rather than at each individual instance. In addition, we also note that this assumption does not limit the scheduling of tasks in any way, as it is really independent of the actual task

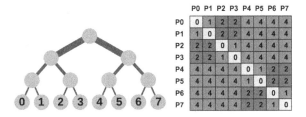

	P0	P1	P2	P3	P4	P5	P6	P7
P0	0	1	2	2	4	4	4	4
P1	1	0	2	2	4	4	4	4
P2	2	2	0	1	4	4	4	4
P3	2	2	1	0	4	4	4	4
P4	4	4	4	4	0	1	2	2
P5	4	4	4	4	1	0	2	2
P6	4	4	4	4	2	2	0	1
P7	4	4	4	4	2	2	1	0

Fig. 3. Fat-tree example (left) and its distance matrix (right)

scheduling enforced by the runtime. The purpose of this closed form is two-fold. First, it will allow to enumeratè most of the possible legal orderings. Second, it essentially serializes the graph and produces a topological sorting of the nodes (tasks) in it.

Our goal is to build a closed form of the set of possible orderings of tasks. For example, if we are given 3 (lexical) tasks, each identified by a number in the set $\{1, 2, 3\}$, and no dependences among them, we want to produce the 6 permutations of the point $[1, 2, 3]$. At a high level, we take 4 steps to build the exploration space: i) define all possible orderings in the space; ii) prune most of the illegal orderings; iii) add legality constraints that do not involve self dependences; iv) add user-provided semantic relations.

Base Exploration Space: Given T lexical tasks, the initial exploration space will consist of T-dimensional tuples, where the value of each dimension must fall in the range $[1..T]$:

$$[i_1, i_2, ..., i_T] : \forall k \in 1..T : 1 \leq i_k \leq T \qquad (1)$$

The purpose of defining the space in this manner, is that each task is identified with a positive integer. By extension, every pair of dimensions in a point represent a synchronization path between two adjacent tasks. Clearly, the constraints used allow for repeated tasks in the set, i.e. two or more dimensions with the same value. We will address this next. This space represents all the possible communication paths among tasks, and will be subsequently pruned. Once we have removed non meaningful and illegal scenarios, the remaining points are viable candidates to exploit the benefits of dynamic task creation, where a specific task instance can be spawned by an instance close to its location, thereby minimizing the latency cost. For instance, the point $[T_3, T_1, T_4, T_2]$ encodes that task instances of T_1 will be created by T_3, instances of T_4 by (some subset) of the instances of T_1, and tasks of T_2 by those of T_4.

Mostly Legal Space: Once the basic bounding constraints are defined we integrate the first type of pruning constraints to remove the bulk of the illegal orderings. This step involves adding a simple sum constraint of the form $\sum_{d=1}^{T} i_k = T \times (T + 1)/2$. This constraint will drastically reduce the exploration space, but will leave a number of undesired (illegal) points. For instance, if T = 4, this constraint will still deem legal the point $\{1, 1, 4, 4\}$. Clearly, this point should not be valid because it is not a permutation of $\{1, 2, 3, 4\}$. However, in exchange for keeping this problem tractable we choose to add a small validation on the iterative optimization stage to guarantee that all entry values in each candidate point are distinct. Effectively, this space will be slightly larger than $T!$.

Adding Legality Constraints: At this point we introduce constraints that model coarse (i.e. not instance-wise) program dependences over the previously designed space. In reality, we do not consider all dependences, as we are interested on the coarse view of the program, we ignore any self dependence at this stage. Now, suppose we are interested in adding the dependence $S[i0, i1] \rightarrow R[i0 + 1, i1]$. This dependence is effectively considered as $S[i0, i1] \rightarrow R[j0, j1]$. In other words, every instance of task R executes after all instances of task S. Now, assume that the identifiers of tasks S and R are $ID^S \in [1..T]$ and $ID^R \in [1..T]$. The way that we model this dependence is by adding a constraint of the type $i_k = ID^S \wedge (\bigvee_{l=k+1}^{T} i_l = ID^R)$. More precisely, we model each dependence $dep = [ID^S \rightarrow ID^R]$ in the following fashion:

$$\bigvee_{d=1}^{T-1} (i_d = ID^S \wedge (\bigvee_{k=d+1}^{T} i_k = ID^R)) \tag{2}$$

In simple terms, the above equation establishes a coarse dependence relation between two lexical tasks. For instance, if a given program has dependences $T_3 \rightarrow T_2 \wedge T_3 \rightarrow T_4$, the previous equation will produce:

$$(i_1 = T_3 \wedge (i_2 = T_2 \vee i_3 = T_2 \vee i_4 = T_2 \vee i_2 = T_4 \vee i_3 = T_4 \vee i_4 = T_4)) \vee$$
$$(i_2 = T_3 \wedge (i_3 = T_2 \vee i_4 = T_2 \vee i_3 = T_4 \vee i_4 = T_4))$$

Pruning the Exploration Space: One last type of dependence that we consider are "non concurrent" or "isolate" relations. The user can provide this new relation as a pruning constraint. In a nutshell, this dependence establishes that the order between the two given tasks is not important, but that they are required to not execute in parallel. This type of relation is modeled almost exactly as a regular dependence, with the addition of an extra disjunction on the constraints previously described for each isolate relation.

4   Finding the Best Candidate

In this section we present the algorithm, in ISL notation, to compute the total cost of each particular task ordering. We assume that the user has provided suitable task affinity mappings and that the candidate exploration space has been constructed. The following iterative algorithm will compute for each point in the candidate space (a task ordering) its associated cost. The total cost results from adding the cost between every pair of adjacent tasks (See Fig. 2 for an example).

Algorithm 1 performs exactly this job. We proceed to break down the different steps of the algorithm for easy digestion. Line 1 builds the mostly legal and pruned exploration space (See Sect. 3). Then, the main computation loop selects a point from the candidate space, computes its cost and adds it to a "big" map (Line 15). Next, in the main loop, Line 3, we initialize the path cost to zero, and proceed to compute the cost between every pair of adjacent tasks, assuming that the point represents a topological sorting of tasks. After this, Lines 5–6 fetch the task domains and affinity maps. Line 7 creates a default synchronization map. In essence, this map penalizes unsynchronized tasks by forcing a point-to-point synchronization among all source and target task instances. The intuition for this is to highly favor orderings where tasks must be ordered by flow dependences (or isolate relations). Once the **sync_map** has been built, we intersect it with the dependences between these two tasks (Line 8); Line 9 then translates the task-to-task dependence to the network coordinate space. This is achieved by plugging the affinity maps of the source and target space to both sides of the dependence relation. Next, we leverage the **isl_deltas_map** function to compute a map of the form $\{[[p_i] \rightarrow [p_j]] \rightarrow [p_j - p_i]\}$. As we saw in Sect. 2, when the topology is either a mesh or a torus, we can simply compose and plug the appropriate distance maps. In contrast, in networks such as fat-trees, a map of the shape $\{[[p_i] \rightarrow [p_j]] \rightarrow [distance(p_i, p_j)]\}$ is built directly. So while in the former case we compose maps, on the latter we take the domain of the **PCD** map and intersect it with the coordinate to distance map. This map is then converted to an ISL quasi-polynomial and aggregated to the path's cost (Lines 12–15), which is added to the main map **M** to be able to compute the minimal cost path in Line 17.

Algorithm 1. Compute Best Ordering

1: space ← compute_closed_form (T, program)
2: **for** each $\boldsymbol{t} = (t_1, t_2, ..., t_N) \in space$ **do**
3: path($\boldsymbol{t}$) ← 0
4: **for** each $(t_i, t_{i+1}) \in (t_1, t_2, ..., t_N)$ **do**
5:    Fetch task domains $T(t_i)$ and (t_{i+1})
6:    Fetch task affinity maps: $A(t_i)$ and $A(t_{i+1})$
7:    Build synchronization map: **sync_map** ← $[T(t_i) \times T(t_{i+1})]$
8:    Intersect dependences $[T(t_i) \Rightarrow T(t_{i+1})]$ with **sync_map**
9:    Compute processor synchronization map (PSM): PSM ← $A(t_i)^{-1} \circ$ **sync_map** $\circ$ $A(t_{i+1})$
10:   Compute "processor coordinate difference" (PCD) with ISL deltas_map (PSM)
11:   Apply network specific coordinate-to-distance map to PCD
12:   edge(i) ← quasi_polynomial_sum(PCD)
13:   path($\boldsymbol{t}$) ← path($\boldsymbol{t}$) + edge(i)
14: **end for**
15: M ← M ∪ path($\boldsymbol{t}$)
16: **end for**
17: result ← lexmin(M)

We make one last observation. The operation on Line 15 does an implicit conversion from a quasi-polynomial to a standard ISL map. Although internally these two objects embody fundamentally different semantics, syntactically the difference between them is minimal, i.e. enclosing the range with '[' and ']' to distinguish between a tuple and a polynomial (a one-dimensional quantity).

5   Conclusion

In this short paper we have presented a novel approach to compute optimal orderings of tasks. We envision the techniques proposed to be useful in applications where long latencies dominate over computation and communication times. As future work, we plan to integrate the abstractions and iterative methods described here into a complete distributed tasking framework that can automatically provide several affinity mappings and task definitions. Other extensions include modeling the abstractions needed for more complex network topologies such as DragonFly and HyperX, where the compositional properties of affinity maps can be fully exploited to model hierarchical networks.

References

1. Ancourt, C., Coelho, F., Irigoin, F., Keryell, R.: A linear algebra framework for static High Performance Fortran code distribution. Sci. Program. **6**(1), 3–27 (1997)
2. Bondhugula, U.: Compiling affine loop nests for distributed-memory parallel architectures. In: Proceedings of the International Conference on High Performance Computing, Networking, Storage and Analysis, SC 2013, pp. 1–12. IEEE (2013)
3. Bondhugula, U., Hartono, A., Ramanujam, J., Sadayappan, P.: A practical automatic polyhedral parallelizer and locality optimizer. In: Proceedings of the 29th ACM SIGPLAN Conference on Programming Language Design and Implementation, PLDI 2008, pp. 101–113. ACM, New York (2008). https://doi.org/10.1145/1375581.1375595
4. Bosilca, G., Bouteiller, A., Danalis, A., Faverge, M., Hérault, T., Dongarra, J.J.: PaRSEC: exploiting heterogeneity to enhance scalability. Comput. Sci. Eng. **15**(6), 36–45 (2013)
5. Budimlić, Z., et al.: Concurrent collections. Sci. Program. **18**(3–4), 203–217 (2010)
6. Dathathri, R., Mullapudi, R.T., Bondhugula, U.: Compiling affine loop nests for a dynamic scheduling runtime on shared and distributed memory. ACM Trans. Parallel Comput. **3**(2), (2016). Article no. 12, 28 pages. https://doi.org/10.1145/2948975
7. Dathathri, R., Reddy, C., Ramashekar, T., Bondhugula, U.: Generating efficient data movement code for heterogeneous architectures with distributed-memory. In: Proceedings of the 22nd International Conference on Parallel Architectures and Compilation Techniques, pp. 375–386. IEEE (2013)
8. Feautrier, P.: Some efficient solutions to the affine scheduling problem. I. One-dimensional time. Int. J. Parallel Program. **21**(5), 313–347 (1992). https://doi.org/10.1007/BF01407835
9. Feautrier, P.: Some efficient solutions to the affine scheduling problem Part II Multidimensional time. Int. J. Parallel Program. **21**(6), 389–420 (1992). https://doi.org/10.1007/BF01379404

10. Griebl, M.: Automatic parallelization of loop programs for distributed memory architectures. Univ. Passau (2004)
11. Kong, M., Pouchet, L.N., Sadayappan, P., Sarkar, V.: PIPES: a language and compiler for task-based programming on distributed-memory clusters. In: Proceedings of the International Conference for High Performance Computing, Networking, Storage and Analysis, SC 2016, pp. 456–467. IEEE (2016)
12. Moreton-Fernandez, A., Gonzalez-Escribano, A., Llanos, D.R.: On the run-time cost of distributed-memory communications generated using the polyhedral model. In: 2015 International Conference on High Performance Computing & Simulation (HPCS), pp. 151–159. IEEE (2015)
13. Ravishankar, M., et al.: Distributed memory code generation for mixed irregular/regular computations. In: ACM SIGPLAN Notices, vol. 50, pp. 65–75. ACM (2015)
14. Vasilache, N., et al.: A tale of three runtimes. arXiv preprint arXiv:1409.1914 (2014)
15. Verdoolaege, S.: *isl*: an integer set library for the polyhedral model. In: Fukuda, K., Hoeven, J., Joswig, M., Takayama, N. (eds.) ICMS 2010. LNCS, vol. 6327, pp. 299–302. Springer, Heidelberg (2010). https://doi.org/10.1007/978-3-642-15582-6_49

SWIRL++: Evaluating Performance Models to Guide Code Transformation in Convolutional Neural Networks

Tharindu R. Patabandi[1]([⊠]) , Anand Venkat[2] , Rajkishore Barik[3] , and Mary Hall[1]

[1] School of Computing, University of Utah, Salt Lake City, UT 84112, USA
{tharindu,mhall}@cs.utah.edu
[2] Parallel Computing Laboratory, Intel Labs, Santa Clara, CA 95054, USA
anand.venkat@intel.com
[3] Uber Technologies Inc., San Francisco, CA 94103, USA
rajbarik@uber.com

Abstract. Convolutional Neural Networks (CNNs) are ubiquitous in applications ranging from self-driving cars to various branches of health care. CPUs with large core counts and wide SIMD support are used in HPC clusters and supercomputers; therefore, high-performance CPU implementations of CNNs are valuable, in addition to the more prevalent GPU implementations. In this paper, we describe *SWIRL++*, an optimization approach for CNNs that incorporates an analytical performance model to identify optimization strategies that minimize data movement overheads of CNN execution. We integrate the model with the *SWIRL* DSL compiler to automatically generate high-performance implementations of CNNs, optimized for cache hierarchies, and both thread-level and SIMD parallelism.

We compare resulting performance of generated code with TensorFlow, integrated with Intel's MKL-DNN library (TF-MKL), and PyTorch on an Intel Xeon 8280 CascadeLake platform. Performance exceeds PyTorch on average by 2×, and is comparable on average for both TF-MKL and the *SWIRL* compiler, showing that an automated code optimization approach achieves performance comparable to hand-tuned libraries and DSL compiler techniques.

Keywords: Optimizing compilers · Convolutional neural networks · Performance models · Autotuning

1 Introduction

Recent advances in deep neural networks (DNNs) have demonstrated equal or even better than human level accuracy for tasks in many domains including

---

R. Barik—Author was affiliated with Intel Labs during the course of this work.

S. Pande and V. Sarkar (Eds.): LCPC 2019, LNCS 11998, pp. 108–126, 2021.
https://doi.org/10.1007/978-3-030-72789-5_9

object recognition, board games, speech recognition, text processing, drug discovery, and genomics, due to the ability of DNNs to learn complex patterns using large neural networks with multiple hidden layers of representation. *Convolutional Neural Networks* (CNNs) are an interesting subset of DNNs, mainly used in computer vision and image recognition. Abundant data parallelism is available in CNN layers including at the granularity of batch size, image dimensions, and feature maps. Although GPU-centric data centers are the most common platforms for such computations, machine learning is being increasingly applied to accelerate scientific simulations on supercomputing facilities [22, 28, 29, 39]. There are lessons from the HPC community on how to optimize CNNs for CPUs since most computations in CNNs can be primarily viewed as multi-dimensional matrix multiplications. As scientific applications must be portable across different target architectures, and not all supercomputers incorporate GPUs, it is important to also consider how to achieve high performance on CPU platforms. Moreover, there is also emerging interest in running CNNs on CPUs [16, 18, 25, 30, 51]. For this reason, Intel recently released MKL with DNN support (MKL-DNN) that provides efficient library implementations for common DNN operations [23].

Several high-level frameworks have emerged to describe neural networks to improve productivity of DNN researchers. All of them can be classified to use one of three approaches: computation graph engines [2, 7, 13, 42], layer-specific libraries [24], and domain-specific languages [45]. A common strategy is to use static libraries for providing efficient implementations. Such high-performance libraries are typically developed in a low-level architecture-specific way; moreover, library calls are not composable with each other.

A compiler-based approach would potentially reduce the programming burden of generating high-performance library code and ease the migration to new architectures. Further, it would enable general cross-layer fusion to reduce data movement across the memory hierarchy. However, parallelization and optimizing data movement give rise to a search space of possible implementations that is prohibitively large given the large dimensionality of the input and output data. Further, the best optimization strategy varies widely across networks, image sizes and batch sizes.

There are two approaches that compilers commonly use to navigate large optimization search spaces: (1) derive a model that allows the compiler to compare different implementations analytically to predict the best implementation; (2) search some or all of the possible implementations and measure performance to identify the best implementation. CNN computations are good candidates for modeling, as they are dense matrix operations with regular memory access patterns, while computation depends on the size of each input and output dimension, which is fixed for each layer. CNNs can use an approach similar to models for matrix multiplication (gemm) [48, 49]. Using a model speeds up compile time, but as architectural complexity continues to grow, inaccuracy in modeling has motivated empirical search-based, or *autotuning*, techniques [47]. This includes using models to prune the search space which then search a more limited space [8, 50].

For optimization search spaces that are very complex, empirical search frameworks can be used to sample a search space to find promising points rather than using exhaustive search [4,6,20,44].

In this paper, we describe *SWIRL++*, an optimization approach for CNNs that incorporates an analytical model designed to be used with or without empirical search. The model navigates the prohibitively large search space of transformations using model-based search, whereby a model predicts the Top$-k$ implementations. *SWIRL++* computes the data footprint at each level of the computation (i.e., loop level), predicting where cache misses are likely and sorting implementations based on estimated memory cost. As compared to the CNN model of Mullapudi et al. in Halide [31], we model more levels of the memory hierarchy and tile interior loops in addition to the parallel ones. We evaluate the effectiveness of this model against an empirical search framework called *Search using Random Forests* (SuRF), which uses a statistical model derived from empirical sampling of the search space with Bayesian optimization of random forests [6].

SWIRL++ is integrated into a domain-specific compiler for CNNs called *SWIRL* [46]. *SWIRL* separates specification from schedule, following the design philosophy of the likes of CHiLL [26] and Halide [35]. A *transformation recipe* [15,19,21] interface activates *SWIRL* transformations and explicitly describes the optimizations to be applied to the computation, which include data layout, loop optimizations, and cross-layer fusion. *SWIRL* provides a code generator that produces high quality vector code via intrinsics.

The paper makes the following key contributions:

- We describe a performance model for CNNs, used in model-based search, that takes into account parallelization, memory footprint, and architectural features to determine a set of parameters for L1/L2 cache tiling and register blocking factors that result in high sustained performance for many-core CPU platforms with AVX-512.
- We show that this model suggests a Top$-k$ collection of predicted best implementations with stable performance. Therefore, we can dial the amount of empirical tuning to tradeoff cost of tuning and resulting performance.
- We evaluate the effectiveness of the analytical model against the best-performing solution found by *SuRF*, an empirical autotuning tool, to demonstrate our model's convergence to optimal regions of the search space. *SWIRL++* Top-1 is always within 1% of SuRF's best variant.
- We provide a performance evaluation on state-of-the-art Intel Xeon Platinum 8280 (CascadeLake) platform, comparing *SWIRL++* against PyTorch (CPU), TensorFlow-MKL and *SWIRL*.

The high-level ideas described in this paper can be applied to other DSLs for CNN such as TensorFlow/XLA [17] and Weld [33]. The rest of the paper is organized as follows. In Sect. 2, we describe some background on CNNs including terminology that will be used throughout the paper. Also, a brief description of the *LATTE* DSL and *SWIRL* compiler framework is provided. Section 3 describes the overall compilation flow of *SWIRL++*. We describe the performance model for CNNs used to automate code variant selection in Sect. 4. Experimental evaluations for both quality of model and resulting performance are presented in Sect. 5. We discuss related work in Sect. 6 and conclude in Section 7.

2 Background

In this section, we briefly describe the concepts of convolutional neural networks, and basic *LATTE* and *SWIRL* terminology necessary for understanding the rest of the paper.

2.1 Convolutional Neural Networks (CNNs)

A CNN is typically trained on large data sets to build a complex model, which is subsequently deployed during online inferencing. Both training and inferencing are time-consuming operations, requiring high performance software implementations. Training, in particular, can span several weeks [40]. A convolution operation can be viewed as a summation of series of multiplications between an *input feature map* ($I \in \mathbb{R}^{NCHW}$) and a set of *filters/weights* (F $\in \mathbb{R}^{KRSC}$). C is the *channel* dimension, H, W are input heights and widths, respectively. K is the number of filters applied to each input. R, S represent the height and width of each filter. Each filter sweeps through the input tensor with horizontal and vertical strides u and v. The padding parameters p_h, p_w specify the number of rows and columns of zeroes that are appended to each input image boundaries. Height (P) and width (Q) of the output field map (output tensor) can be expressed as functions of input parameters, $P = \frac{H-R+2p_h}{u} + 1$, $Q = \frac{W-S+2p_w}{v} + 1$.

A simple C-like implementation of forward convolution, used in inferencing, is shown in Fig. 1a. Usually, convolutions are computed in mini batches, hence the dimension N. CNNs compute two additional tensors `grad-inputs` ($\nabla I \in \mathbb{R}^{NCPQ}$) and `grad-weights` ($\nabla W \in \mathbb{R}^{KCRS}$) during the training phase of a network. These two computations are described by the two loop nests provided in Figs. 1b and 1c.

2.2 *LATTE* DSL

LATTE is a DSL for generating optimized CNN codes for CPU backends. We use *LATTE* as our compiler front-end and the *SWIRL* code generator, which is capable of generating CPU code with ×86 vector intrinsics.

A network in *LATTE* consists of a collection of connected ensembles. An *ensemble* is a collection of neurons. Ensembles are connected using a *mapping function* that specifies the connections between the neurons in the ensembles.

LATTE initially demonstrated performance improvements over Caffe [24] using the matrix multiplication formulation (**gemm**). We redirect the voracious reader to the original *LATTE* paper for further details on the language implementation, *LATTE* syntax, semantics, and performance results [45].

```
for(n=0; n<N; n++)  // minibatch size
  for(k=0; k<K; k++)  // output feature map
    for(c=0; c<C; c++)  // input feature map
      for(p=0; p<P; p++)  // output height
        for(q=0; q<Q; q++) // output width
          for(r=0; r<R; r++) // filter height
            for(s=0; s< S; s++) // filter width
              O(n,k,p,q)+=I(n,c,u·p+r,v·q+s)*W(k,c,r,s)
```

(a) Convolution Forward Propagation

```
for(n=0; n<N; n++)
  for(k=0; k<K; k++)
    for(c=0; c<C; c++)
      for(p=0; p<P; h++)
        for(q=0; q<Q; q++)
          for(r=0; r<R; r++)
            for(s=0; s< S; s++)
              ∇I(n,c,u·p+r,v·q+s)+= ∇(n,k,p,q)*F(k,c,r,s)
```

(b) Convolution Backward Pass

```
for(n=0; n<N; n++)
  for(k=0; k<K; k++)
    for(c=0; c<C; c++)
      for(p=0; p<P; p++)
        for(q=0; q<Q; q++)
          for(r=0; r<R; r++)
            for(s=0; s< S; s++)
              ∇W(k,c,r,s)+= ∇(n,k,p,q)*input(n,c,u·p+r,c·q+s)
```

(c) Convolution Weight Update

Fig. 1. Phases of CNN computation as represented in *SWIRL*.

3 *SWIRL* and *SWIRL++* Overview

SWIRL is an optimizing compiler infrastructure that extends *LATTE* [46]. A user of *SWIRL* describes a convolutional neural network in *LATTE*. Internally, this description is first lowered to a standard Python AST and is subsequently transformed using program synthesis and compiler transformations. The *SWIRL* compiler implicitly builds a dataflow graph using the mapping functions specified in the DSL to connect an ensemble to its inputs.

To facilitate adapting the compiler transformation approach to the variety of networks that arise in practice, the *SWIRL* compiler exposes a *transformation recipe* abstraction, which permits a programmer or higher levels of the compiler to explicitly direct the transformations to be applied to the network. A compiler organization that takes transformation recipes as input makes it possible to

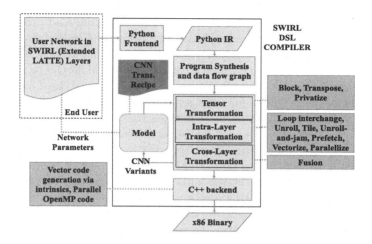

Fig. 2. High-level system diagram of *SWIRL++*.

employ autotuning to decide on which and tune the parameters of layer-specific transformations [15,19,21].

- *Data Layout Transformation Commands* are used to modify the way tensors are stored in memory. Different code optimization choices such as vectorization, parallelization, and locality enhancements decide optimal data layout for each tensor.
- *Layer Transformation Commands* affect code transformations targeting a specific layer. The layer transformations defined in *SWIRL* are standard transformations for parallelism and locality for modern architectures, and all are vital to achieving high performance for DNN code. Most of these loop transformations closely follow the definitions used to in the polyhedral framework for loop transformations.
- *Cross-layer Fusion Commands* improve cache locality and reduces memory footprint by removing unnecessary intermediate storage. Fusion is performed after individual layer-specific transformations are applied.

SWIRL++ extends *SWIRL* with an analytical performance model that evaluates the memory footprint of each convolution variant, given the reuse characteristics of the individual layer and taking cross-layer fusion into account. The model identifies the Top−k code variants; *SWIRL++* can be configured to pick the Top−1 variant, or use empirical tuning to search a small number of variants. The analytical performance model is discussed in detail in the next section.

4   Automation Through Analytical Models

As described earlier, *SWIRL* provides the programmer with a rich set of transformations to generate high performance CNN code. However, tailoring an optimal sequence of transformations for a given network structure could prove difficult for a programmer due to the complexity of finding the right transformation sequence that simultaneously optimizes for parallelism and locality. We propose instead an automated approach where an analytical model derives parameters to an implementation that leads to high performance. The analytical model quantifies the memory access costs for a given parallelization strategy and loop tiling scheme. Algorithm 1 ranks different solutions based on the associated model. Either the Top-1 solution provided by the model can be selected, or some small subset of Top$-k$ can be empirically evaluated.

In the remainder of this section, we first describe a set of heuristics we use to a priori limit the implementations considered by the model. We then describe how Algorithm 1 iterates over proposed implementations and ranks code variants based on the memory cost. Finally, we explain in detail how to estimate memory access costs for each code variant as proposed by Algorithm 2.

4.1 Notation

In this work, we derive an analytical model that approximates the memory costs of a given loop nest computation. We introduce the notation required to describe the model in this section. The loop nest computations we consider have the form of Fig. 3, which is general enough to capture all three phases of CNN computations, forward, backward, and weight-update.

An n-deep loop nest is $L = \langle l_1, l_2, ..., l_n \rangle$. We assume iteration counts for each loop l_i are normalized to start at 0 and have unit stride (i.e., $\forall_i, 0 \le l_i < ub_i$ and $l_i \in \{0\} \cup \mathbb{Z}^+$). Loop nest L can be tiled for locality optimization, to reduce the data footprint at inner loop levels and exploit data reuse. We denote the subset of tiled loops by T_L, the loops chosen for parallelization as P_L, and the vectorized loops as V_L.

Also, for a given tensor X, a loop level l_i is said to be a *reuse dimension* if the reference to X is nested inside loop l_i and l_i does not contribute to an index calculation in X. The set of reuse dimensions are denoted by R_X.

```
for (l_1 = 0;  l_1 < ub_1;  l_1++)
    for (l_2 = 0;  l_2 < ub_2;  l_2++)
        ⋮  ⋱
        for (l_n = 0;  l_n < ub_n;  l_n++)
            O(Refs_O)  += A(Refs_A) · B(Refs_B)
```

Fig. 3. Tensor Computation involving input tensors A, B, and output tensor O

4.2 Initial Pruning Heuristics

The model exploits a set of heuristics inspired by the domain-specific behavior of the computation and the knowledge of the target platforms. Most of these heuristics are derived following the structure of tensors and possible data layout transformations. These heuristics are used to prune the search space which otherwise allows sub-optimal variants and renders the search impractical.

Based on *SWIRL*'s native data layouts for each tensor, K and C loops, which exhibit parallelism in the innermost dimension, are assumed to use the SIMD vector instructions for parallelization. Therefore, their tile size is assumed to be the SIMD width, SW (see [46] for details). In the `forward` phase of the computation, if we consider the 7-deep loop nest of Fig. 1, the N, K, P and Q loops do not carry dependences and are candidates for parallelization, individually or in combination.

We limit parallelization strategies by selecting the N and K loops for thread-level parallelism using OpenMP. N is the mini batch dimension, which has the least reuse and the most parallelism, but parallelizing only N provides insufficient parallelism for the large number of cores in modern systems. The K loop also has high levels of parallelism due to larger loop bounds. We also use two levels of parallelism to match the target architectures' core count. H and W loops are also valid candidates for thread-level parallelization but not explored in this paper.

Similarly, in the `backward` (Fig. 1b) and `weight update` (Fig. 1c) phases of the computation, we choose inner C dimension for SIMD vectorization, and N, K, C as candidates for OpenMP thread parallelism. If a dependence-carrying loop needs to be parallelized, *SWIRL* privatizes corresponding output tensors and accumulates the result using a parallel reduction.

Given a fixed parallelization strategy and loop order, Algorithm 1 seeks to identify the best tile sizes for a given parallelization strategy, architecture's core count, and the structure of the memory hierarchy.

4.3   Code Variants

Algorithm 1 generates a space of code variants S_L whose tiling, parallelizing, and vectorizing schemes are governed by T_L, P_L, and V_L respectively.

The *transform* function takes as input the original loop nest L, a parallelization strategy t, a tiling scheme p, and a vectorization strategy v; and returns the corresponding code variant if the input transformations are legal, else *null* is returned. Each t may include multiple levels of tiling. Note that a tiling transformation can also result in multiple variants due to varying tile factors. In addition, *transform* will utilize a set of search-space pruning heuristics H_L to limit the number of variants returned.

For each L' in S_L, memory cost of the variant is computed by calling Algorithm 2. All variants are ranked by the associated memory cost and Top-k variants are returned.

4.4   Memory Cost

The goal of the memory cost model is to identify code variants that minimize the memory access costs by evaluating alternative tile sizes in the context of

Algorithm 1. GenerateVariants(L, T_L, P_L, V_L, H_L, k)

1: $S_L = \{\}, variants = \{\}$
2: **for** $p \in P_L$ **do**
3:     **for** $t \in T_L$ **do**
4:         **for** $v \in V_L$ **do**
5:             $S_L = S_L \cup \{transform(L, p, t, v, H_L)\}$
6: **for** $L' \in S_L$ **do**
7:     $cost = ComputeCost(L')$
8:     $variants = variants \cup \{(L', cost)\}$
9: **return** $sort(variants, k)$

Algorithm 2. ComputeCost(L)

1: $fp_X = 1, \forall X \in \{O, A, B\}$ //footprint for each tensor
2: $ll = 0$ // last loop level
3: **for** i in $\{|L|, ..., 2, 1\}$ **do** //from innermost to outermost loop
4:     **for** $X \in \{O, A, B\}$ **do**
5:         **if** $i \notin P_L \wedge i \notin R_X$ **then**
6:             $fp_X = fp_X \cdot ub_i$
7:     $fp = fp_O + fp_A + fp_B$ //total footprint at level i
8:     **if** $fp > cache\_size$ **then**
9:         $ll = i$
10:         **break** //cache eviction occurs at level i
11: $oic = \prod_{k=1}^{ll-1} ub_k$ //outer iterations count
12: **for** $X \in \{O, A, B\}$ **do**
13:     $fp_X = fp_X \cdot oic$
14:     **if** $ll \in R_X$ **then**
15:         $fp_X = fp_X \cdot ub_{ll}$
16: $reloads = \dfrac{(FM \cdot fp_O + fp_A + fp_B)}{CLS}$
17: $cost = t \cdot reloads$ //cache latency
18: **return** $cost$

each parallelization strategy. A convolution variant is characterized by its tensor references ($Refs_A$, $Refs_B$, $Refs_O$), associated tiled loops T_L, parallel loops P_L, and vectorized loops V_L.

ComputeCost function estimates the cost of memory accesses incurred during the computation a given convolution variant.

Given a loop order, the model traverses the loop structure in an outward direction starting from the innermost loop. At this stage, Algorithm 2 quantifies the increase of data footprint for each tensor (fp_O, fp_A, fp_B). More precisely, this is the footprint per thread, hence the omission of parallel dimensions P_L (line 5). At each loop level, the model computes the memory footprint required by each memory reference while taking available reuse along R_X dimensions into account. As long as a memory reference can be satisfied by the target cache level, reuse dimensions R_X, by definition, do not add to the overall footprint of a tensor.

However, if at some point (i.e., loop level ll), the footprint exceeds the capacity of the cache level that is being considered, we start attributing the subsequent memory accesses to the next cache level. This leads to the eviction of resident cache lines by the incoming data and as a result, further exploitation of available reuse along R_X is denied.

Outer iterations count (oic) keeps track of the size of the iteration space outside the current loop level. This is later used to estimate the cache reloads per tensor (line 13). Once a cache limit is reached, the reuse achieved along reuse dimensions R_X can no longer be exploited at that cache level. As a result, the footprint along R_X is increased penalizing the current loop variant (line 15). We use this information to compute the number of total cache reloads required to bring in the total footprint of each tensor.

During the forward computation, the model accommodates the fusion of consecutive layers (Conv-Bias-ReLU fusion) with identical dimensions or loop bounds. The fusion multiplier (FM), whose default value is 1, is the number of layers that are to be fused together. For example, for Convolution-Bias fusion this would be 2, and for Convolution-Bias-ReLU fusion this would be 3. This fusion multiplier is incorporated into the tiled *output* footprint (fp_O) of the convolution layer since the shape of the inputs of subsequent fused layers are the same as that of the output of the convolution layer. Since the fused footprint is now increased, the tile factors chosen would be smaller than that of the un-fused loop nest. These tile factors are then used for cache blocking the fused loop nest.

Once the amount of data movement between the target cache level and the rest of the memory hierarchy is quantified, we estimate the number of cache lines that are transferred, using cache line size of the target cache level, CLS (line 16). Finally, cache load latency t (cycles per cache line) is used to estimate the cost of accessing the full data footprint required by the computation (line 17). This estimated memory cost is then used to rank convolution variants against each other.

In summary, the `ComputeCost` function evaluates the data transfer costs for each tensor (A, B, and O) across the memory hierarchy by taking into account the number of reloads between each reuse and the latencies associated with fetching data from one memory level to another. Memory cost computation of Algorithm 2 can be extended to any target cache level of interest without loss of generality.

4.5   Final Code Generation

With the ideas presented in Sects. 4.2, 4.3, and 4.4, we are ready to generate variants for the CNN code of Fig. 1 by sweeping over the tiled loops and determining how tile sizes impact the cost calculation. Beyond what has already been described, the algorithm selects tile sizes that fully utilize the register file. Outside of this algorithm, we also derive loop unroll factors by taking tile structure, T_L, tile sizes, and the number of available registers into consideration.

When target unroll dimensions are tiled in Algorithm 1, we also make sure the tile factors are large enough to fully hide FMA (Fused Multiply-Add) latency upon unrolling (Eg. if P, Q are candidates for unrolling, corresponding tile factors p, q are determined such that $p \cdot q \geq REGS$). These constraints are incorporated into the heuristics set, H_L.

5   Experimental Evaluation

We now present an evaluation of the performance benefits of *SWIRL++* using well-known CNNs on state-of-the-art many-core CPU platforms with AVX-512 support, Intel Xeon Platinum 8280 (CascadeLake) and Intel Xeon Platinum 8180 (SkyLake).

We evaluate the quality of the performance model by comparing resulting performance against manually-tuned solutions and existing frameworks.

5.1   Methodology

Hardware Platforms: The AVX-512 platform we use is a high performance server class dual socket Intel Xeon Platinum 8280 CascadeLake Processor with 2×28 turbo-enabled cores with 192 GB of memory running at 2.7 GHZ (max 4.0 GHz). The processor is equipped with 32 KB of instruction and L1 data caches apart from 1 MB of L2 caches. Additionally, CascadeLake has a massive 38.5 MB of L3 cache to reduce memory latency. The processor is also equipped with 32 512-bit vector registers.

An Intel Xeon Platinum 8180 platform (SkyLake) with 2×28 cores running at 2.3 GHz was used to evaluate *SWIRL++* against an empirical autotuning tool, SuRF.

Benchmarks: For our evaluation, we used three well-known ImageNet models [37] including AlexNet [27], Overfeat [38], and VGG [41] using standard publicly available configurations [12], and GoogLeNet-v1 [43]. GoogLeNet-v1 has the largest number of layers among the four networks with 197 layers, whereas AlexNet and Overfeat use 25 layers, and VGG uses 36 layers. We report throughput results in terms of (a) images per second for CNN inferencing and training and (b) Gflops per second for individual layer evaluations. In our evaluation, AlexNet and GoogLeNet-v1 use a mini-batch size of 128, whereas VGG and Overfeat use a mini-batch size of 64. Please note that GoogLeNet-v1 with 197 layers presents an interesting test case since it offers a wide range of values for the parameters of the layers, presenting a lot of opportunities for compiler models (described in Sect. 4) and cross layer optimization.

Environment: We use the Intel Compiler (ICC) version 18.0.1 with -O3 -qopenmp for compiling *SWIRL* generated C++ code with NUM_OMP_THREADS=56.

5.2   Performance Comparison with Other Frameworks

We compare the Top−1 code variant generated by *SWIRL++* with TensorFlow integrated with Intel's MKL-DNN (aka TF-MKL) and PyTorch (CPU v1.1.0)

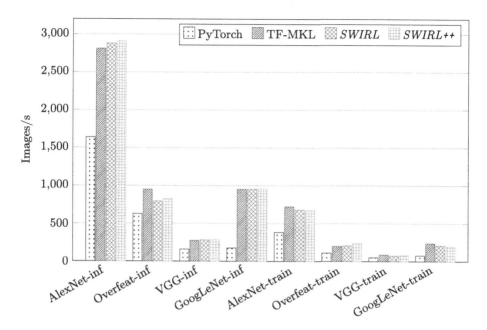

Fig. 4. Performance comparison of *SWIRL++* with PyTorch (CPU), TF-MKL, and *SWIRL* on Intel Xeon CascadeLake for CNN Inference and Training.

library. TF-MKL optimizations are provided through MKL-DNN library and PyTorch uses a JIT IR to perform transformations. Furthermore, we compare *SWIRL++* performance against *SWIRL* compiler which utilizes a manually-tuned transformation recipe.

As shown in Fig. 4, for CNN inference, *SWIRL++* achieves comparable performance for all networks, an average speedup of 0.99× over `TF-MKL` and 1.02× over *SWIRL*, both are hand-tuned implementations. For training, *SWIRL++* achieves 0.96× and 1.02× over `TF-MKL` and *SWIRL*, respectively.

5.3 Performance Model Evaluation

In this section, we provide an evaluation of the quality of the analytical performance model in selecting high-performing CNN code variants. This evaluation will focus on per-layer results on Intel Xeon Platinum 8180 (SkyLake), focusing on the individual convolution layers of the input networks. The *SWIRL++* model is designed to rank order the variants that are explored analytically by the model, and return the ordered Top$-k$ variants, where parameter k is set to default to 30 but could be specified by the user. Top-k variants are ranked based on the evaluation of the cost model, i.e., k variants with the least per-thread memory footprint. The effect of returning only the Top-k variants is to aggressively prune the massive search space resulting from varying tile sizes and unroll factors for the high-dimensional convolution loop nest. If desired, a user could empirically evaluate all k variants by executing each to identify the best-performing variant. With k set by the user, the search space can be constrained to limit the cost of search and exhaustively search only a small number of variants that are likely to perform well. Our initial evaluation compared the Top-1 solution, which can be derived analytically without executing the variant, to the best empirical variant among the Top-k variants, for varying values of k.

An alternative approach to tuning variants in a large search space is to sample points in the search space, possibly randomly, and evaluate them empirically to locate promising regions of the search space that can be further explored. By limiting the number of points, or search time, the cost of this exploration can be constrained. To compare such an approach against the analytical model, we integrated the *Search using Random Forests* (SuRF) technique with *SWIRL++*, and encoded the same search space as explored by the analytical model. SuRF derives a statistical model by sampling points in the search space and measuring their performance [9,32], using Bayesian optimization of random forests. We compare *SWIRL++*'s Top-1 variant to the best code variants identified by SuRF.

Performance of Top-1 Variant. The objective of the evaluation is to observe whether empirical search, whose evaluation is based on actual feedback of code variants, is capable of significantly outperforming *SWIRL++*, which is purely analytical. We first compare the forward convolution variants explored by SuRF within the search quota (q=500 points) against the Top-1 variant attained by *SWIRL++* and the results for select network layers are shown in Fig. 5.

From these results, several interesting observations can be drawn. The horizontal series (orange) represents the Top-1 prediction of *SWIRL++*. In all evaluated cases, we observe that measured performance of *SWIRL++*'s Top-1 falls among the best variants found by SuRF with a generous search budget $q = 500$. In cases such as (b), (c), (k), (l), the best variant can be distinctly identified from the other variants, and *SWIRL++* successfully converges to find that code variant. Also, in cases (a), (e), (i), (j), the search space is densely populated with high performing configurations and the Top-1 of *SWIRL++* is consistent with candidate variants in the region. In none of the cases, SuRF finds significantly superior configurations to outperform *SWIRL++*, signalling the potential convergence to the globally optimal regions in the given search space. In this regard, we can observe that *SWIRL++* Top-1 is chosen from a universally profitable region in the search space.

It is also noteworthy that empirical autotuners are often oblivious to the non-trivial inter-dependencies among search parameters, especially in discrete search domains like the one we encountered in this paper. As a result, performance-similar variants with seemingly different configurations may fall in different regions of the search space making empirical evaluation less effective unless we increase the search budget which is often expensive.

Table 1 compares the *SWIRL++* Top-1 solution to the best-performing variant among the Top-k versions for different values of k and also to the best-performing implementation identified by SuRF. We observe a minimum variance across the

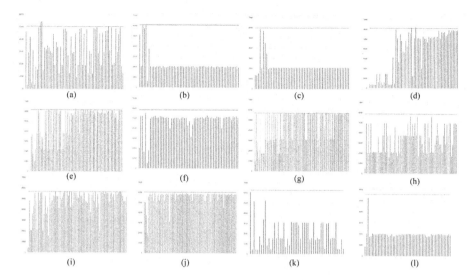

Fig. 5. Comparison between *SWIRL++* and SuRF empirical autotuning framework across select convolutional layers on Intel Xeon SkyLake. (a) vgg2_1, (b) vgg3_1, (c) vgg3_2, (d) vgg4_1, (e) vgg4_2, (f) vgg5_2 , (g) overfeat3, (h) overfeat4, (i) overfeat5, (j) inception_3a_3 × 3 , (k) inception_3b_3 × 3, (l) inception_4a_3 × 3. Vertical axis is throughput measured in Gflops/s and horizontal axis represents each code variant generated and explored by SuRF. Horizontal series (orange) represents the best throughput attained by the Top-1 *SWIRL++* variant for the particular layer.

top predictions made by *SWIRL++* implying the stability of the analytical memory model presented earlier. This behavior allows us to simply use *SWIRL++* Top-1, which is purely analytical, without resorting to often expensive iterative compilation based Top-k empirical evaluation without significant performance compromise.

Cost of Deriving Variant. Both *SWIRL++* and SuRF traverse the same search space but *SWIRL++* being an analytical solution, computes Top−1 in $\mathcal{O}(1)$ compared to an empirical search tool such as SuRF, in theory, would take $\mathcal{O}(q)$ in the worst case if it ever converges within the given quota q. Even Top−k, which is presumably exploring only promising variants, has an average cost of about 100 ms per variant.

Therefore, we can conclude that *SWIRL++* achieves convergence with consistently robust Top−1 predictions and using either Top−k or SuRF empirical search yields at best modest performance gains at substantial increase in code generation costs.

Table 1. Performance impact of empirical search: Top-1 is normalized to 1, and other versions show speedup over Top-1. Top-k represents the best variant's speedup compared to Top-1. Top-SuRF is the speedup of the best variant found by SuRF against *SWIRL++* Top-1.

Layer	Top-1	Top-5	Top-10	Top-30	Top-SuRF
vgg2_1	1	1.0097	1.0185	1.0185	0.9228
vgg3_1	1	1.0031	1.0031	1.0031	1.0111
vgg3_2	1	1.0086	1.0265	1.0639	0.9919
vgg4_1	1	1.0000	1.0193	1.0248	1.0497
vgg4_2	1	1.0107	1.0414	1.0467	1.0786
vgg5_2	1	1.0033	1.0033	1.0033	0.8977
overfeat3	1	1.0760	1.0760	1.0760	1.0310
overfeat4	1	1.0165	1.0232	1.0232	0.9328
overfeat5	1	1.0160	1.0161	1.0174	0.9459

6   Related Work

Programmer productivity, performance portability, and the ability to generate high performance code have been responsible for the popularity of many, if not all, of the modern high-level deep learning frameworks [2,3,7,9,13,24, 42,45]. For performance reasons, most of these frameworks resort to statically tuned libraries, sometimes with multiple implementations that are dynamically selected, e.g., cuDNN [11], TensorRT [1] on GPUs and Intel MKL-DNN [23]/OpenBLAS on CPUs.

Modern tensor optimization frameworks are determined to automate the optimization process due to the complexity of the manual optimization. To this end, both high level IR transformations as well as device specific low level optimizations are explored. The likes of Glow [36], nGraph [14], and TVM[10] are capable of performing graph level optimizations. More recently, Tiramisu [5] proposed a multi-tier IR for decoupling various aspects of tensor optimization through separate IR layers.

A number of efforts have been made to model the behavior of tensor computations. Compared to earlier models for dense matrix computations [8,48,50], modeling the CNN computations is more difficult and the search space has more degrees of freedom since it consists of a 7 dimensional loop nest operating on multiple 4 dimensional data tensors. In an attempt to model computational and communication costs associated with deep learning, Paleo presents an analytical model for DNN training [34]. Paleo models convolution layers using SGEMM and FFT based implementations whereas *SWIRL* uses direct convolution.

7 Conclusion

In this paper, we presented *SWIRL++*, an analytical performance model to optimize CNN payloads for CPU backends. The model uses *transformation recipes* provided by *SWIRL*, a DSL compiler for CNN implementation and optimization. The model automates the process of tailoring optimizing transformation sequences for convolutional layers. *SWIRL++* model is based on the memory footprint of convolution variants, and achieves high performance by finding variants that minimize the memory costs associated with each variant.

We evaluate performance gains achieved by *SWIRL++* over PyTorch, TF-MKL, and *SWIRL* native optimizations. We conduct performance evaluations using 4 popular CNNs; AlexNet, VGG, Overfeat, and GoogLeNet-v1 on an Intel Xeon CascadeLake platform. *SWIRL++* constantly achieves performance comparable with hand-tuned libraries and hand-written transformation recipes across all four benchmarks used in the experiments.

Finally, we empirically validate *SWIRL++*, using two approaches, (a) evaluating Top-k variants predicted by *SWIRL++*, (b) with the help of SuRF to demonstrate that *SWIRL++* actually converges to the optimal search region within the defined search space. In (a), *SWIRL++* shows internal consistency among the predicted top-k variants with minimal performance variance, and in case (b), *SWIRL++* demonstrates convergence to optimal regions of the search space.

Acknowledgement. This research was supported by the Exascale Computing Project (17-SC-20-SC), a collaborative effort of the U.S. Department of Energy Office of Science and the National Nuclear Security Administration, by the Department of Energy Scientific Discovery through Advanced Computation program, and by the National Science Foundation under CCF-1564074.

References

1. NVIDIA GPU Inference Engine (2016). https://devblogs.nvidia.com/parallelfor all/production-deep-learning-nvidia-gpu-inference-engine/. Accessed 6 July 2020
2. Abadi, M., et al.: TensorFlow: Large-scale machine learning on heterogeneous systems (2015). http://tensorflow.org/
3. Agarwal, A., et al.: An introduction to computational networks and the computational network toolkit. Technical Report MSR-TR-2014-112 (2014). http://research.microsoft.com/apps/pubs/default.aspx?id=226641
4. Ansel, J., et al.: Opentuner: an extensible framework for program autotuning. In: International Conference on Parallel Architectures and Compilation Techniques. Edmonton, Canada (2014). http://groups.csail.mit.edu/commit/papers/2014/ansel-pact14-opentuner.pdf
5. Baghdadi, R., et al.: Tiramisu: a code optimization framework for high performance systems. arXiv preprint arXiv:1804.10694 (2018)
6. Balaprakash, P., et al.: Autotuning in high-performance computing applications. Proc. IEEE **106**(11), 2068–2083 (2018). https://doi.org/10.1109/JPROC.2018.2841200
7. Bergstra, J., et al.: Theano: a CPU and GPU math expression compiler. In: Proceedings of the Python for Scientific Computing Conference (SciPy) (2010)

8. Chen, C., Chame, J., Hall, M.: Combining models and guided empirical search to optimize for multiple levels of the memory hierarchy. In: International Symposium on Code Generation and Optimization. CGO 2005, pp. 111–122. IEEE (2005)

9. Chen, T., et al.: Mxnet: A flexible and efficient machine learning library for heterogeneous distributed systems. arXiv preprint arXiv:1512.01274 (2015)

10. Chen, T., et al.: TVM: an automated end-to-end optimizing compiler for deep learning. In: 13th USENIX Symposium on Operating Systems Design and Implementation (OSDI 2018), pp. 578–594 (2018)

11. Chetlur, S., et al.: cuDNN: Efficient Primitives for Deep Learning. CoRR abs/1410.0759 (2014). http://arxiv.org/abs/1410.0759

12. Chintala, S.: Convnet Benchmarks (2015). https://github.com/soumith/convnet-benchmarks. Accessed 6 July 2020

13. Collobert, R., Kavukcuoglu, K., Farabet, C.: Torch7: A MATLAB-like environment for machine learning. In: BigLearn, NIPS Workshop. No. EPFL-CONF-192376 (2011)

14. Cyphers, S., et al.: Intel® nGraph™: an intermediate representation, compiler, and executor for deep learning. arXiv preprint arXiv:1801.08058 (2018)

15. Donadio, S., et al.: A language for the compact representation of multiple program versions. In: Workshop on Languages and Compilers for Parallel Computing (LCPC) (2005)

16. Dukhan, M.: NNPACK (2016). https://github.com/Maratyszcza/NNPACK. Accessed 6 July 2020

17. Google: TensorFlow XLA (2016). https://www.tensorflow.org/xla/. Accessed 6 July 2020

18. Google: Improving the speed of neural networks on CPUs (2011). https://research.google.com/pubs/pub37631.html. Accessed 6 July 2020

19. Hall, M.W., Chame, J., Chen, C., Shin, J., Rudy, G., Khan, M.M.: Loop transformation recipes for code generation and auto-tuning. In: Proceedings of the 22nd International Workshop on Languages and Compilers for Parallel Computing (2009)

20. Hartono, A., Norris, B., Sadayappan, P.: Annotation-based empirical performance tuning using orio. In: 2009 IEEE International Symposium on Parallel Distributed Processing, pp. 1–11 (2009). https://doi.org/10.1109/IPDPS.2009.5161004

21. Hartono, A., Norris, B., Sadayappan, P.: Annotation-based empirical performance tuning using Orio. In: IPDPS (2009)

22. Hezaveh, Y.D., Levasseur, L.P., Marshall, P.J.: Fast automated analysis of strong gravitational lenses with convolutional neural networks. Nature **548** (2017)

23. Intel: Intel MKL-DNN. https://github.com/01org/mkl-dnn. Accessed 6 July 2020

24. Jia, Y., et al.: Caffe: Convolutional Architecture for Fast Feature Embedding. arXiv preprint arXiv:1408.5093 (2014)

25. Jin, L., Wang, Z., Gu, R., Yuan, C., Huang, Y.: Training large scale deep neural networks on the intel xeon phi many-core coprocessor. In: 2014 IEEE International Parallel Distributed Processing Symposium Workshops, pp. 1622–1630 (2014). https://doi.org/10.1109/IPDPSW.2014.194

26. Khan, M., Basu, P., Rudy, G., Hall, M., Chen, C., Chame, J.: A script-based auto-tuning compiler system to generate high-performance CUDA code. ACM Trans. Archit. Code Optim. **9**(4), 31:1–31:25 (2013). https://doi.org/10.1145/2400682.2400690

27. Krizhevsky, A., Sutskever, I., Hinton, G.E.: ImageNet classification with deep convolutional neural networks. In: Advances in Neural Information Processing Systems, pp. 1097–1105 (2012)

28. Kurth, T., et al.: Deep learning at 15PF: supervised and semi-supervised classification for scientific data. In: Proceedings of the International Conference for High Performance Computing, Networking, Storage and Analysis, New York, NY, pp. 7:1–7:11. SC 2017, ACM (2017). https://doi.org/10.1145/3126908.3126916

29. Liu, Y., et al.: Application of deep convolutional neural networks for detecting extreme weather in climate datasets. CoRR abs/1605.01156 (2016). http://arxiv.org/abs/1605.01156

30. Milova, E., Sveshnikova, S., Gankevich, I.: Speedup of deep neural network learning on the mic-architecture. In: 2016 International Conference on High Performance Computing Simulation (HPCS), pp. 989–992 (2016). https://doi.org/10.1109/HPCSim.2016.7568443

31. Mullapudi, R.T., Adams, A., Sharlet, D., Ragan-Kelley, J., Fatahalian, K.: Automatically scheduling halide image processing pipelines. ACM Trans. Graph. **35**(4), 83:1–83:11 (2016). https://doi.org/10.1145/2897824.2925952

32. Nelson, T., et al.: Generating efficient tensor contractions for GPUs. In: 2015 44th International Conference on Parallel Processing, pp. 969–978. IEEE (2015)

33. Palkar, S., et al: Weld: a common runtime for high performance data analytics. In: Biennial Conference on Innovative Data Systems Research (CIDR). CIDR 2017 (2017)

34. Qi, H., Sparks, E.R., Talwalkar, A.: Paleo: a performance model for deep neural networks (2016)

35. Ragan-Kelley, J., Barnes, C., Adams, A., Paris, S., Durand, F., Amarasinghe, S.: Halide: a language and compiler for optimizing parallelism, locality, and recomputation in image processing pipelines. ACM SIGPLAN Notices **48**(6), 519–530 (2013)

36. Rotem, N., et al.: Glow: Graph lowering compiler techniques for neural networks. arXiv preprint arXiv:1805.00907 (2018)

37. Russakovsky, O., et al.: ImageNet large scale visual recognition challenge. Int. J. Comput. Vis. (IJCV) **115**(3), 211–252 (2015). https://doi.org/10.1007/s11263-015-0816-y

38. Sermanet, P., Eigen, D., Zhang, X., Mathieu, M., Fergus, R., LeCun, Y.: OverFeat: Integrated Recognition, Localization and Detection using Convolutional Networks. CoRR abs/1312.6229 (2013). http://arxiv.org/abs/1312.6229

39. Shashank Kaira, C., et al.: Automated correlative segmentation of large transmission x-ray microscopy (TXM) tomograms using deep learning. Mater. Characterization **142**, 203–210 (2018). https://doi.org/10.1016/j.matchar.2018.05.053

40. Silver, D., et al.: Mastering the game of Go with deep neural networks and tree search. Nature **529**(7587), 484–489 (2016). https://doi.org/10.1038/nature16961

41. Simonyan, K., Zisserman, A.: Very Deep Convolutional Networks for Large-Scale Image Recognition. CoRR abs/1409.1556 (2014)

42. Systems, N.: NEON (2016). https://github.com/NervanaSystems/neon. Accessed 6 July 2020

43. Szegedy, C., et al.: Going deeper with convolutions. CoRR abs/1409.4842 (2014). http://arxiv.org/abs/1409.4842

44. Tapus, C., I-Hsin Chung, Hollingsworth, J.K.: Active harmony: towards automated performance tuning. In: SC 2002: Proceedings of the 2002 ACM/IEEE Conference on Supercomputing, pp. 44–44 (2002). https://doi.org/10.1109/SC.2002.10062

45. Truong, L., et al.: Latte: A language, compiler, and runtime for elegant and efficient deep neural networks. In: Proceedings of the 37th ACM SIGPLAN Conference on Programming Language Design and Implementation, New York, NY, pp. 209–223. PLDI 2016. ACM (2016). https://doi.org/10.1145/2908080.2908105

46. Venkat, A., Rusira, T., Barik, R., Hall, M., Truong, L.: SWIRL: high-performance many-core CPU code generation for deep neural networks. Int. J. High Perform. Comput. Appl. 1094342019866247. https://doi.org/10.1177/1094342019866247

47. Whaley, R.C., Dongarra, J.J.: Automatically tuned linear algebra software. In: Proceedings of the 1998 ACM/IEEE Conference on Supercomputing, Washington, DC. SC 1998, pp. 1–27. IEEE Computer Society (1998). http://dl.acm.org/citation.cfm?id=509058.509096

48. Wolf, M.E., Lam, M.S.: A data locality optimizing algorithm. In: ACM SIGPLAN Notices, vol. 26, pp. 30–44. ACM (1991)

49. Yotov, K., et al.: A comparison of empirical and model-driven optimization. In: Proceedings of the ACM SIGPLAN 2003 Conference on Programming Language Design and Implementation, New York, NY. PLDI 2003, pp. 63–76. ACM (2003). https://doi.org/10.1145/781131.781140

50. Yotov, K., et al.: Is search really necessary to generate high-performance blas? Proc. IEEE **93**(2), 358–386 (2005)

51. Zlateski, A., Lee, K., Seung, H.S.: ZNN - A fast and scalable algorithm for training 3D convolutional networks on multi-core and many-core shared memory machines. CoRR abs/1510.06706 (2015). http://arxiv.org/abs/1510.06706

A Structured Grid Solver with Polyhedral+Dataflow Representation

Eddie C. Davis[1]($\boxtimes$), Catherine R. M. Olschanowsky[1]($\boxtimes$),
and Brian Van Straalen[2]

[1] Boise State University, Boise, ID 83702, USA
{eddiedavis,catherineolschan}@boisestate.edu
[2] Lawrence Berkeley National Laboratory, Berkeley, CA 94720, USA
bvstraalen@lbl.gov

Abstract. Proto is a C++ embedded Domain Specific Library for stencil-based computations. Proto is augmented in this work with a polyhedral dataflow intermediate representation (IR). The IR exposes several promising transformations. Each IR instances produces a performance model, and source code in C++. Generated code is annotated with OpenMP or OpenACC pragmas for shared-memory or accelerator parallelism. Performance is measured on modern multicore CPU and GPU platforms.

Keywords: Stencil · Mesh · Polyhedral · Dataflow · Compiler

1 Introduction

Finite difference and finite volume methods for solving partial differential equations are the core of many scientific applications, spanning scientific disciplines including biology, engineering, physics, and geography. Several frameworks exist that support scientific application development with these requirements combined with adaptive mesh refinement (AMR). However, current solutions struggle to realize performance across the range of compute architectures currently available.

The demands of exascale computing require performance portability across CPU and GPU architectures. Many existing legacy scientific applications are implemented in Fortran or other aging technologies. Refactoring these codes to achieve portability across modern, heterogeneous architectures poses a significant challenge for the scientific computing community.

`Proto` is a lightweight library designed for efficient solution of differential equations on domains that are composed of unions of structured, logically rectangular grids. The DSL improves the productivity of computational scientists through an intuitive programming interface that seamlessly integrates with an

© Springer Nature Switzerland AG 2021
S. Pande and V. Sarkar (Eds.): LCPC 2019, LNCS 11998, pp. 127–146, 2021.
https://doi.org/10.1007/978-3-030-72789-5_10

existing AMR framework. The goal of `Proto` is to decouple the precise description of a finite-difference discretization of a partial differential equation, and how that algorithm is executed on a specified computer architecture. The `Proto` library includes support for CPU and GPU computations.

This paper describes `Proto` and how it was coupled with a polyhedral+dataflow intermediate language (`PDFL`) to achieve performance portability for shared memory, multi-core CPU and GPU backends. The DSL improves productivity of computational scientists through an intuitive programming interface that seamlessly integrates with an existing AMR framework.

Embedded domain specific languages allow developers to add functionality to an existing language like C++ with mature compiler infrastructures such as GCC, Clang, and Intel (ICC). However, it can be difficult to optimize codes implemented in a high-level representation, since the compiler cannot easily optimize code across several layers of abstraction. Challenges include limited data reuse, large quantities of temporary storage, and low arithmetic intensity in many small kernels. Parallelizing such kernels for multi-threaded architectures can suffer from the excessive overhead of fork/join calls in the case of OpenMP, or kernel launches in CUDA.

The intermediate polyhedral+dataflow representation [14] addresses this challenge by collecting computation information in a dataflow graph, then fusing nodes to increase AI, minimize fork/join overhead, perform storage reductions to minimize memory traffic, SIMD vectorization, and apply tiling to improve data locality. The dataflow representation is combined with a performance model that estimates FLOPs and memory throughput to guide optimizations and generate code variants. The experimental results indicate that performance speedups of up to 3X for CPU, and 2.6X for GPU are achievable.

This paper provides the following contributions:

1. Specification of computations as high-level constructs as an eDSL.
2. Dataflow-based intermediate representation designed for optimizations.
3. Performance model to predict the profitability of transformations based on FLOP estimates and memory read/write traffic.
4. Compiler infrastructure with multi-pass architecture using graph visitors.
5. Auto-parallelized loops with OpenMP, OpenACC, or SIMD pragmas.
6. Temporary storage reductions based on reuse distance.
7. Memory allocation heuristic that only allocates sufficient memory for data that are alive at any point during the computation.

2   Background

This section provides background information on Chombo, as an example of an application framework that solves partial differential equations (PDEs), and the Euler equations that will be used as a motivating example in this paper.

2.1   Chombo and AMR

The Chombo [1,11,17] package supports conservative discretizations of complex PDEs. It provides programming abstractions for iterations spaces, data spaces, and more. The discretized problem domain comprises a set of boxes that each comprise a subset of the points in the domain. Chombo is used in a variety of scientific applications and is designed to perform well on many compute resources ranging from laptops to leadership class supercomputers [13,16,40,41,44,47].

Adaptive mesh refinement saves time and energy by refining sections of the problem domain based on the complexity of the phenomena modeled in that area. Areas where little change is taking place remain at a courser granularity and, therefore, require fewer compute resources to include in the simulation. The Chombo C++ Library is designed to support these kind of applications running across all modern supercomputing platforms. `Proto` is intended to support the same applications types as Chombo with a high-level programming model that can be executed on heterogeneous architectures.

2.2   Euler Equations

Our running example is an implementation of the Euler equations. They provide a manageable example of a PDE system that requires the properties of SAMR discretization methods (over time highly localized in space or time features develop due to nonlinearities). The Euler equations in fluid dynamics are quasilinear hyperbolic equations that are a special case of the Navier-Stokes with zero viscosity (inviscid), and zero thermal conductivity (adiabatic). They can be applied to both compressible and incompressible fluid flows [39]. The method described in this work is an implementation of the 4th-order Method Of Lines published in [28] and written in the `Proto` DSL.

A fourth order Runge-Kutta method is applied to solve for $\mathbf{u}$, the flow velocity vector. The solution is advanced by integrating over multiple time steps until some target time is reached, or a maximum number of iterations has been performed. The current state becomes the input to compute the next output state after each time increment. The step function is executed four times, forming the bottleneck of the solver.

Each point in the grid contains a component vector (ρ, p_x, p_y, p_z, e) where ρ is the density, p is momentum in each direction, and e is energy. These are the conserved values. The first operation in the step function is to convert the conserved values into their primitive counterparts, performed by the *consToPrim* function. A deconvolution stencil is applied to the input box, and the result is also converted to primitives. These two are added together and a Laplacian stencil is applied to compute the average. Interpolation is then performed for each dimension, with both a high and low wave speed calculated. This operation includes two stencils, an upwind state computation, a deconvolution, two flux calculations, a Laplacian, and a divergence with each added to the final result to produce the new state.

3 Proto Overview

`Proto` derives from earlier work on `AMRStencil`, a domain-specific language developed as part of the D-TEC project [33]. That effort relied upon a true augmentation of the underlying C++11 language specification with stencil-based language features. Learning a lesson from the transition of UPC [18] to UPC++ [3], it was determined that C++ is now powerful enough to describe language semantics from within a C++ template library itself, thus separating DSL development from compiler semantics.

`Proto` is a lightweight C++ library developed to efficiently solve differential equations over domains formed from the union of structured, rectangular grids. The goal is to decouple the complexities of *designing* an algorithm from the *scheduling*. The `PDFL` language and IR share this as a common goal. `Proto` contains a number of high-level constructs for achieving this goal. A `Point` represents a point $\in \mathbb{Z}^D$, a D-dimensional integer space. A `Box` encloses a subset, B, of $\mathbb{Z}^D$, a rectangular domain over an array. Each is described by a pair of points, (l, h), for example bottom-left, and top-right in the 2D case. `Proto` boxes support many transformations that lend themselves to be supported by the polyhedral model, such as intersection, shifting, and coarsening or refinement.

Boxes describe a discretization of physical space, while data represent components in the state space. Data are encapsulated with boxes in a `BoxData` object. `Proto` uses C++ templates to an arbitrary type $\mathbb{T}$, that can either be the real numbers, $\mathbb{R}$, complex numbers, $\mathbb{R}$, or integers $\mathbb{Z}$. The data associated with each point can be a scalar value, a component vector of length, C, a component matrix ($C \times D$), or a tensor ($C \times D \times E$). Box ranges are computed at runtime, while component indices are known at compile time.

There are two primary ways to represent computations in `Proto`. The `forall` operation receives as inputs a function pointer, `F`, `Box`, and an arbitrary (variadic) number of parameters, including data boxes or scalars. If the box is omitted, the operation will be applied to each point in the intersection of the supplied `BoxData` objects. Finally, `Proto` supports the creation of arbitrary stencil objects at runtime, where each consists of a set of offsets (as points) and corresponding weights. Stencils can be added, multiplied by scalars, or composed to create new stencils. Class methods in `BoxData` enable other pointwise operations via operator overloading, e.g., addition or scalar multiplication.

3.1 Euler in Proto

The `Proto` implementation to solve for velocity using the Euler equations is given in Fig. 1. The input vector, **U** is the flow velocity vector. The `consToPrim` function converts the conserved quantities, i.e., momentum, into primitives, i.e., velocities in each direction. The input data is deconvolved into a local vector with the `deconvolve` stencil. The `laplacian` stencil computes the average velocity, and the deconvolved primitives are added to the result. Lower and upper interpolations are performed on the average velocity for each dimension. The fluxes for each dimension are then computed, and the divergence of the average is added to the output vector. Finally, each point is multiplied by the negative inverse of the step size (dx). Stencils are applied to each point in the data space including the component space. A forall statement executes the function on each point in the data space by operating on the component space. Arithmetic operations (e.g., +=) are applied to all points in the data and component spaces.

```
1  Vector W_bar = forall<double,C>(consToPrim,U_in,gamma);
2  Vector U = deconvolve(U_in);
3  Vector W = forall<double,C>(consToPrim,U,gamma);
4  Vector W_ave = laplacian(W_bar,1.0/24.0);
5  W_ave += W;
6
7  for (int d = 0; d < DIM; d++) {
8    Vector W_aveL = interpL[d](W_ave);
9    Vector W_aveH = interpH[d](W_ave);
10   Vector W_ave_f = forall<double,C>(upwind,W_aveL,W_aveH,d,gamma);
11   Vector F_bar_f = forall<double,C>(getFlux, W_ave_f,d,gamma);
12   Vector W_f = deconvolve_f[d](W_ave_f);
13   Vector F_ave_f = forall<double,C>(getFlux,W_f,d,gamma);
14   F_bar_f *= (1 / 24);
15   F_ave_f += laplacian_f[d](F_bar_f,1.0/24.0);
16   U_out += divergence[d](F_ave_f);
17 }
18 U_out *= -1 / dx;
```

Fig. 1. Proto implementation of the step function from the Euler solver.

4   Compiler Approach

Computations in Proto are executed directly in the C++ code of the algorithm specification at run time. This paper proposes a compiler-based approach that collects the details of the computation, builds a dataflow graph intermediate representation, applies loop transformations and storage reductions, then generates optimized code to perform the same computation in less time.

4.1   Intermediate Representation

The Proto code is translated into the polyhedral+dataflow intermediate representation via the PDFL embedded DSL that defines computations in the IR. This eDSL consists of four primary constructs: spaces, functions, iterators, and computations. Spaces represent points in space, either iteration spaces or data. Iteration spaces are collections of integers, describing the points of a polyhedron. Data spaces can have any primitive data type.

Iterators are values that traverse a space. The space are bounded by constraints on the corresponding iterators. A space representing an $N \times M$ matrix, for example can be described by two iterators (i, j) with constraints, $0 \leq i < N$ and $0 \leq j < M$, where $M, N \in \mathbb{Z}$

Functions can represent uninterpreted functions, symbolic constants, or relations that map points in one space to those in another. An access function maps an iterator tuple referenced in a computation to the corresponding location of the data in memory. Similarly, a scattering function maps an iteration space tuple to a location in an execution schedule. Computations are executed in lexicographic order.

A computation is defined by an iteration space, combined with an ordered set of executable statements to be performed at each point. Each statement can be assigned a conditional expression (*guard*) that must be satisfied for the statement to be executed. Conditions that depend on the iterators are affine. Otherwise, the guard is non-affine and handled with a control or exit predicate [8]. A computation performed over an iteration space with two iterators (i, j), with three statements $(s0, s1, s2)$, would have the scattering function, $([i, j] \rightarrow s0(i, j, 0)$, $s1(i, j, 1)$, and $s2(i, j, 2))$. A space can also be scalar, consisting of a single point to execute statements, or an individual data point is located.

Loop fusion is one of the primary transformations applied to the dataflow graph IR. Fusing two statement nodes results in the union of their iteration spaces and computations. An additional data structure is introduced to represent the internal execution schedule within a group of fused nodes to ensure that all producer-consumer relationships are maintained correctly.

Each computation node has a corresponding iterator tree that describes the execution schedule. The root node connects all of the iterators. The internal nodes are iterators, and the leaf nodes statements. Edge labels indicate the order of the iterator in the resulting schedule. A scattering function for each statement is derived by performing a depth first traversal of the iterator tree. The global schedule for the entire dataflow graph is determined by combining these individual trees as subtrees of a single root.

4.2   Mapping Proto to Polyhedral+Dataflow IR

The entities defined in `Proto` are analogous to those in the PDFG-IR. A point in `Proto` is equivalent to an instance of an iterator tuple in `PDFL`. Collections of points are represented by `Box` objects. These are equivalent to iteration spaces in `PDFL`. `BoxData` objects in `Proto` correspond to data spaces.

The `forall` operation is represented by a computation in `PDFL`. The PDFG representation of a `Proto` kernel is transformed into C code before running. Function pointers are not directly supported since the compiler cannot determine the source of the original code. `Proto` kernel functions are expressed in the `PDFL` eDSL. The corresponding iteration space is built by adding the spatial dimensions in reverse order. In the 2D case, the x-dimension would become the inner loop, with y as the outermost loop.

Stencils in `Proto` are also mapped to computations in `PDFL`. A stencil, S, is represented by a point matrix, P of size $n \times d$ where n is the number of stencil points, and d the dimensions, and a coefficient vector, $\mathbf{c}$ of size n. The five-point Laplacian stencil, for example, would be represented by the offset points $\{(0,0), (1,0), (-1,0), (0,1), (0,-1)\}$ and coefficient weights $(-4, 1, 1, 1, 1)$.

A stencil is applied to all components, so the iteration space includes the component space. Component loops are initially placed as the outermost loops. A 2D stencil over a box of N cells with component vector of length C would produce the following iteration space.

$$S = \{[c, y, x] \mid 0 \leq c < C \wedge 0 \leq y < N \wedge 0 \leq x < N\}$$

The offsets and weights in the stencil are unrolled to become a weighted sum expression. Applying the stencil to a data space, W, produces this expression:

$$\bar{W}(c, y, x) = -4W(c, y, x) + W(c, y, x + 1) + W(c, y, x - 1)$$
$$+ W(c, y + 1, x) + W(c, y - 1, x)$$

Data accesses are denoted by a data space followed by an iterator tuple (e.g., $W(y, x)$). Accesses on the right hand side of an assignment are assumed to be reads, and the associated statement node a consumer. Those on the left are considered writes and the statement node a producer. The default data mapping is a linearization of the data as a one dimensional array, e.g., $W(y, x) \rightarrow W[N * y + x]$.

`Proto` objects are transformed into PDFG-IR by an interface layer. As each `Proto` method is executed, the corresponding `PDFL` objects are generated while the PDFG-IR is constructed. Each time a function is called, an automatically incrementing identifier is assigned to prevent conflicts (e.g., $getFlux1$, $getFlux2$, etc.). After a single pass through the `Proto` kernel has been completed, the initial, serial dataflow graph is created. The PDFG for the two-dimensional Euler step function is given in Fig. 2.

Representing control flow in a dataflow language is challenging. Some `Proto` functions, e.g., `upwind`, require control flow. This has been supported in `PDFL` by the inclusion of a conditional expression that implements the ternary operator. Intermediate computations in temporary variables are replaced with the actual expression. This is a form of redundant computation, and can help relieve register pressure or reduce memory traffic.

4.3 Performance Modeling

A performance model is generated for each graph variant. Floating point operations (FLOPs) are counted from eDSL operations. Read/write traffic is estimated from iteration space sizes and producer/consumer access mappings. The total number of bytes allocated are computed from the size of each data space. The number input/output streams active at any point in the execution is determined from the incoming and outgoing dataflow graph edges.

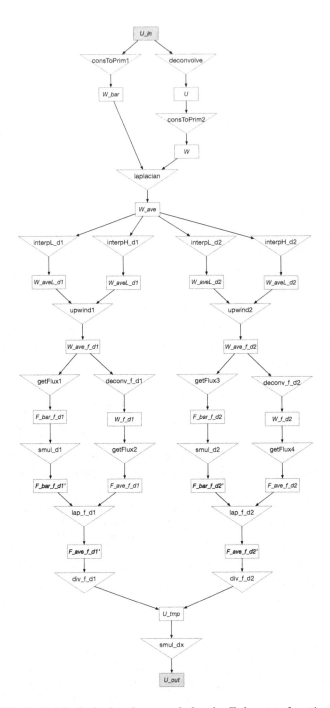

Fig. 2. Polyhedral+dataflow graph for the Euler step function.

Arithmetic intensity is computed from FLOPs and memory traffic estimates. Estimates are correlated to the results of the Intel VTune/SDE and LIKWID [42] performance modeling tools. The model is applied to predict the profitability of IR transformations, and computes estimates that are hardware independent, i.e., an application signature.

4.4   Shift and Fuse Algorithm

The automatic fusion of loop nests requires that data dependences be satisfied to ensure correctness. The fusion algorithm consists of three steps. The iteration spaces of the computation nodes are first compared to determine whether loop interchange is required. Interchange is necessary when pointwise methods (i.e., `forall` operations) are fused with stencils, for example, because the pointwise methods do not have component loops. The component loops are moved to the inside as their bounds are known at compile time (the e.g., C, D, E template parameters), and are relatively small with respect to the spatial loops (i.e., $C \ll N$). These innermost loops become candidates for unrolling, allowing the innermost spatial loop (e.g., x) to be vectorized. Interchange is performed by exchanging the nodes within the iterator tree.

The next step calculates any iterator shifts that may be necessary. This requires finding the computation nodes within the current fusion group that produce data required by the node being fused. The data access mappings for each producer are processed to determine the maximum reuse distance. This distance is then added to the difference between the loop start bounds of the fused node and the current node. The result becomes the shift tuple, one per iterator, of the node being fused.

Finally, the iterator tree must be updated to position the new node within the fusion group. A depth first search of the iterator tree is performed for each of the producer nodes in the previous step, returning the path through the tree. The fused node is then inserted into iterator tree at a position one greater than the maximum position of its producers, ensuring that it is not executed until the data it must read have been written.

As a motivating example, fusing the `laplacian` node with `consToPrim1` from Euler demonstrates each of the three steps. The component loop iterator, c in the `laplacian` node is interchanged before fusing. Each of the spatial iterators is shifted by 1 as the reuse distance of the stencil is $1 - (-1) = 2$, and the loop bounds differ by -1 in each direction. In the last step, the `laplacian` node is inserted after `consToPrim1` because it produces the `W_bar` data that `laplacian` consumes. Figure 3(a) contains the original iterator trees for the two statement nodes, the interchanged and shifted `laplacian` tree is displayed in (b), and the resulting fused iterator tree in (c).

Once the serial version of a graph has been generated, additional variants are generated by applying transformations to the original. This can be done manually using eDSL methods such as `fuse`, `split`, or `tile`, or variants can be generated automatically.

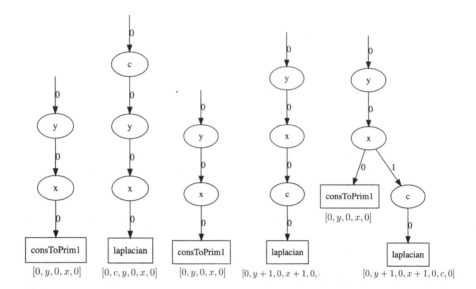

Fig. 3. Iterator trees for the (a) original `consToPrim1` and `laplacian` computations, (b) `laplacian` after interchange and shift applied, and (c) final fused tree.

The PDFG infrastructure consists of a multi-pass system. Passes are implemented as visitors on the dataflow graph, that either annotate nodes with attribute values such as iterator shifts or tile sizes, or can produce a new transformed graph. The system is extensible, a new pass can be added by implementing a new visitor. The original graph is not modified, so the passes can be applied in an arbitrary order.

The passes are performed in a particular order by default. The schedule visitor traverses the computation nodes, then walks the iterator trees of each to produce the scattering functions needed by the polyhedral compiler. The performance model visitor traverses the graph to build the model, annotating the nodes with FLOPs, data reads and writes, and the number of input and output streams.

The data reduce visitor minimizes the temporary storage within fused node groups based on the reuse distance between data nodes. The distances are inferred from the data accesses in the statement nodes that read or write the data nodes. A data space is reducible if it is produced and consumed within the same fusion group. A reuse tuple is generated that contains the distance for each iterator. Iterators with a reuse of zero can be reduced to the size of a scalar, a component vector, or one spatial dimensions. The data space size and access mappings are updated accordingly.

The memory allocation visitor traverses the graph in reverse order and assigns each data space a memory location using liveness analysis, further reducing data allocation. This ensures that only as much memory as is required for the most live data spaces needs to be allocated. This leads to a balance between loop fusion and memory allocation.

The parallel visitor decorates the iterator tree of each statement node with either thread level parallelism for outer loops, or SIMD parallelism for innermost loops. These tags are converted into pragmas during code generation. Loops that have been automatically shifted are not parallelized.

The transformation visitor attempts to produce an optimal version of the graph using the performance model that reduces control flow and temporary storage, and enables vectorization opportunities. Decisions include whether to fuse two nodes or sets of nodes, perform loop interchange, unroll inner loops, or apply tiling.

5   Code Generation

Code generators are implemented as visitors on the dataflow graphs. Statement nodes are output as loop nests, data nodes as memory allocation statements, and data mappings as macros. The default generator also includes any necessary headers, and defines any other functions required in the code body. Data nodes that have no incoming edges (sources) become input parameters, and those without outgoing edges (sinks) become outputs, unless otherwise specified. Internal data nodes are assumed to be temporary storage and subject to reduction. Loop nests are generated by the *Omega+ polyhedral compiler*, and modified or annotated as needed by the code generator.

OpenMP pragmas are inserted into the loop nests as previously determined by the parallel visitor. The memory allocation statements and access functions are modified so that dedicated memory spaces are assigned to each thread. The maximum number of active threads is computed from the upper bound of the loop being parallelized. The remaining threads are applied over boxes.

Code variants can optionally be validated after generation against the data produced by the execution of the `Proto` code that produced the initial dataflow graph. Variants that do not match the desired output within a given error threshold are discarded.

6   Experimental Evaluation

Performance results were collected using an implementation of the Euler fluid equations [12] solver in `Proto`. The step function applied by the fourth order Runge-Kutta method at each time step is the most computationally intensive method. An initial version of the graph was generated from one pass through the Euler step function. Several code variants were produced by manipulating the dataflow graph IR and generating the resulting code. The performance results indicate that scheduling transformations are more effective when coupled with dataflow optimizations. The performance model predicts that the fastest variants are those that increase arithmetic intensity, while reducing the data sufficiently to keep the working set size within the L3 cache.

6.1   Experimental Setup

The Euler step function was evaluated by computing boxes of size 64^3, with one box allocated to each parallel thread. Each experimental run was performed nine times with the mean time reported. Execution times are normalized with respect to the Proto implementation and output data were validated against the same to ensure correctness.

The CPU experiments were performed on single nodes of the Cori cluster at NERSC. Each Haswell node consists of a dual socket, Intel Xeon E5-2698 v3 CPU clocked at 2.30 GHz, each with 32 physical cores, 16 per socket, and 64 logical cores with hyperthreading. There are 64K of L1, 256K of L2, respectively, with 40960K of shared L3 cache. Each node contains 128 GB of DRAM distributed over two NUMA domains, with a 2 GB block size. The code variants were compiled using Intel compiler (ICC) v19.0.3 at optimization level -O3.

The GPU data were collected on an NVIDIA Quadro P1000 with 4 GB of GDDR5 with an Intel Xeon Silver 4114 CPU at 2.20 GHZ. The OpenACC code was compiled with version 19.4 of the PGI compiler using the CUDA 9.2 toolkit, also with the -O3 flag, and managed memory enabled. Memory transfer times between host and device are included.

6.2   Code Variants

The first code variant is a series of loop nests, each representing one Proto kernel. This version has the lowest arithmetic intensity per loop, but also the least amount of allocated memory. The fully fused version fuses all loop nests into one. This has the effect of maximizing arithmetic intensity, but also the quantity of live data. This variant also contains increased control flow due to the guards inserted to ensure that data dependences are satisfied. The added control flow limits SIMD vectorization.

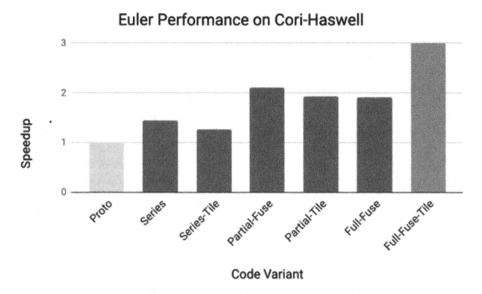

Fig. 4. Performance results for the Euler step function on a Cori Haswell CPU node.

The third variant is partial fusion. Statement nodes are grouped using a greedy approach that increases arithmetic intensity while reducing memory traffic within each group. When the working set size for a group exceeds a given threshold, a new group is created. The threshold is approximately based on the L3 cache size of the target architectures. This variant strikes a balance between AI and memory traffic.

Tiled versions of each variant are also generated. Tile sizes are set to 8 in each dimension, as 4 is too small for the applied stencils, and no performance benefit is observed at size 16. Performance results are given in Fig. 4. Speedup is computed relative to the baseline execution time of the Euler implementation in Proto. The fully fused and tiled code variant is fastest as it maximizes arithmetic intensity, while reducing the active memory footprint to a single tile size (8^3). data space.

A scalability study was performed by sweeping the number of threads from 1 to 64 by powers of two on each of the three code variants for three different box sizes, small ($N = 16$), medium ($N = 32$), and large ($N = 64$). The number of boxes computed are set to ensure a constant number of cells (1536) for each run. The data are displayed in Fig. 5. The Proto variant is excluded from these

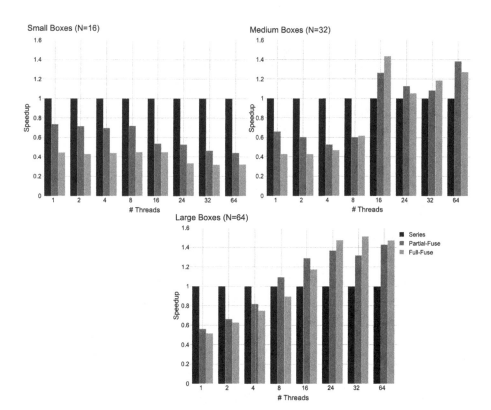

Fig. 5. Comparison of code variants for each box size with thread sweep from 1 to 64.

results as it does not implement OpenMP parallelism. The series of loops variant is used as the baseline. This variant is the fastest in all cases for small boxes. The fused and tiled variants do not outperform it until 16 threads for medium sized boxes, and 8 threads for large boxes.

The series of loops, partially fused, and fully fused variants were generated for the GPU with OpenACC pragmas. These variants are similar to those on the CPU, except component loops are interchanged and unrolled for vectorization. Figure 6 contains the performance results. Only the series of loops variant outperforms the original `Proto` implementation. This is possibly because the loop shifts required for fusion introduce additional control flow, that causes thread divergence.

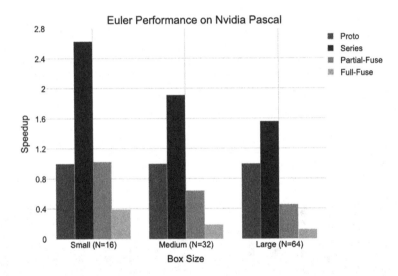

Fig. 6. Performance results for the Euler step function on a NVIDIA Pascal GPU.

7   Related Work

7.1   Polyhedral Compilers

PENCIL [4], Pluto [9], and LoopChains [37] are automatic polyhedral compilers that rely on code annotation with pragmas to identify static control parts (SCoPs). Polly [21] is another that works at the level of the LLVM-IR. These rely on the Integer Set Library (ISL) [46] and the ClooG compiler [6] for code generation. CHiLL [38] provides a scheduling language for transforming code, using Omega+ and Codegen+ [10] for code generation. Other approaches that use scheduling languages are AlphaZ [49] and URUK [45]

This paper provides an eDSL to represent computations and perform automatic transformations, rather than augmenting existing code or implementing a scheduling language to manipulate it. The iterator trees described here are similar in purpose to schedule trees [22] in ISL, or iteration graphs in the tensor algebra compiler (TACO) [25]. The redundant computation for conditionals is similar to polyhedral expression propagation [15].

7.2 Embedded DSLs

Developing a compiler requires a considerable engineering investment, so embedded languages are provide a means to add new functionality to existing languages. Other eDSLs that follow a similar approach include Halide [32], PolyMage [29], and TIRAMISU [5]. Halide is a functional language embedded in C++ and implemented as a library, much like `Proto`. The goal is to decouple the algorithm from the underlying implementation. Halide is focused on image processing pipelines that are often implemented as a stream of stencil operations. It does not support the polyhedral model, but rather relies on interval analysis.

PolyMage is an eDSL implemented in Python, that also targets image processing pipelines, but differs from Halide in that it supports the polyhedral model. Both rely on autotuning to select optimal code variants, however a dynamic programming model for loop fusion and tiling was added to PolyMage [24].

TIRAMISU is also a C++ eDSL and library that also provides a multi-layer intermediate representation. The polyhedral model is supported using ISL and code is lowered to the Halide-IR. The IR levels include algorithm specification, computation, data management, and communication. Code generation supports OpenMP, CUDA, and MPI. However, neither a performance model nor autotuning are provided to automate transformations, rather they are manually specified in the eDSL. `Proto` differs from these existing DSL's in its specialization on structured grid applications. The basic abstractions are boxes of data acted upon by for-all functions point-wise operations, and stencils.

7.3 Dataflow Languages

PolyAST [35] presents an optimization flow that combines the polyhedral model with AST transformations to improve parallelism, but does not specifically target dataflow. The Data-Flow Graph Language (DFGL) [34] is an optimization framework that allows graph based dataflow dependences to be represented in the polyhedral model. TIDeFlow [30] is an execution model that schedules computations using Petri nets, with the transitions and places used to determine the availability of data. LIFT [36] is a data parallel IR language that performs control and dataflow optimizations. The ΣC language [20] applies the polyhedral model to dataflow programs in the context of agent-oriented programming. The dataflow graphs used in this work most closely resemble the modified macro-dataflow graphs (M^2DFGs) described in [14].

7.4 Memory Optimizations

Memory optimization in the polyhedral model was implemented in [31] with the Alpha functional language. Array privatization [43] is a technique for enhancing parallelism by privatizing variables per thread by applying dataflow analysis both inter- and intraprocedurally. Array contraction [2] optimizes code by scalarizing array variables inside a loop, saving memory by removing temporary arrays and increasing data locality.

7.5 Stencil Parallelization

Automatic parallelization in the polyhedral model was introduced in [19]. Overlapped tiling as an approach to improve the parallelism of skewed and tiled stencil applications are described by Krishnamoorthy et al. [26]. Data layout transformations for stencils were developed in [23]. CHiLL has also been applied to optimize higher-order stencil computations [7].

7.6 Adaptive Mesh Refinement

Block-structured adaptive mesh refinement (SAMR) is a computational technique for solving large-scale hyperbolic, parabolic, or elliptic PDE equations, computing different regions of the problem domain with different spatial resolutions, while maintaining the blocks in a logically organized hierarchy [17]. The Chombo library [11] consists of a set of C++ classes designed to support SAMR and is part of the BoxLib toolkit [51]. The `Proto` library is an extension of this work, that provides performance portability by supporting CPU and GPU backends. AMREx [50] is another SAMR framework in C++, designed for PDEs with complex boundary conditions with support for heterogenous architectures.

7.7 Performance Modeling

The Roofline performance model [27, 48] was developed for multicore machines. Operational intensity (Flops/byte) is plotted on the x-axis, versus the attainable (GFlops/second) on the y-axis. Attainable performance is defined as the minimum of peak floating point performance and peak memory bandwidth times operational intensity. These lines intersect at peak computational performance and peak memory bandwidth. The performance model in this work was inspired by the need to maximize arithmetic intensity and memory bandwidth to achieve peak performance.

LIKWID [42] provides an API and a set of command line utilities for modeling performance on multicore x86 architectures, making use of hardware performance counters. It is one of the tools used in this work to verify the estimates produced by the performance model.

8   Conclusion

This paper presented `Proto`, an eDSL for structured grid PDE solvers, combined with a polyhedral+dataflow language (`PDFL`) that combines execution schedule transformations with dataflow optimizations. `Proto` statements and data are translated into the PDFG-IR by an interface layer and then optimized by applying a combination of loop fusion, tiling, parallelization, vectorization, and temporary storage reductions. A performance model including FLOP and memory throughput estimates is incorporated to automatically guide optimizations by maximizing arithmetic intensity while reducing the working set size. Performance improvements of up to 3X were demonstrated with a CPU implementation of the Euler equations, and up to 2.6X for the GPU version.

Acknowledgments. This material is based upon work supported by the US Department of Energy's Office of Advanced Scientific Computing Research under contract number DE-AC02-05- CH11231. Any opinions, findings, and conclusions or recommendations expressed in this material are those of the authors and do not necessarily reflect the views of the Department of Energy.

References

1. Adams, M., et al.: Chombo software package for AMR applications-design document. Technical report (2015)
2. Alias, C., Baray, F., Darte, A.: Bee+ cl@ k: an implementation of lattice-based array contraction in the source-to-source translator rose. In: ACM SIGPLAN Notices, vol. 42, pp. 73–82. ACM (2007)
3. Bachan, J., et al.: The UPC++ PGAS library for exascale computing. In: Proceedings of the Second Annual PGAS Applications Workshop, p. 7. ACM (2017)
4. Baghdadi, R., et al.: PENCIL: a platform-neutral compute intermediate language for accelerator programming. In: 2015 International Conference on Parallel Architecture and Compilation (PACT), pp. 138–149. IEEE (2015)
5. Baghdadi, R., et al.: Tiramisu: a polyhedral compiler for expressing fast and portable code. In: Proceedings of the 2019 IEEE/ACM International Symposium on Code Generation and Optimization, pp. 193–205. IEEE Press (2019)
6. Bastoul, C.: Generating loops for scanning polyhedra: Cloog users guide. Polyhedron **2**, 10 (2004)
7. Basu, P., Hall, M., Williams, S., Van Straalen, B., Oliker, L., Colella, P.: Compiler-directed transformation for higher-order stencils. In: 2015 IEEE International Parallel and Distributed Processing Symposium (IPDPS), pp. 313–323. IEEE (2015)
8. Benabderrahmane, M.-W., Pouchet, L.-N., Cohen, A., Bastoul, C.: The polyhedral model is more widely applicable than you think. In: Gupta, R. (ed.) CC 2010. LNCS, vol. 6011, pp. 283–303. Springer, Heidelberg (2010). https://doi.org/10.1007/978-3-642-11970-5_16
9. Bondhugula, U., Hartono, A., Ramanujam, J., Sadayappan, P.: PLuTo: a practical and fully automatic polyhedral program optimization system. In: Proceedings of the ACM SIGPLAN 2008 Conference on Programming Language Design and Implementation (PLDI 2008), Tucson, AZ, June 2008. Citeseer (2008)

10. Chen, C.: Polyhedra scanning revisited. ACM SIGPLAN Not. **47**(6), 499–508 (2012)
11. Colella, P., et al.: Chombo software package for AMR applications design document (2009). http://seesar.lbl.gov/ANAG/chombo/. Accessed Sept 2008
12. Colella, P., Woodward, P.R.: The piecewise parabolic method (PPM) for gas-dynamical simulations. J. Comput. Phys. **54**(1), 174–201 (1984)
13. Cornford, S., Martin, D., Lee, V., Payne, A., Ng, E.: Adaptive mesh refinement versus subgrid friction interpolation in simulations of Antarctic ice dynamics. Ann. Glaciol. **57**(73), 1–9 (2016)
14. Davis, E.C., Strout, M.M., Olschanowsky, C.: Transforming loop chains via macro dataflow graphs. In: Proceedings of the 2018 International Symposium on Code Generation and Optimization, pp. 265–277. ACM (2018)
15. Doerfert, J., Sharma, S., Hack, S.: Polyhedral expression propagation. In: Proceedings of the 27th International Conference on Compiler Construction, pp. 25–36. ACM (2018)
16. Dorr, M.R., Colella, P., Dorf, M.A., Ghosh, D., Hittinger, J.A., Schwartz, P.O.: High-order discretization of a gyrokinetic Vlasov model in edge plasma geometry. J. Comput. Phys. **373**, 605–630 (2018)
17. Dubey, A., et al.: A survey of high level frameworks in block-structured adaptive mesh refinement packages. J. Parallel Distrib. Comput. **74**(12), 3217–3227 (2014)
18. El-Ghazawi, T., Smith, L.: UPC: unified parallel C. In: Proceedings of the 2006 ACM/IEEE Conference on Supercomputing, p. 27. ACM (2006)
19. Feautrier, P.: Automatic parallelization in the polytope model. In: Perrin, G.-R., Darte, A. (eds.) The Data Parallel Programming Model. LNCS, vol. 1132, pp. 79–103. Springer, Heidelberg (1996). https://doi.org/10.1007/3-540-61736-1_44
20. Fontaine, R., Gonnord, L., Morel, L.: Polyhedral dataflow programming: a case study. In: International Symposium on Computer Architecture and High Performance Computing (SBAC-PAD) (2018)
21. Grosser, T., Groesslinger, A., Lengauer, C.: Polly: performing polyhedral optimizations on a low-level intermediate representation. Parallel Process. Lett. **22**(04), 1250010 (2012)
22. Grosser, T., Verdoolaege, S., Cohen, A.: Polyhedral AST generation is more than scanning polyhedra. ACM Trans. Program. Lang. Syst. (TOPLAS) **37**(4), 12 (2015)
23. Henretty, T., Stock, K., Pouchet, L.-N., Franchetti, F., Ramanujam, J., Sadayappan, P.: Data layout transformation for stencil computations on short-vector SIMD architectures. In: Knoop, J. (ed.) CC 2011. LNCS, vol. 6601, pp. 225–245. Springer, Heidelberg (2011). https://doi.org/10.1007/978-3-642-19861-8_13
24. Jangda, A., Bondhugula, U.: An effective fusion and tile size model for optimizing image processing pipelines. In: Proceedings of the 23rd ACM SIGPLAN Symposium on Principles and Practice of Parallel Programming, pp. 261–275. ACM (2018)
25. Kjolstad, F., Kamil, S., Chou, S., Lugato, D., Amarasinghe, S.: The tensor algebra compiler. Proc. ACM Program. Lang. **1**(OOPSLA) (2017). Article no. 77
26. Krishnamoorthy, S., Baskaran, M., Bondhugula, U., Ramanujam, J., Rountev, A., Sadayappan, P.: Effective automatic parallelization of stencil computations. In: ACM SIGPLAN Notices, vol. 42, pp. 235–244. ACM (2007)
27. Lo, Y.J., et al.: Roofline model toolkit: a practical tool for architectural and program analysis. In: Jarvis, S.A., Wright, S.A., Hammond, S.D. (eds.) PMBS 2014. LNCS, vol. 8966, pp. 129–148. Springer, Cham (2015). https://doi.org/10.1007/978-3-319-17248-4_7

28. McCorquodale, P., Colella, P.: A high-order finite-volume method for conservation laws on locally refined grids. Commun. Appl. Math. Comput. Sci. **6**(1), 1–25 (2011)
29. Mullapudi, R.T., Vasista, V., Bondhugula, U.: PolyMage: automatic optimization for image processing pipelines. In: ACM SIGARCH Computer Architecture News, vol. 43, pp. 429–443. ACM (2015)
30. Orozco, D.: TIDeFlow: a parallel execution model for high performance computing programs. In: 2011 International Conference on Parallel Architectures and Compilation Techniques (PACT), p. 211. IEEE Press, New York (2011)
31. Quilleré, F., Rajopadhye, S.: Optimizing memory usage in the polyhedral model. ACM Trans. Program. Lang. Syst. (TOPLAS) **22**(5), 773–815 (2000)
32. Ragan-Kelley, J., Barnes, C., Adams, A., Paris, S., Durand, F., Amarasinghe, S.: Halide: a language and compiler for optimizing parallelism, locality, and recomputation in image processing pipelines. ACM SIGPLAN Not. **48**(6), 519–530 (2013)
33. Sadayappan, P.: Domain specific language support for exascale. Technical report, The Ohio State University, Columbus, OH, United States (2017)
34. Sbîrlea, A., Shirako, J., Pouchet, L.-N., Sarkar, V.: Polyhedral optimizations for a data-flow graph language. In: Shen, X., Mueller, F., Tuck, J. (eds.) LCPC 2015. LNCS, vol. 9519, pp. 57–72. Springer, Cham (2016). https://doi.org/10.1007/978-3-319-29778-1_4
35. Shirako, J., Pouchet, L.N., Sarkar, V.: Oil and water can mix: an integration of polyhedral and AST-based transformations. In: Proceedings of the International Conference for High Performance Computing, Networking, Storage and Analysis, pp. 287–298. IEEE Press (2014)
36. Steuwer, M., Remmelg, T., Dubach, C.: LIFT: a functional data-parallel IR for high-performance GPU code generation. In: 2017 IEEE/ACM International Symposium on Code Generation and Optimization (CGO), pp. 74–85. IEEE (2017)
37. Strout, M.M., et al.: Generalizing run-time tiling with the loop chain abstraction. In: 2014 IEEE 28th International Parallel and Distributed Processing Symposium, pp. 1136–1145. IEEE (2014)
38. Tiwari, A., Chen, C., Chame, J., Hall, M., Hollingsworth, J.K.: A scalable auto-tuning framework for compiler optimization. In: 2009 Processing of the IEEE International Symposium on Parallel & Distributed, IPDPS 2009, pp. 1–12. IEEE (2009)
39. Toro, E.F.: Riemann Solvers and Numerical Methods for Fluid Dynamics: A Practical Introduction. Springer, Heidelberg (2013)
40. Trebotich, D., Graves, D.: An adaptive finite volume method for the incompressible Navier-Stokes equations in complex geometries. Commun. Appl. Math. Comput. Sci. **10**(1), 43–82 (2015)
41. Trebotich, D., Shen, C., Miller, G., Molins, S., Steefel, C.: An adaptive embedded boundary method for pore scale reactive transport
42. Treibig, J., Hager, G., Wellein, G.: LIKWID: a lightweight performance-oriented tool suite for x86 multicore environments. In: 2010 39th International Conference on Parallel Processing Workshops, pp. 207–216. IEEE (2010)
43. Tu, P., Padua, D.: Automatic array privatization. In: Pande, S., Agrawal, D.P. (eds.) Compiler Optimizations for Scalable Parallel Systems. LNCS, vol. 1808, pp. 247–281. Springer, Heidelberg (2001). https://doi.org/10.1007/3-540-45403-9_8
44. Van Straalen, B., Trebotich, D., Ovsyannikov, A., Graves, D.T.: Scalable structured adaptive mesh refinement with complex geometry. In: Exascale Scientific Applications: Scalability and Performance Portability, p. 307 (2017)
45. Vasilache, N., Bastoul, C., Cohen, A.: Polyhedral code generation in the real world. In: Mycroft, A., Zeller, A. (eds.) CC 2006. LNCS, vol. 3923, pp. 185–201. Springer, Heidelberg (2006). https://doi.org/10.1007/11688839_16

46. Verdoolaege, S.: *isl*: an integer set library for the polyhedral model. In: Fukuda, K., Hoeven, J., Joswig, M., Takayama, N. (eds.) ICMS 2010. LNCS, vol. 6327, pp. 299–302. Springer, Heidelberg (2010). https://doi.org/10.1007/978-3-642-15582-6_49

47. Vogman, G., Colella, P.: Continuum kinetic plasma modeling using a conservative 4th-order method with AMR. In: APS Meeting Abstracts (2012)

48. Williams, S., Waterman, A., Patterson, D.: Roofline: an insightful visual performance model for floating-point programs and multicore architectures. Technical report, Lawrence Berkeley National Lab. (LBNL), Berkeley, CA, United States (2009)

49. Yuki, T., Gupta, G., Kim, D.G., Pathan, T., Rajopadhye, S.: AlphaZ: a system for design space exploration in the polyhedral model. In: Kasahara, H., Kimura, K. (eds.) LCPC 2012. LNCS, vol. 7760, pp. 17–31. Springer, Heidelberg (2013). https://doi.org/10.1007/978-3-642-37658-0_2

50. Zhang, W., et al.: AMReX: a framework for block-structured adaptive mesh refinement (2019)

51. Zhang, W., Almgren, A., Day, M., Nguyen, T., Shalf, J., Unat, D.: BoxLib with Tiling: an adaptive mesh refinement software framework. SIAM J. Sci. Comput. **38**(5), S156–S172 (2016)

CubeGen: Code Generation for Accelerated GEMM-Based Convolution with Tiling

Amarin Phaosawasdi[1(✉)], Christopher Rodrigues[2], Long Chen[2], and Peng Wu[2]

[1] University of Illinois at Urbana-Champaign, Champaign, IL, USA
`phaosaw2@illinois.edu`
[2] Futurewei Technologies, Santa Clara, CA, USA
{`christopher.rodrigues,long.chen,peng.wu`}`@futurewei.com`

Abstract. In a convolutional neural network (CNN), the convolution layers typically dominate the execution time. Hardware accelerators have been designed to speed up convolution. One class of accelerators provide hardware support for matrix multiplication (matmul), allowing the reduction of convolution to matmul, a previously known approach we refer to as GEMM-based convolution. Manually writing and tuning tiled GEMM-based convolution is time consuming and error prone, especially in the presence of hardware constraints such as tensor layout. We propose a kernel compiler called CubeGen that generates fast convolution code and an auto-tiling tool that generates well-performing tiling plans. Our experiments show that for one large convolution problem, we generate code performing up to 93% compared to hand-tuned code. For various other convolution problems, we show that among the automatically generated plans, we are able to find plans with 2.02× speed up on average compared to the median tiling plan.

Keywords: Convolution · Code generation · Tiling · Blocking · DMA · im2col · Matrix multiplication · Hardware acceleration · Performance

1 Introduction

A convolutional neural network (CNN) is a deep neural network architecture widely used in image processing applications. The execution time of a CNN inference is typically dominated by the time taken to evaluate the convolution layers. Convolution uses spatial information to infer useful data, such as edges in an image. Formally, convolution computes the following.

$$O[h, w, g] = \sum_{c=0}^{C-1} \sum_{i=0}^{H_k-1} \sum_{j=0}^{W_k-1} I[hS_h + iD_h - P_t, wS_w + jD_w - P_l, c] K[g, i, j, c] \quad (1)$$

This material is based in part upon work supported by Futurewei Technologies and by the National Science Foundation under Award 1533912.

S. Pande and V. Sarkar (Eds.): LCPC 2019, LNCS 11998, pp. 147–163, 2021.
https://doi.org/10.1007/978-3-030-72789-5_11

where O is the output tensor with size $[H_o, W_o, C_o]$, I is the feature map with size $[H_i, W_i, C]$, and K are N_k kernels, each with size $[H_k, W_k, C]$. The 2D convolution has the stride $[S_h, S_w]$, dilation factor $[D_h, D_w]$, and top/bottom/left/right padding $[P_t, P_b, P_l, P_r]$. Out of bound indices in I are treated as zeros. An optional bias array B, not shown in the equation, may be added to O after the computation. The tensor sizes are typically known ahead of time in machine learning applications. One can view convolution as dividing I into equal-sized windows, and storing the dot product of each window and each kernel K as an element of O.

Hardware accelerators have been proposed to speed up convolution. Some include matmul units to support high intensity computations [9,13]. Of equal importance is efficient use of memory bandwidth [7,17]. Our work is based on the DaVinci architecture [16], which was designed for better control of memory bandwidth (through explicit DMA instructions) while supporting high intensity computations (through the matmul unit).

An overview of the architecture is shown in Fig. 1. It has a cube unit for carrying out matmul operations. The cube unit may only access data in the L0 caches. Additionally, the matmul instruction requires that the matrices be stored in block layout [19]. All memory movements are explicit and done through DMA instructions that optionally support data re-organization during transfer, including im2col, padding, and dilation.

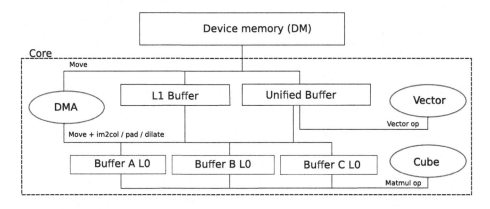

Fig. 1. Target architecture

Convolution can be reduced to matmul by transforming the tensors to matrices through an operation called im2col [5]. We will refer to this algorithm as GEMM-based convolution. It has been shown that GEMM-based convolution provides consistent performance for many convolution problems [8]. To fully utilize the cube unit, our work focuses on dense tensors and GEMM-based convolution.

With limited L0 caches and explicit memory movement, software-level tiling is neccessary when handling large tensors. While tiled matrix multiplication has been well studied, tiled GEMM-based convolution on DaVinci poses unique problems. Firstly, im2col may result in duplicate data. In order to reduce memory overhead, im2col should only be performed at the L0 level tiling. Because of this, calculating the tile sizes is not as straightforward as tiled matrix multiplication. Secondly, padding, dilation, and strides all affect the tile offset and tile size calculation. This problem is not present in matrix multiplication. Thirdly, the cube unit requires the matrices to be stored in block layout [19]. When the tile size is not divisible by the problem size, there will be partial tiles left. These partial tiles need to be 2D-padded to conform with the layout requirements of the cube unit. A typical vector operation in a CPU, for example, would only need 1D padding. Finally, we need to carefully choose a tile size to minimize latency, as its effect on this architecture is significant.

Manually writing tiled GEMM-based convolution code is a complex task. Calculating the tile offset and tile size is not straightforward and error-prone. When tuning for performance, each tile size affects the loop structure, allowing even more room for error. Even though the problem size is typically known ahead of time in machine learning applications, the combination of ways in which the tiling plan can interact with the problem size makes it infeasable to manually implement convolution. We propose a kernel compiler called *CubeGen* and an accompanying auto-tiler. The overall code generation process is shown in Fig. 2. The system's parameters consists of two parts: the convolution problem parameters and the tiling specification. A user may interact directly with CubeGen or through the auto-tiler.

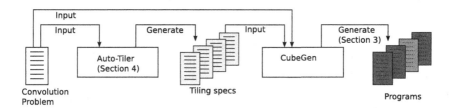

Fig. 2. System overview

At a high level, **CubeGen** generates code through hierarchical tiling [4], while the problem's complexity lies in the details. CubeGen uses a recursive process involving loop tiling and software-managed caching. In loop tiling, the iteration space is broken down into smaller tiles. When a dimension can be padded, CubeGen also keeps track of padding (as described in Sect. 3.1). In software-managed caching, CubeGen allocates enough space to hold the tile data, calculates the correct region of memory to be copied into a memory level, and generates the correct DMA instruction that takes into account the (block) layout between each tiling level (as described in Sect. 3.3). Data re-organization such as im2col, padding, and dilation is done at the same time as memory movement. Double-buffering is used to hide latency. The **auto-tiler** reduces the search space for good tiling plans by tiling convolution only once, pruning invalid tiling plans that do not conform to the hardware's layout requirements, and making an assumption that the larger the tile size the better performance (as described in Sect. 4).

The main contributions of this work are (1) A **code generation algorithm** that generates fast GEMM-based convolution for the DaVinci architecture. We show that CubeGen can generate code comparable, up to 93% to hand-tuned code for a convolution problem, (2) A **tiling specification scheme** that specifies how to tile both convolution and matmul for GEMM-based convolution, and (3) **auto-tiling heuristics** for reducing the space of available tiling plans. In our experiments, we were able to find good tiling plans that perform up to 14.79× better than bad tiling plans and with a geometric mean of 2.02× better than the median tiling plans.

The paper is structured as follows. Section 2 describes how we map convolution onto DaVinci. Section 3 describes the code generation algorithm. Section 4 describes how we automatically choose tile sizes. Section 5 describes our evaluation. Section 6 describes related work. Finally, Sect. 7 concludes.

2 Mapping Convolution onto the Architecture

The main strengths of the DaVinci architecture lies in the matmul and DMA operations. Both operations set the constraints on the tensor layouts, which in turn affects how the loops are tiled and how the arrays are allocated. This section describes how to tile GEMM-based convolution on this architecture.

In GEMM-based convolution, I, K, and O are converted to their GEMM format, I_{virtual}, K_{virtual}, and O_{virtual}. The process of converting tensors to their GEMM format is called *im2col*, and its reverse is called *col2im*. GEMM-based convolution and the logical GEMM formats are defined below. The hardware requires that the physical GEMM formats be blocked in both dimensions. Partial blocks are padded with zeros for the correctness of the matmul instruction.

$$\text{flatten\_outer}(h, w) = hW_o + w \tag{2}$$

$$\text{flatten}(i, j, c) = iW_k N_c + jC + c \tag{3}$$

$$I_{\text{windowed}}[h, w, i, j, c] = I[hS_h + iD_h - P_t, wS_w + jD_w - P_l, c] \tag{4}$$

$$I_{\text{windowed}}[h, w, i, j, c] = I_{\text{virtual}}[\text{flatten\_outer}(h, w), \text{flatten}(i, j, c)] \tag{5}$$

$$K[g, h, w, c] = K_{\text{virtual}}[\text{flatten}(h, w, c), g] \tag{6}$$

$$O[h, w, g] = O_{\text{virtual}}[\text{flatten\_outer}(h, w), g] \tag{7}$$

$$O = col2im(matmul(im2col(I), im2col(K))) \tag{8}$$

In summary, Eq. 2 linearizes the 2D space of windows. Equation 3 linearizes the 3D space within a 3D window. Equations 4 views the tensor I in terms of the window position and the index within that window. Equation 5 flattens the 2D space of windows and the 3D space within a window into I_{virtual}'s rows and columns, respectively. Equation 6 shows how K_{virtual} is derived by flattening the H, W, and C dimensions of K. Equation 7 shows how O_{virtual} is derived by flattening the H and W dimensions of O. Finally, Eq. 8 summarizes how convolution can be reduced to matmul by using im2col and col2im.

The L0 caches are much smaller than typical tensors, so we tile the convolution algorithm to fit subarrays into each memory level. We tile convolution by taking the tile sizes from a tiling specification (Sect. 4), computing the shape and location of the tile used in each tensor, invoking DMA and the im2col transformation to move data, and formulating the remainder of the work as a modified convolution problem which can be handled recursively. The details of an implementation depend on the problem's tensor size, padding, filter window size, stride, and dilation as described below.

Conversion between convolution and GEMM format happens at two levels of tiling. The im2col transformation is delayed until moving a tile of I into L0. By doing so, the replicated data that is created by the transformation can be read by the cube unit without further copying, which would waste memory bandwidth. On the other hand, it is more efficient to precompute K_{virtual} before the algorithm begins. Kernel values are typically reused to evaluate many convolutions. Precomputing it amortizes the overhead of changing the tensor's data layout. The col2im transformation on O has minor overhead, and it is performed in L0 as a matter of convenience. The bias array plays no role in the GEMM part of the algorithm. Thus, tiling brings I, K_{virtual}, B, and O from an outer memory level to an inner one. At L0, it converts I and O to or from GEMM format.

As with tiled matmul, a tile of a convolution problem is itself a smaller convolution problem. For a given problem size $[H_o, W_o, C, C_o]$, we select a tile offset $[h, w, c, c_o]$ and size $[H'_o, W'_o, C', C'_o]$ in each dimension according to a given tiling specification. In generating code, we must translate tile offsets and sizes into other coordinate spaces, as related by Eqs. 2–8, in order to compute instruction operands and access arrays. We must also account for ISA-imposed size constraints, such as the layout of the matrices in L0 that must have block sizes be multiples of a fixed data size. These aspects of GEMM-based convolution make tiling more complex.

As an example of how tensors are tiled, consider tiling a convolution problem of size $H_o = 38, W_o = 10, C = 28, C_o = 20$ for a tile size of ten in all four dimensions. Stride and dilation are 1, the filter size is 3×3, and padding is $P_t = P_b = 1, P_l = P_r = 0$. Figure 3 illustrates how the tensors are divided into tiles. The output tensor's tile size, $10 \times 10 \times 10$, derives directly from the chosen tile size. Since H_o is not evenly divisible by 10, the bottom set of tiles is smaller. Since the kernels are in virtual matrix format, each tile is expanded by the filter size (Eq. 6), and thus the tile size is 90 in the C dimension. To get the feature map's tile size, we convert the tile size from GEMM to direct convolution format by computing the part of I corresponding to the chosen $10 \times 10 \times 10$ tile of I_{virtual}. This yields a tile size of $12 \times 12 \times 10$, with neighboring tiles overlapping. Because zero-padding is explicitly stored in GEMM format but not in direct convolution format, the top and bottom tiles are smaller by the size of this zero-padding.

Furthermore, the last tile in two dimensions is smaller because H_o and C are not divisible by the tile size.

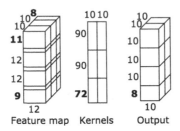

Fig. 3. Tensors tiled for a tile size of 10 in each dimension. The size of each tensor tile in each dimension is labeled. Tile sizes that are different due to boundary conditions are highlighted in bold.

This tiling scheme yields 24 tiles, with six different sets of tile shapes. The first and last tiles in the H dimension are different from the middle tiles, and the last tile in the C dimension is different from the others. We treat each set of shapes as a different subproblem and generate code for each. By doing so, tile sizes are known constants at each step of the process, which simplifies code generation. The different codes are combined, shown in pseudocode in listing 4. This listing is simplified to show only loops and data movement used for tiling. The outer loop is over the H dimension, and its first and last iterations are peeled off to handle padding. Thus, three similar loop nests are created for the three different tile shapes in this dimension. The next loop would be over the W dimension, but no loop is created because there is only one tile. The next loop is over the C_o dimension. In the body of this loop, part of B is copied into local memory at the beginning and part of O is copied out of local memory at the end. The innermost loops are over the C dimension, and the final loop iteration is peeled off to handle the smaller final tile. Within the inner loop body, tiles of I and K are copied in and convolution is evaluated.

The tile size calculation for tensor I is particularly complex, as it depends on the chosen tile size, stride, dilation, and padding. Equations 4 and 5 constitute the mapping between elements of I and I_{virtual}. The tile size in I is computed as the image of a tile in I_{virtual} under this mapping, excluding out-of-bounds elements (which correspond to padding). For a tile offset h and tile size H'_o, we first determine the tile's padding, P'_t and P'_b according to whether the tile is at the top, bottom, or middle of I_{virtual}. Then, the tile origin in I is $hS_h + P'_t - P_t$ and the tile size is $(H'_o - 1)S_h + (K_h - 1)D_h - (P'_t + P'_b) + 1$.

To perform the im2col transformation, we select a tile of I as above, then call an intrinsic function that both transforms data layout and performs DMA. The intrinsic function takes pointers to the input and output arrays, their sizes, and other convolution parameters. It fills the output array with the initial part of the im2col-transformed input. Section 3.3 describes this intrinsic in more detail.

```
for  0 <= gi < 2,                    // Top tile
  DMA for B[10*gi:10]
  for  0 <= ci < 2,
    DMA for I[0:11][0:12][10*ci:10]
    DMA for K[90*ci:90][0:10]
    Convolution tile (0, 0, 10*ci, 10*gi)
  DMA for I[0:11][0:12][20:8]
  DMA for K[180:72][0:10]
  Convolution tile (0, 0, 20, 10*gi)
  DMA for O[0:10][0:10][10*gi:10]

for  1 <= hi < 3,                    // Middle tiles
  for  0 <= gi < 2,
    DMA for B[10*gi:10]
    for  0 <= ci < 2,
      DMA for I[10*hi−1:12][0:12][10*ci:10]
      DMA for K[90*ci:90][0:10]
      Convolution tile (10*hi, 0, 10*ci, 10*gi)
    DMA for I[10*hi−1:12][0:12][20:8]
    DMA for K[180:72][0:10]
    Convolution tile (10*hi, 0, 20, 10*gi)
    DMA for O[10*hi:10][0:10][10*gi:10]

for  0 <= gi < 2,                    // Bottom tile
  DMA for B[10*gi:10]
  for  0 <= ci < 2,
    DMA for I[29:9][0:12][10*ci:10]
    DMA for K[90*ci:90][0:10]
    Convolution tile (30, 0, 10*ci, 10*gi)
  DMA for I[29:9][0:12][20:8]
  DMA for K[180:72][0:10]
  Convolution tile (30, 0, 20, 10*gi)
  DMA for O[30:8][0:10][10*gi:10]
```

Fig. 4. Pseudocode for one level of tiling in a convolution algorithm, showing location and size of tensor tiles and index of first element of convolution tiles. Slices shown in [start:size] notation.

3 Compilation

The code generation algorithm creates an implementation of Eq. 1 through hierarchical tiling [4]. The overall code generation task is recursively broken down into *loop tiling* and *software-managed caching* steps, each of which fulfills a convolution task by generating a small amount of code and reducing the rest of the problem to simpler convolution subtasks, solved recursively. The innermost loops perform matmul, which is recursively broken down in the same way.

For ease of presentation, instead of showing code that builds a compiler internal representation, we embed the generated IR into the compiler algorithm. For example, instead of showing code for constructing a for loop, we show the loop that it constructs. It is convenient to interpret these algorithms as functions to be partially evaluated, leaving a residual program to be executed at run time. In fact, the "residual program" is generated as IR and subsequently compiled.

3.1 Loop Tiling

The code generation algorithm tiles and peels multiple loops in order to generate appropriate code for the loop's boundary cases. When a loop is peeled, the remainder of code generation is run for the main loop body and again for each peeled part.

We define a loop tiling function below. Tiling in the H and W dimensions needs to handle padding in the initial and final iterations, as discussed in Sect. 2. The function partitions an N-iteration loop into tiles of size T. For a chosen tile offset x, size M, and the padding on each side P_i, P_f, it calls $f(x, M, P_i, P_f)$ to generate code for processing the tile. It first handles the special case where $N \leq T$ and only a single tile is created. Otherwise, it creates code for an initial tile with initial padding, interior tiles with no padding, and a final tile with final padding.

Padding cannot straddle a tile boundary. Since padding is normally much smaller than the loop tile size, this is not a limitation in practice.

```
function PARTITION(N, T, Pinitial, Pfinal, f)
    if N ≤ T then
        f(0, N, Pinitial, Pfinal)                              ▷ Single tile
    else
        x ← 0
        if Pinitial > 0 then
            f(x, T, Pinitial, 0)                              ▷ Initial boundary tile
            x ← x + T
            N ← N − T
        end if
        m ← ⌊(N − Pfinal)/T⌋
        if m > 0 then
            for (int j = 0; j < m; j++)
                f(x + Tj, T, 0, 0)                            ▷ Non-boundary tiles
            x ← x + Tm
            N ← N − Tm
        end if
        if N > 0 then
            f(x, N, 0, Pfinal)                                ▷ Final boundary or partial tile
        end if
    end if
end function
```

Note that the floor operation is used to count the number of non-boundary tiles. This is to ensure that all non-boundary tiles have size T. The remaining final boundary or partial tile will be handled subsequently.

Since the C dimension does not need to handle padding, we overload another partition function that does not accept padding parameters and assumes $P_{\text{initial}} = P_{\text{final}} = 0$.

3.2   Tensor Representation

The code generator represents each tensor with a compile-time object holding its address, logical size, and data layout. For a tensor object A, we write A.pointer for the run-time expression representing the tensor's address. In general, this expression refers to run-time variables such as loop counters. We write A.size for the tensor's logical size, which is a list of integers. Tiling decisions are made using the logical size. We write A.layout for the tensor's data layout, which is used when creating memory accesses and array index calculation.

A tensor's data layout consists of, for each dimension, a list of block sizes and strides. For example, suppose tensor I has logical size $[56, 56, 64]$ and its elements are stored in a flat array with index (h, w, c) residing at the flattened index $560h + 56w + c \bmod 10 + 31360 \lfloor c/10 \rfloor$. As a list of sizes and strides, the layout is $[[(56, 560)], [(56, 10)], [(10, 1), (7, 31360)]]$. The first two dimensions, which are not blocked, have a single size and stride. The last dimension has two sizes and strides, one for the intra-block part and one for the inter-block part. The sizes in this dimension, 10 and 7, incorporate padding that is added to make an integral number of blocks. This format represents the size of a block and the size of the whole array in a uniform way, which simplifies some algorithms.

When we compute the address of a tensor's tile, we use the data layout to create an index expression similar to the example in the previous paragraph. Because we always choose tile sizes that are multiples of the block size, the block size can be factored out of the resulting expression, so that computing a tile's address does not require evaluating division and modulus operations.

We define a helper function A.tile($offset$, $size$) that returns a new tensor tile referring to the region of A at the given offset and size. It converts the given logical $offset$ as described above and it uses $size$ directly.

3.3 Software-Managed Caching

For each tensor that is cached, the code generator statically allocates storage and creates data movement code. Since the DMA unit works more efficiently when moving data as blocks in burst mode, it is neccessary for the code generator to handle data movement between different block layouts and to minimize the number of bursts by moving consecutive memory together when possible. Additionally, to hide latency, double buffering may is also used.

We introduce a helper function copyIn(A, f) for caching an input tensor A, which is generally a tile of a larger tensor in the upper memory level, and call the function f on the tile. We also introduce a similar helper function copyInOut(A, f) for caching a tile of the output tensor, moving data in and out as needed.

To create a DMA call, the code generator gathers together the sizes and strides from all tensor dimensions, producing a list of (size, source stride, destination stride) tuples, sorts them in order of increasing destination stride, and collapses consecutive elements that represent contiguous regions.

The code generator has a specialized function to do the im2col transformation described in Sect. 2 on blocked feature map data layouts. The reverse process, col2im, does not need data re-organization since moving O_{virtual} out from L0 simply removes the padded data in from the 2D blocked layout. It generates a DMA call normally as described above.

When loop tiling creates several subproblems, software-managed caching allocates storage space separately for each subproblem. To use storage more efficiently, the arrays used to store tensor data are merged, keeping only one array per tensor per memory space. The merged array's size is that of the largest array that was merged.

3.4   Computation

Once all data movement is taken care of, two steps of computation remain. The bulk of the work consists of matmul. The cube unit provides a matmul intrinsic that operates on arrays in blocked layout. We write $matmul(C, A, B)$ for the intrinsic function call that multiplies A and B and accumulates the result into output C. The tensor sizes do not have to be a multiple of the block size; when arrays are padded to fit the block size, the padding is ignored appropriately.

When the bias array is used, it is added to the output using vector addition, updating the output in-place. We write $vecadd(B, A)$ for adding bias vector A to output C, updating C in-place. C is in blocked HWC format.

3.5   Main Structure

The main code generation algorithm consists of a series of calls for tiling loops and software-managed caching. We group these calls into two functions for tiling across the two levels of the memory hierarchy. The outer level is tiled by convolution. The inner level is tiled by convolutionIm2Col, which also converts to GEMM format and calls the matmul intrinsic function. The overall structure of the algorithm is shown in Fig. 5.

The first function, convolution, is shown below. This function keeps track of all parameters representing the convolution problem and passes the appropriate values to other functions. Calls to partition, pass the current tensor size, the tile size from the tiling specification, the current padding, and a function that receives new values and generates the partitioned loop body. Calls to copyIn and copyInOut take a tensor, which identifies a region of a tensor at an outer memory level, and caches that region at an inner level of memory. Tile sizes in I and K are calculated as described in Sect. 2. The bias is added at the same loop level where O is copied out.

The loop nest ordering is chosen to minimize the number of accesses to the output array. This ordering avoids saving and reloading partially computed output data. Thus, the outer tiled loops correspond to the output tensor's dimensions: h, w, and g for convolution, and j and i for matmul. Tensor O, as well as B if present, is copied across memory levels. Within this loop level, the loop over c or k is tiled, and within that, tensors I and K are copied.

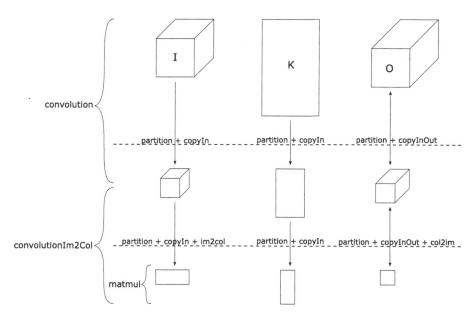

Fig. 5. Main structure of the algorithm. Cache levels descend from top to bottom and are separated by dotted lines. Each tensor is tiled into smaller ones as they are moved into lower level caches. The arrows represent the directions of data movement. Tensor I becomes a matrix through im2col, tensor K maintains its matrix representation throughout the algorithm, and tensor O is converted back to its 3D representation through col2im. Tensor B is omitted for simplicity.

function CONVOLUTION(N_h, N_w, N_c, N_g, P_t, P_b, P_l, P_r, O, I, K, B)
    partition($N_h, H_o^1, P_t, P_b, \lambda(h', N_h', P_t', P_b')$ {   ▷ Image H
      partition($N_w, W_o^1, P_l, P_r, \lambda(w', N_w', P_l', P_r')$ {   ▷ Image W
        partition($N_g, C_o^1, \lambda(g', N_g')$ {   ▷ Channel out
          copyIn(B.tile($\{g'\}, \{N_g'\}), \lambda(B')$ {   ▷ Bias
            copyInOut(O.tile($\{h', w', g'\}, \{N_h', N_w', N_g'\}), \lambda(O')$ {   ▷ Output
              partition($N_c, C_i^1, \lambda(c', N_c')$ {   ▷ Channel in
                $H \leftarrow (N_h' - 1)S_h + (K_h - 1)D_h - P_t' - P_b' + 1$ ▷ Feature map
                $W \leftarrow (N_w' - 1)S_w + (K_w - 1)D_w - P_l' - P_r' + 1$
                copyIn(I.tile($\{h'S_h + P_t' - P_t, w'S_w + P_l' - P_l, c'\}, \{H, W, N_c'\}), \lambda(I')$ {
                  copyIn(K.tile($\{K_hK_wc', g'\}, \{K_hK_wN_c', N_g'\}), \lambda(K')$ {   ▷ Filters
                    convolutionIm2Col($N_h', N_w', N_c', N_g', P_t', P_b', P_l', P_r', O', I', K', B'$)
            })})})
          vecadd(O, B, N_h', N_w', N_g')
  })})})})})
end function

The second function, convolutionIm2Col, works in a similar way to create tiles in GEMM layout. At each call to partition, it converts the current tile sizes into virtual matrix tile sizes before tiling the loop. For the im2col transformation, it needs to copy a chosen virtual matrix tile out of I. It converts the tile's index back to convolution format to find the tile's starting index in I, then it calls im2col to copy and transform data. In the inner loop, it calls the matmul intrinsic to multiply matrices.

function CONVOLUTIONIM2COL(N_h, N_w, N_c, N_g, P_t, P_b, P_l, P_r, O, I, K, B)
  partition($N_h N_w$, M_a, $\lambda(j', N_j')$ {   ▷ Virtual matrix J
   partition(N_g, M_b, $\lambda(i', N_i')$ {   ▷ Virtual matrix I
    copyInOut(O.col2im().tile($\{j', i'\}, \{N_j', N_i'\}$), $\lambda(O')$ {   ▷ Output
     partition($N_c K_h K_w$, M_c, $\lambda(k', N_k')$ {   ▷ Virtual matrix K
      $I' \leftarrow$ allocate($\{N_j', N_k'\}$)   ▷ Feature map
      $h', w' \leftarrow$ flatten_outer$^{-1}(j')$
      $H_i, W_i, C_i \leftarrow I$.size
      im2col(I', I.tile($\{h', w', k'/(K_h K_w)\}, \{H_i - h', W_i - w', C_i - k'/(K_h K_w)\}$), P_t, P_l)
       copyIn(K.tile($\{k', i'\}, \{N_k', N_i'\}$), $\lambda(K')$ {   ▷ Filters
        matmul(O', I', K')
})})})})})
end function

4   Automatically Choosing Tile Sizes

As mentioned in Sect. 2, we can tile convolution with sizes $[H_o', W_o', C', C_o']$. Once convolution is in matmul form, we can further tile it with sizes $[M_a, M_b, M_c]$. It follows that a natural tiling specification for GEMM-based convolution would be a 7-tuple $[H_o', W_o', C_o', C', M_a, M_b, M_c]$.

Simply generating all possible tile sizes results in a state explosion: the state space is the product of the maximum possible values for each parameter. We employ several methods and heuristics to reduce this space Firstly, constraints imposed by the hardware and the algorithm can reduce the search space. For example, because of the block layout restrictions of the tensors and matrices, the tiling parameters, $[C_o', C', M_a, M_b, M_c]$ only need to be multiples of the block sizes. Secondly, we prefer a larger tile size when it can fit into the available memory, a technique generally used in practice. For simplicity, we use a greedy algorithm, maximizing only 1–3 tiling parameters at a time, while fixing other parameters. With this strategy, tiling plans are generated based on the order of parameters that we choose to optimize. We further reduce the search space by always optimizing convolutional tiling parameters before matmul's. Doing so, we can further check that the matmul tile is at most the size of the convolution tile and not generate tiling plans that waste L0 space. It is worth mentioning that because we double-buffer the matrices in the matrix scratchpads, the space available when optimizing $[M_a, M_b, M_c]$ is cut in half.

For our experiments, it sufficed to use adhoc heuristics to reduce the state space and find good tiling plans. Using a quantitative cost model would arguably reduce the tile size selection time and is considered future work.

5   Evaluation

5.1   Experimental Setup

We evaluate CubeGen and the auto-tiler through a hardware simulator, which measures execution time, the number of issued matmul/DMA instructions and the matmul/DMA unit utilization and idle time. Since the majority of the computation happens in the matmul unit, the peak throughput of the accelerator can be approximated by the matmul unit utilization. The convolution problems were drawn from various neural network architectures [1,11,14,20,21,23,25]. The problems were chosen with diversity of problems in mind. All problems we generate assume half-precision floating point tensors. CubeGen is able to handle other element types as well. To reduce the tiling plan search time, during tiling plan selection, the generated code is not validated. If the chosen tile size produces incorrect code, that tiling plan will not be used. If this happens, it is likely an error in CubeGen. We set an arbitrary timeout to 20 min on the simulator. Typically, when the simulator runs long, the measured execution time is also long. Once a tile size is found, the code is generated. If the tile size is not supported, such as a tile size that causes padding to straddle the tile boundary, CubeGen will report an error. Finally, to ensure correctness of the generated code, we compare the output tensor of the generated code to that from a naive implementation written in Python using a random input.

5.2   Performance of Generated Code

We compared the execution time of a hand-tuned convolution program by an expert and a generated program. The hand-tuned code reached up to 88% matmul unit utilization. The convolution problem instance was a slightly modified problem from the ResNet architecture. It was chosen because the problem size does not fit in memory and hence the many possible tiling plans. The problem parameters are $[I_h, I_w, I_c] = [225, 225, 16]$, $K_n = 64$, $[K_h, K_w] = [7, 7]$, $[S_h, S_w] = [2, 2]$, $[P_t, P_b, P_l, P_r] = [0, 0, 0, 0]$, and $[D_h, D_w] = [1, 1]$.

Performance is measured by dividing the hand-tuned execution latency over the generated code's latency. For this problem, the generated code performs 93% compared to the hand-tuned code[1]. The tiling plans of both versions are similar and differ in only dimension H_o^l, for which the hand-tuned version has a larger size and is explained later below.

Upon closer inspection, we found that the hand-tuned code performed an additional loop-invariant code motion that CubeGen did not handle. The best tiling plan for this problem is one that holds all kernels in the convolution tile. The hand-tuned code loads the kernels into L1 only once and uses it throughout

---

[1] While we use the matmul unit utilization to quantify the difference between the hand-tuned code's performace and the hardware's theoretical peak performance, we believe that users are generally concerned about latency, which we use to quantify the generated code's performance. From our experiments, we found that high matmul unit utilization correlates with low latency.

the whole convolution. CubeGen loads the same data over and over for each convolution tile. We manually hoisted the DMA instruction in the generated program which increased the performance to 97% of the hand-tuned code.

5.3   Effect of Tile Size on Performance

To show that a choice of tile size can dramatically affect performance, we compare the performance of all 10 tiling plans that run to completion out of the 18 that our auto-tiler generates for the convolution problem above. The tiling plans generated had performance ranging from 27–93% compared to the hand-tuned version, which signifies the effect of a tiling plan on the performance of the generated code. The execution of a convolution program is dominated by the matmul and DMA instructions. This suggests that a cost model based on number of matmul and DMA instructions issued may be appropriate.

5.4   Quality of Automatically-Chosen Tile Size

We experimented further on a more diverse set of convolution problems to see how well our auto-tiler selects the tile sizes. From about 100 convolution problems, we hand picked 12 convolution problems that represent the different parameters of convolution. We did not have enough time to implement hand-tuned versions for these problems.

For these problems, we generate convolution code and generate tiling plans. We show the speed up of the best available tiling plan against the worst and median tiling plan. When there are an even number of tiling plans, the median is the better performing one so that any bias in performance is against our favor. Since our selection criteria try to maximize memory usage, even the worst tiling plans maximize the size for at least one dimension such that increasing it further will result in a tile that cannot fit in memory.

The problems and speed ups are shown in Fig. 6. The geometric mean of best over median tiling plan speed up is 2.02×. Note that this speed up is conservative, as for many problems, the simulator timed out, indicating even worse tiling plans

Convolution parameters						Best plan speed up (x times)		Unique generated plans	
$[F_h, F_w, F_c]$	K_n	$[K_h, K_w]$	$[S_h, S_w]$	$[P_t, P_b, P_l, P_r]$	$[D_h, D_w]$	Versus worst	Versus median	# total	# timed out
$[7, 7, 32]$	128	$[5, 5]$	$[1, 1]$	$[2, 2, 2, 2]$	$[1, 1]$	14.79	4.32	5	0
$[7, 7, 576]$	576	$[3, 3]$	$[1, 1]$	$[1, 1, 1, 1]$	$[1, 1]$	5.75	2.50	10	3
$[7, 7, 832]$	32	$[1, 1]$	$[1, 1]$	$[0, 0, 0, 0]$	$[1, 1]$	1.72	1.59	5	0
$[14, 14, 528]$	128	$[1, 1]$	$[1, 1]$	$[0, 0, 0, 0]$	$[1, 1]$	5.16	1.81	4	0
$[28, 28, 192]$	96	$[1, 1]$	$[1, 1]$	$[0, 0, 0, 0]$	$[1, 1]$	1.23	1.20	5	0
$[61, 46, 32]$	32	$[21, 11]$	$[2, 1]$	$[0, 0, 0, 0]$	$[1, 1]$	2.02	2.02	5	2
$[112, 112, 128]$	128	$[3, 3]$	$[1, 1]$	$[1, 1, 1, 1]$	$[1, 1]$	1.88	1.05	40	30
$[128, 128, 32]$	32	$[3, 3]$	$[1, 1]$	$[8, 8, 8, 8]$	$[8, 8]$	11.60	2.97	32	0
$[161, 81, 16]$	32	$[41, 11]$	$[2, 2]$	$[0, 0, 10, 10]$	$[1, 1]$	1.93	1.93	5	2
$[224, 224, 16]$	64	$[7, 7]$	$[2, 2]$	$[3, 2, 3, 2]$	$[1, 1]$	3.31	2.08	18	8
$[224, 224, 16]$	96	$[11, 11]$	$[4, 4]$	$[2, 1, 2, 1]$	$[1, 1]$	4.73	4.28	20	8
$[224, 224, 64]$	64	$[3, 3]$	$[1, 1]$	$[1, 1, 1, 1]$	$[1, 1]$	1.72	1.17	34	22

Fig. 6. Various convolution problems

possible. We believe this suffices to demonstrate that the auto-tiler helps us avoid bad tiling plans, even though it does not neccessarily mean it chooses an optimal one.

6   Related Work

Our work is focused on GEMM-based convolution [5]. There are other approaches for convolution such as FFT-based [18,22], Winograd-based [15], and direct convolution [24].

CubeGen is specialized to generate convolution code for DaVinci. There are existing models to help specify hierarchical memory layers and tasks, such as Sequoia [10] and HTAs [2,3]. Our work does not need such flexibility.

Because how the tile size can significantly affect the performance and the combinatory ways it can interact with the convolution problem size, we chose a code generation approach. Previous work using a code generation approach also exists, including CaffePresso [12]. Their work tunes the performance on different accelerators using knobs such as patch sizes, DMA burst lengths, storage choices in the memory hierarchy, and compiler options. It is unclear how those parameters would affect the performance in the presence of a matmul unit. TVM [6] is a flexible computation model, that supports data layout transformation and arbitrary computations, including convolution. However, it requires the user to specify how to transform loop nests such that the resulting inner loops correspond exactly to hardware primitives. Additionally the block layout confounds TVM's caching and GEMM primitive recognition. Contrasing the code generation approach, libraries such as cuDNN [8] have been developed. We did not compare the performance with existing libraries in this work.

7   Conclusion

We have presented a code generator called CubeGen that generates code for GEMM-based convolution with padding and dilation for the DaVinci architecture. CubeGen tiles the computation, correctly computes tile offsets and sizes and produces intrinsic calls that conform to the layout and locality requirements of the hardware. We have shown the impact the tile sizes have on performance. We have separated out the code generation problem from the tiling problem and have proposed a heuristic-based auto-tiler that generates well-performing tiling plans. CubeGen, together with the auto-tiler, produces code with execution time comparable to hand-tuned code, suggesting that a code generation approach is suitable for implementing convolution on this hardware.

References

1. Amodei, D., et al.: Deep speech 2: end-to-end speech recognition in English and Mandarin. In: International Conference on Machine Learning, pp. 173–182 (2016)

2. Bikshandi, G., et al.: Programming for parallelism and locality with hierarchically tiled arrays. In: Proceedings of ACM SIGPLAN Symposium on Principles and Practice of Parallel Programming, pp. 48–57. ACM (2006)

3. Bikshandi, G., et al.: Design and use of htalib – a library for hierarchically tiled arrays. In: Almási, G., Caşcaval, C., Wu, P. (eds.) LCPC 2006. LNCS, vol. 4382, pp. 17–32. Springer, Heidelberg (2007). https://doi.org/10.1007/978-3-540-72521-3_3

4. Carter, L., Ferrante, J., Hummel, S.F.: Hierarchical tiling for improved superscalar performance. In: Proceedings of 9th International Parallel Processing Symposium, pp. 239–245. IEEE (1995)

5. Chellapilla, K., Puri, S., Simard, P.: High performance convolutional neural networks for document processing. In: International Workshop on Frontiers in Handwriting Recognition. Suvisoft (2006)

6. Chen, T., et al.: TVM: an automated end-to-end optimizing compiler for deep learning. In: USENIX Symposium on Operating Systems Design and Implementation, pp. 578–594 (2018)

7. Chen, T., et al.: DianNao: a small-footprint high-throughput accelerator for ubiquitous machine-learning. In: ACM SIGPLAN Notices, vol. 49, pp. 269–284. ACM (2014)

8. Chetlur, S., et al.: cuDNN: efficient primitives for deep learning. arXiv preprint arXiv:1410.0759 (2014)

9. Choquette, J., Giroux, O., Foley, D.: Volta: performance and programmability. IEEE Micro **38**(2), 42–52 (2018)

10. Fatahalian, K., et al.: Sequoia: programming the memory hierarchy. In: Proceedings of ACM/IEEE Conference on Supercomputing, p. 83. ACM (2006)

11. He, K., Zhang, X., Ren, S., Sun, J.: Deep residual learning for image recognition. In: Proceedings IEEE Conference on Computer Vision and Pattern Recognition, pp. 770–778 (2016)

12. Hegde, G., Ramasamy, N., Kapre, N., et al.: CaffePresso: an optimized library for deep learning on embedded accelerator-based platforms. In: International Conference on Compliers, Architectures, and Synthesis of Embedded Systems, pp. 1–10. IEEE (2016)

13. Jouppi, N.P., et al.: In-datacenter performance analysis of a tensor processing unit. In: ACM/IEEE International Symposium on Computer Architecture, pp. 1–12. IEEE (2017)

14. Krizhevsky, A., Sutskever, I., Hinton, G.E.: ImageNet classification with deep convolutional neural networks. In: Advances in Neural Information Processing Systems, pp. 1097–1105 (2012)

15. Lavin, A., Gray, S.: Fast algorithms for convolutional neural networks. In: Proceedings of IEEE Conference on Computer Vision and Pattern Recognition, pp. 4013–4021 (2016)

16. Liao, H., Tu, J., Xia, J., Zhou, X.: DaVinci: a scalable architecture for neural network computing. In: 2019 IEEE Hot Chips 31 Symposium (HCS), pp. 1–44. IEEE (2019)

17. Liu, D., et al.: PuDianNao: a polyvalent machine learning accelerator. In: ACM SIGARCH Computer Architecture News, vol. 43, pp. 369–381. ACM (2015)

18. Mathieu, M., Henaff, M., LeCun, Y.: Fast training of convolutional networks through FFTs. arXiv preprint arXiv:1312.5851 (2013)

19. Park, N., Hong, B., Prasanna, V.K.: Tiling, block data layout, and memory hierarchy performance. IEEE Trans. Parallel Distrib. Syst. **14**(7), 640–654 (2003)

20. Simonyan, K., Zisserman, A.: Very deep convolutional networks for large-scale image recognition. arXiv preprint arXiv:1409.1556 (2014)
21. Szegedy, C., et al.: Going deeper with convolutions. In: Proceedings of IEEE Conference on Computer Vision and Pattern Recognition, pp. 1–9 (2015)
22. Vasilache, N., Johnson, J., Mathieu, M., Chintala, S., Piantino, S., LeCun, Y.: Fast convolutional nets with fbfft: a GPU performance evaluation. arXiv preprint arXiv:1412.7580 (2014)
23. Yu, F., Koltun, V.: Multi-scale context aggregation by dilated convolutions. arXiv preprint arXiv:1511.07122 (2015)
24. Zhang, J., Franchetti, F., Low, T.M.: High performance zero-memory overhead direct convolutions. In: Proceedings of International Conference on Machine Learning, pp. 5771–5780 (2018)
25. Zhang, X., Zhou, X., Lin, M., Sun, J.: ShuffleNet: an extremely efficient convolutional neural network for mobile devices. In: Proceedings of IEEE Conference on Computer Vision and Pattern Recognition, pp. 6848–6856 (2018)

Author Index

Ancourt, Corinne   74

Barik, Rajkishore   108

Chen, Dong   89
Chen, Long   147

Damani, Sana   64
Davis, Eddie C.   127
Ding, Chen   89

Hall, Mary   108
Haller, Philipp   49
Han, Wei   32

Kasahara, Hironori   1
Kiepas, Patryk   74
Kimura, Keiji   1
Kong, Martin   98
Koźlak, Jarosław   74

Ma, Lin   32
Mawhirter, Daniel   32
Mikami, Hiroki   1

Nishida, Hikaru   1

Oki, Yoshitake   1
Olschanowsky, Catherine R. M.   127

Patabandi, Tharindu R.   108
Patru, Dorin   89
Phaosawasdi, Amarin   147
Porpodas, Vasileios   15

Ratnalikar, Pushkar   15
Rodrigues, Christopher   147

Sarkar, Vivek   64

Tadonki, Claude   74
Tian, Chen   32

Umeda, Dan   1

Van Straalen, Brian   127
Venkat, Anand   108

Wu, Bo   32
Wu, Peng   147

Zhao, Xin   49

Printed in the United States
by Baker & Taylor Publisher Services